THE BEST OF RECLAIMING KIN

"If you don't know history, then you don't know anything. You are a leaf that doesn't know it is part of a tree."

-Michael Crichton

"If you look deeply into the palm of your hand, you will see your parents and all the generations of your ancestors. All of them are alive in this moment. Each is present in your body. You are the continuation of each of these people."

-Thich Nhat Hanh

THE BEST OF RECLAIMING KIN

HELPFUL TIPS ON RESEARCHING YOUR ROOTS

by Robyn N. Smith

Forward By Tim Pinnick

Published by Robyn N. Smith

2015

First Printing: 2015

ISBN: 978-0-578-15707-8

Published by Robyn N. Smith
Elkridge, MD 21075
email: msualumni33@verizon.net

To purchase more copies, go to:
"Reclaiming Kin" Blog at: http://www.reclaimingkin.com
Also available at Lulu.com and Amazon.com

Ordering Information:
Special discounts are available on quantity purchases by corporations, associations, educators, and others. For details, contact the publisher at the above email address.

Cover photograph: Celestine Prather and her soon-to-be husband Jesse Hebron, of Rockville, Maryland, dated ca. 1935, from the author's collection.

THE BEST OF RECLAIMING KIN

In honor of all my ancestors, those known and yet to be discovered.
I stand on your shoulders.

For Sebastian, my Greatest Love.
With a special dedication to my beloved grandmothers shown below , Mattie Mae Springer
Holt and Pauline Celeste Waters Smith. They were both gateways to discovering myself.

TABLE OF CONTENTS

TABLE OF FIGURES

It seems like a million years since I first started my research and the discoveries are still just as powerful as they've always been. I want to thank the readers of my blog first and foremost. I am humbled that you honor me with your readership amidst the thousands of genealogy blogs. I look forward to reading your comments and you demonstrate the community spirit that *is* family history research. This book took over a year to complete, and many times I did not think I would finish.

There are a few special people I must recognize. I want to first thank my daddy Paul Smith for his never-ending love and support for anything I do. I appreciate that my entire family endured endless rounds of questioning over the years and that they shared their stories about their lives. The Family Griot is surely what I was meant to be.

This journey wouldn't be half as fun without my friend Aaron Dorsey, who gave me the idea to turn my blog into a book. Our conversations have continually brought me new insights and more than a few times have been the impetus behind a blog post. Carole Hyman, my "mamacita," has nurtured me from the moment we met and I still thank her for being my first official "genealogy client" but more importantly my friend. It is such a joy to know Andrea Ramsey and I want to be like her when I grow up! I want to give a special shout-out to Marion Simmons, for her constant support and our constant laughter. I also thank Michael Hait, who I met many years ago as we both were navigating Maryland's records at the Archives. Our endless "debates" keep me sharp. And last but not least, to my long time friend Tim Pinnick, who loves history and knows how to make it exciting. He inspires me to excellence and is doing groundbreaking work on newspaper research and the role of coal miners in our nation's history. Thank you for writing the Forward for this book.

I also to express my sincere gratitude to my Afro-American Genealogical and Historical Society (AAHGS) family for providing a wonderful space for genealogists to meet, share and learn. I thank the National Genealogical Society (NGS) and the Association for Professional Genealogists (APG) for keeping high standards in the field and offering communities of professional genealogists always ready to assist. All of these groups offer publications and conferences that have contributed to making me a better researcher.

Let's keep uncovering and telling the stories of our families.

Robyn

Genealogical research has been a part of my life for over 30 years. In the beginning it was all about me—and my people, as I learned how to use the Soundex, waited weeks for my chance to view microfilm census records at the National Archives and Record Administration branch in Chicago, and corresponded with the county clerk in Fluvanna county, Virginia, and other far flung locations.

However it was not long before it became about other people—those in the communities in which my ancestors were living their lives. And, it became about the community of researchers that I was becoming attached to as I joined genealogical and historical societies, and attended conferences.

It became my calling to go down the road less traveled in the world of genealogical research. Those seeking to unravel the mysteries of their heritage will eventually come to the stark reality that in order to do thorough and successful genealogical research, the historical record must be consulted. So it was on this road, at the intersection of history and genealogy that Robyn and I met. We shared a passion

for scholarly literature related to the African American experience such as theses, dissertations, books, and articles, along with African American newspapers.

What has made Robyn's contribution to the African American genealogical community much more substantial than my own is the skillful way that she uses her blog as an instrument of instruction. Although I am not a blogger, thankfully it does not disqualify me from paying homage to the author of an outstanding one. I could hardly contain my excitement when my colleague and dear friend revealed her plans to publish a selection of writings from *Reclaiming Kin*, and was humbled beyond words when asked to write the foreword. I suspect this will be the first of several special printings of her work as she continues to blaze a path of noteworthy achievement in the blogosphere and beyond.

Having served in the teaching profession for over ten years, I can say without any hesitation that Robyn is the consummate teacher. As her lessons begin to reach an ever growing audience, Robyn and I will eagerly look forward to our road less traveled being a bit more crowded.

Timothy N. Pinnick

http://blackcoalminerheritage.net

Author of *Finding and Using African American Newspapers*

"History, despite its wrenching pain,
cannot be unlived, but if faced with courage,
need not be lived again."
-Maya Angelou

Every since my friend Aaron Dorsey proposed the idea to publish a book based upon my genealogy blog, *Reclaiming Kin*, the idea has been taking shape in my mind.

Creating a blog is a very different undertaking than publishing a book. As a form of social media, blog posts invite responses that in turn drive new blog posts. When I started *Reclaiming Kin* its primary purpose was to serve as a record of my research thoughts, ideas and findings. It quickly morphed into a more educational realm, as the teacher in me wanted a louder voice. In every post, I always want to find a way to use a new discovery to illustrate methods and assist other researchers. If I can get someone to think about a genealogy problem differently or introduce a new set of records and how to use them, then the spirit of my blog has been served.

After six years and over a hundred and fifty posts, the idea to publish a book of posts from *"Reclaiming Kin"* had its own advantages. Physical books allow for easier reading. New readers can more easily access older posts. As an avid book reader myself, books allow one to bookmark or highlight favorite thoughts and write notes in the margins. Posts can be combined based upon subject matter into "chapters," essentially groupings of similar posts. With that I concluded that a published "blog book" had its own value.

There are drawbacks that I have tried to address. Blogs have hotlinks to other websites not easily recreated in print. For this book, I have underlined words and phrases that are linked in the original online post. I have included the original title and post dates so that readers can go online, find the original posts and explore those links if desired. With the internet in constant flux, no guarantee can be made that the links are still valid, although all were verified before publication date of this book. Original posts were also edited for clarity and length. I provide references for selected images in Appendix A. You'll find a list of recommended book in Appendix B, and tips for beginners in Appendix C.

It is my sincere hope that the ideas and research communicated through *Reclaiming Kin* are an inspiration to those who have chosen to take the genealogy journey, and that it serves to assist those interested in honing critical research skills and sharing their family's story with a wider audience. The mysteries of the past are still ripe for discovery.

1A. THE JOY OF PROBATE

21 AUGUST 2010

FIGURE 1, ESTATE SALE

Probate records hold a wealth of information about our ancestors. But when exploring these records, do you limit yourself to the will and inventory, and neglect all of the other documents that are part of the probate process? *All* parts of probate hold potential clues. Here's a breakdown of some of the other steps involved in the typical probate process:

✓ **Petition:** A petition to the court usually starts the probate process. This could be submitted by a relative or perhaps a creditor.

✓ **Hearing:** A hearing date is set by the court to prove the will, if one exists (in "testate" cases). The hearing date is usually published in the local newspaper so all interested parties can have a chance to weigh in. If no one contests the will, it was considered "proved" and ordered recorded. In the case where there was no will ("intestate"), an administrator was named. Remember that original wills were usually retained by the court. Always examine *original* wills if they exist for your locality instead of the will transcribed by the clerk in the court books. Transcribing always presents opportunities for error.

✓ **Relinquishments/ Renunciations:** These records show an executor or.

✓ administrator relinquishing the duties he or she has been assigned. A renunciation for one of my Prather ancestors listed *every living heir and where they lived.*

✓ **Bonds:** The executor or administrator posted bond guaranteeing his performance of the duties associated with the estate. Bonds are valuable; they name individuals who served as securities who are often relatives.

✓ **Letters Issued:** Once the bond is accepted, the court issues Letters Testamentary (or Letters of Administration in intestate cases). This represents the court's authority for that person to perform their appointed duties with regard to the estate.

✓ **Inventory:** These are familiar records for those doing slave research. Usually the court will appoint three disinterested parties to inventory the estate. If the case drags on through the years, additions and subtractions are often made to the inventory. The household items can be powerful measures of social history for that family and provide insight into what kind of life your ancestor may have led.

✓ **Accounts and Sales:** Depending on the size of the estate, probate may end within a year, while others may drag on for 15 or 20 years, especially if there were minor children involved.

✓ During that time, periodic accounting is made to the court by the executor or administrator about the financial status of the estate. *Don't overlook these documents with regard to slave research—you can find slave sales and the name of the purchaser as well.* The sales account in Figure 1 shows numerous slaves, whom they were sold to and for what price. You may also find slaves being hired out to others while the estate is being probated.

✓ **Accounts** in the court books may be titled "First account," "Second Account," "Third and final accounting," "First and final accounting," and so on. Pay close attention to the names of the individuals who are purchasing items from the estate. Many are relatives or neighbors.

✓ **Petitions for Sale:** Executors or administrators may petition the court to sell real estate or personal property, such as slaves. Many estates that need to sell property are either going broke or cannot otherwise divide the estate among heirs easily. The next page shows an example of a slave sale as the result of a petition made to the court during probate.

Remember that the steps involved in the probate process are *determined by the law in place at that time in that State.* So don't limit yourself to just wills and inventories-look at the entire probate process. Also check original probate papers might be found in collections called "Loose Papers" or "Probate Packets" if they exist.

Note: See Christine Rose's book, "Courthouse Research for Family Historians" for more detailed information on the probate process and other courthouse records.

List of sales of negroes belonging to the Estate of the late Nathaniel Beall sold this 5th day of June 1836.

Purchasers names}	Servants names	
John S. Manakee	Bot Hanson serve 20 year	$325:00
John Gassaway	Do. Harry Do. 24 year	325:00
William S. Hays	Do. Betty Do. 19 year	250:00
D. H. Candler	Do. Rachel Do. 12 year and Jane her child to serve 25 year	250:00
		$1150:00

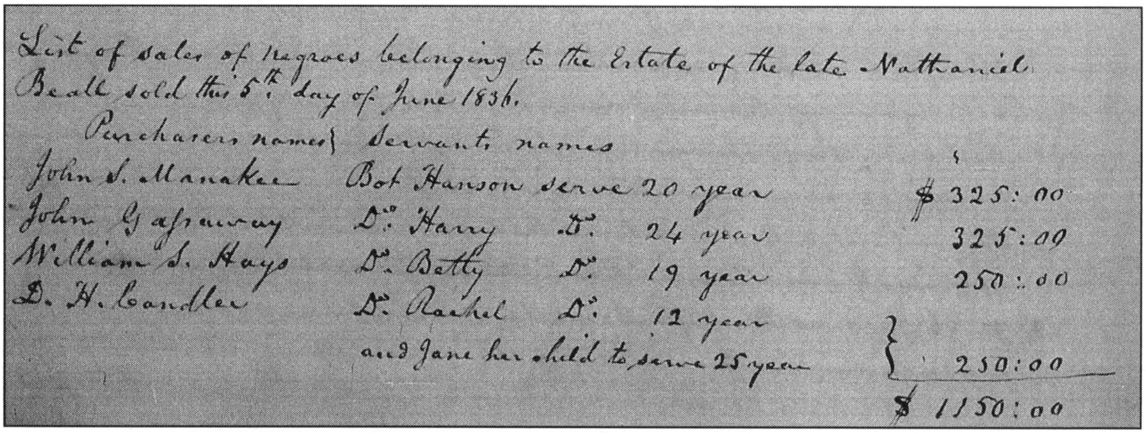

FIGURE 2, SALE OF NEGROES

24 JANUARY 2011

I've been given some gifts lately by the genealogy spirits. I think they are designed to gently ease me back into the fray after my maternity break of several months.

Last year, I spoke with a new cousin (Jahrod) and we discovered we share the same roots in Somerset County, Maryland. Recently, he shared with me the website for *The Inventory of Historic* *Properties,* which is a part of the Maryland Historical Trust. It's a beautifully designed website but the data is the true goldmine: it contains applications from historic places in Maryland and offers these files as downloadable files. I stayed up until 2:00AM, which is not advisable with a new baby! This is the homepage:

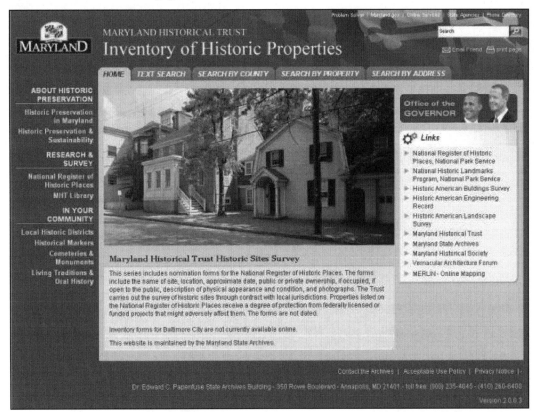

FIGURE 3, INVENTORY OF HISTORIC PROPERTIES WEBPAGE

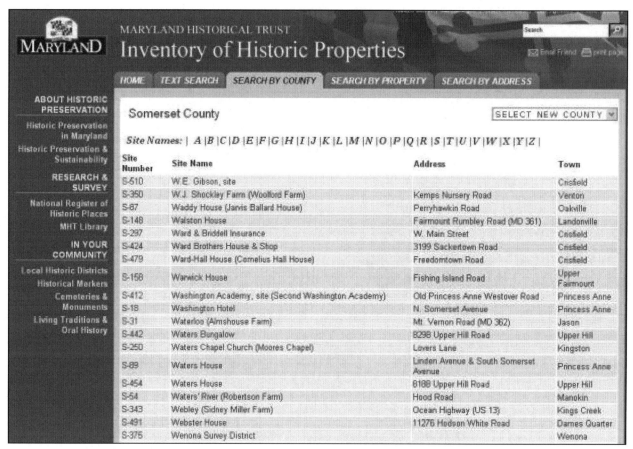

You can search by county, address, property or do a simple text search. Since I have two major ancestral counties in Maryland (Somerset and Montgomery) I was thrilled.

Many of these files have pictures of the properties, which may not be standing today. Many files also include a brief historical background, a chain of title to the property, and maps showing specific locations. The quality of each application varies; some are sparse with just a few pages, and some run more than 50 pages.

The jewel for Jahrod and I was that the entire community in Somerset County where our ancestors lived, which is called "Upper Hill", was designated a historic site. Using these files, it is possible to recreate almost the entire neighborhood from right around the turn of the century. One application mentioned one of my ancestors, the

Rev. Daniel James Waters. He apparently owned land in Somerset County when he died intestate in Delaware in 1899. The land was awarded by circuit court decree to a man named John Waters. I ordered a copy of the court case, hoping that it will illuminate the relationship between the two men.

The community of Upper Hill, in the early 19th century, was called "Freetown." This is likely a nod to the fact that the area was populated mostly by freed blacks, many of whom carried the surname Waters. The white Waters family was a large, multi-generational slaveowning family. A few family members freed slaves in the late 1790s and early 1800s, one of whom was my ancestor Joshua Waters, who was freed in 1819.

I did a short walk around the web trying to see if a resource like this exists for other states. Pennsylvania, Texas, Ohio and Arkansas are just a few of the states that seem to have similar databases online.

Here are some links you can explore at your leisure:

- ✓ The National Register for Historic Places (NRHP) has started to digitize their over 80,000 files. Their site also had a terrific link to other states' inventories that may be online.

- ✓ Virginia has a 72 page PDF file of its list of properties and the files themselves are

available to view at the Library of Virginia. For Virginia, there was a website hosted at the Virginia Department of Historic Resources.

- ✓ North Carolina only has a list of historical preservation links, but may be something hidden here. Same for South Carolina.

Every resource counts. This database gave me a significant lead on several ancestors as well as provided lots of good historical information for the entire community. Thanks cousin Jahrod!

FIGURE 5, THE RIDGE, COOKE HOME

24 JANUARY 2011

FIGURE 6, LOLA HOLT

Today I want to share the possibilities for genealogical research that are buried in theses and dissertations.

Footnotes are usually the first thing I look at when I'm reading a historical article or book. I'm looking to see if there are any resources for that subject that I have missed, and I'm also just curious about what sources the author is using. Ph. D students are master researchers. Their theses and dissertations (including those for students pursuing Master degrees) can be a boon for genealogical research.

In addition to pointing the way to hidden resources, I like the fact that many of these documents provide social context, as well as an understanding of the lives and times the ancestors lived in. After all, one of my biggest passions is trying to encourage us all to step away from digging awhile in order to actually write up a narrative on your family lineages (fully sourced of course). Once we've gotten the names/dates/places,

many of us are stuck about how to craft an interesting story. Theses and dissertations are just one more way to find that kind of information.

The Internet now provides instant access to many of these documents. In fact, many universities now mandate that these works be submitted electronically.

I especially love websites like the <u>Networked Digital Library of Theses and Dissertations</u> which provides a repository of theses from many different colleges. Other websites are PQDT Open at pqdtopen.proquest.com and Open Access at oatd.org.

I suggest searching for keywords like your county or city of interest and for African-Americans search for terms like **slave, slavery, African-American, freed blacks,** etc. Search for institutions; I've found several on the Methodist Church. Be creative. Here are some of the documents I found at the University of Maryland website:

- ✓ *"There Slavery Cannot Dwell': Agriculture and Labor in Northern Maryland, 1790-1860,"* by Max L. Grivno

- ✓ *"A Tradition of Struggle: Preserving Sites of Significance to African American History in Prince George's County, Maryland, 1969-2007,"* by Courtney Elizabeth Michael

- ✓ *"Capital Constructions: Race and the Reimagining of Washington, D.C.'s Local History in the Twentieth Century,"* by Megan Elizabeth Harris. Look at this title from <u>Pennsylvania State University</u>:

- ✓ *"On the Edge of Freedom: The Fugitive Slave Issue in South Central Pennsylvania, 1820-1870,"* by David Grant Smith

Most are available immediately as downloadable PDF documents. Also remember:

- ✓ Check elite ivy-league schools, large state schools and smaller local colleges, but don't forget Historically Black Colleges and Universities (HBCUs) which may have a higher proportion of theses and dissertations with emphasis on African-American history.

- ✓ Many websites won't allow full access to all theses and dissertations, but all should be available in hardcopy at that institution.

- ✓ Think in broad terms. We want to understand our ancestors lives from the 1800s (and before, if possible) right up until today, so a dissertation about the lives of blacks in your city in the 1960s is going to be just as meaningful from a story-telling perspective as an article about freed blacks in the 1850s in your city.

Be mindful of plagiarism and copyright issues as you utilize information found in these documents. Many dissertations are easily 500 pages, so don't plan on printing them out unless you have plenty of paper!

FIGURE 7, JULIUS ROSENWALD

The *Rosenwald Rural School Building Program* has been one of the most amazing chapters of history I have discovered while on this genealogical journey. It perfectly illustrates how the efforts of a few visionary people can have results that positively affect hundreds of thousands of lives. This story should be told in all U.S. high school history textbooks.

Julius Rosenwald (Figure 7) made a fortune as a former owner of Sears, Roebuck, and Company Inc., and in the early 1910s, he began a collaboration with Booker T. Washington at Tuskegee that eventually gave millions to building schools for black children across the South. By 1932, the "Rosenwald Fund" (as the program was called) had contributed to building almost 5,000 schools, teacher's homes and shop buildings. It's a remarkable accomplishment.

The program in most cases required the local black community to raise an amount

equal to what the Fund provided, in addition to requiring local public funding. It is no small feat and deserves amplification that largely impoverished black people of the early 20th century were committed enough to education to raise the amounts of money they did. Our ancestors knew education was the key to future success.

I believe almost all African-Americans have a relative who attended one of these schools. We as their descendants are still reaping the benefits of schools that were built when local governments didn't have the will or desire to do it themselves. Early in my research I wanted *so badly* to see these schools, most of which are no longer standing. I found photos for my Tennessee branch at the Tennessee State Library and Archives. However, resources online today have made researching this important part of our collective history just a little bit easier.

Fisk University has a wonderful database of Rosenwald schools, searchable by county and state among other variables. Many (though not all) will pull up with pictures of the school, information about the funding and what year the school was built. South Carolina and North Carolina also both have Rosenwald school databases.

The National Trust for Historic Preservation awarded Rosenwald schools its *National Treasure status* in 2011, which means these buildings have been identified as a critical part of the story of who we are as Americans. The Trust resources have coalesced around trying to save 100 of these schools. The Trust also offers a very nice downloadable PDF pamphlet about their Rosenwald program.

There is good historical information at their website including background on its origins at Tuskegee, building architectural plans, case studies and links to resources on how to get involved to save a school. The beautifully restored Highland School was preserved in Prince George's County, Maryland, which is where I grew up.

The Jackson-Davis Collection at the University of Virginia has long been one of my favorite websites. It contains over 6000 photographs of African-American schools, many of which were Rosenwald Schools. I particularly like this website because it shows teachers and students in addition to the buildings.

We should include this information when writing up our family histories. These issues are still relevant, as we continue to struggle with educating our poorest. I recommend two books about Rosenwald:

✓ *"Julius Rosenwald: the Man Who Built Sears, Roebuck and Advanced the Cause of Black Education in the South,"* by Peter Ascoli.

✓ *"You Need a Schoolhouse: Booker T. Washington, Julius Rosenwald and the Building of Schools for the Segregated South,"* by Stephanie Deutsch

FIGURE 8, CHESTER COUNTY TRAINING SCHOOL

I remain convinced that there are thousands of documents that contain information on our enslaved ancestors that aren't being widely used. Sometimes it's because we can't easily get access to the information, and sometimes it's because the information itself is difficult to peruse and understand (<u>court records</u> and <u>freedmen's bureau records</u> come to mind).

One of the best sources on enslaved families can be found within the manuscripts that are stored in research libraries, historical societies, state archives and local libraries. Families donated personal papers, letters, business papers, receipts, diaries, account books and many other types of documentation and ephemera. Many of these families owned slaves, and historians have long relied on these sources to understand "the political,

economic and cultural life of the South as a whole." These Plantation Records (as they are collectively called) give readers an inside view of plantation life.

I want to highlight the collection known as the *Records of Antebellum Southern Plantations*. This historic effort to compile a selection of plantation records from all over the country in one microfilm publication was undertaken by Kenneth Stampp, one of our foremost slavery historians. Though its original purpose was more scholarly in nature, this microfilm series is a boon to genealogists. Still, you'll have to locate a major research library in your area to find one that houses this enormous microfilm collection.

FIGURE 9, VICKSBURG, MS

Slave Birth Record, 1807–1861, Russell (now Lee) County, Alabama

Description of the Collection

This collection comprises five pages from a medical manual entitled, "A Compendium of the Theory and Practice of Midwifery Containing Practical Instructions for the Management of Women During Pregnancy, in Labour, and in Child-bed," by Samuel Bard, 1817. Records of slave births and deaths from 1807 to 1861 are written in the margins. The pages appear to be from a volume belonging to P. Philips and read by A. C. Phillips. No location is indicated.

N.B. A related collection among the holdings of the Southern Historical Collection is the Tillman and Norwood Ledgers. That collection, which follows this collection in this edition concerns Russell (now Lee) County, Alabama, physicians, in which entries for Mrs. P. Phillips and for the estate of P. Phillips appear, and in which some of the names of slaves in this collection are duplicated.

The records in this collection were created in "Series" from A-N, with each letter representing a particular archives or library. For example, Series D covers the Maryland Historical Society while Series E covers the University of Virginia Library. Start your research in these records by utilizing the detailed Series Guides that are available online .The University of Virginia Library website hosts an online guide that includes links to each microfilm roll.   I have scoured every one for data not just about my specific family, and any others living in the same county. Finding information about what was happening in the county is a great way to add more detail to any narrative about your genealogical research. Also, most of the guides contain brief biographies about the particular individual or family that is covered.

As an example(Figure 10), there is a "Slave Birth Record, 1801-1861" contained within the Thompson Family Papers, and housed at the Southern Historical Collection at the University of North Carolina, Chapel Hill. The detail in Series J, Part 7 relates

to the State of Alabama, and it says that this Slave Birth Record covers Russell County, Alabama (now Lee).

Author Jean L. Cooper created a printed index to this material titled *"Index to Records to Ante-bellum Southern Plantations: Locations, Plantations, Surnames and Collections," (2nd. ed)*. Her printed index is expensive, but a quick search at Worldcat (add your zip code) will tell you what nearby library has it.

This book is an invaluable resource because Ms. Cooper created it for family historians and the way that we research. The records in the Series Guides are listed in each Table of Contents by family surname, for example, *"The Robert King Carter Papers."* It is not always obvious what county that family lived in until you get down to the Reel Index sections. Ms. Cooper's book makes it easier to find records by county.

Of course, most historical societies, archives or research libraries have their own guides to their manuscript collections. The Virginia Historical Society has a voluminous 200+-page guide specifically created for African-American-related manuscripts and the Tennessee State Library and Archives has a similar Guide available.

Another way to use these Series Guides is as pointers. I can use Series D, and run right up the road to the Maryland Historical Society. Even though they have their own manuscript guides, it may or may not provide the detail about slaves and slaveowning families that I need.

Certainly, these records are not exhaustive, and the records chosen for inclusion are often the larger, more prominent citizens and families—as the Introduction indicates, "mostly from the larger tobacco, cotton, sugar and rice plantations." However, some smaller estate papers are represented in the collection.

My readers, how many of you have been successful finding information about your ancestors within these records? Please tell me where you viewed your collection and how you were able to find it. If you haven't used these records yet, I hope this post will encourage you to take a look.

I was at the <u>Reginald Lewis Museum in Baltimore</u> recently, presenting my first lecture on using land records effectively. Because it's a museum dedicated to African-American history, I wanted to focus not just on genealogical use of the records, but also the unique history between land and African-Americans and its relevance to our family histories.

I begin my lecture with the failure of <u>Reconstruction</u> to provide former enslaved laborers with land ownership, dooming many to decades of sharecropping and tenant farming. In spite of that, by 1910, African-Americans had amassed 15 million acres of land, a figure that astonishes me still today. <u>The great migration north,</u> along with continual discrimination in agricultural subsidies and loans have decimated those numbers today. President <u>Obama signed the law</u> in December 2010 that fully funded the <u>landmark Pigman vs. Glickman case,</u> which we should all know about. The Department of Agriculture admitted to historical discrimination, and black farmerswere awarded billions in the largest class action settlement ever.

As an agricultural nation, land was central to our experience. It's why enslaved people were brought here to begin with. In some of my slavery studies, I have found that some former slaves felt emotionally tied to the land they worked and some determined that it was as much theirs as their owners.

For former slaves, to even approach independence after emancipation was a difficult prospect. It wasn't enough to just buy the land: who was going to provide seed & fertilizer? How were you going to get animals and tools? Like everywhere else, the South moved on credit. Never mind the racism and violence and illiteracy on top of all that.

I think about my 3rd great grandfather, John W. Holt, who was the largest black landowner in Hardin County, TN in the early 20th century. His first land purchase was only six years out of slavery. Also, consider that many families who later migrated North lost family land to taxes or sale because they were simply not as connected to the land as their parents.

One thing that struck me was <u>the use of partition sales </u>by speculators and developers to wrest control of inherited land from heirs. The majority of black farmers who owned land did not leave wills, so their land was inherited by spouses and children according to the laws of the state. All someone had to do was buy <u>one share</u> from one of those parties, and they could *force a sale* of all the land.

I don't think I'll ever think about land the same way again. **Take a look at some of the links below, but more importantly, think about the history of land as it relates to your family. In** what ways did it make or break their fortunes? Did some choose to stay on land owned by previous owners? For how long? Which lines were able to eventually purchase land? Did anyone end up losing land? Do you have pictures of the old homeplaces that no longer stand? What crop did your ancestors grow?

✓ <u>Black Farmers Win Settlement; Congress passes legislation</u>

✓ <u>Black Farmers Losing Land</u>

✓ <u>Homecoming: Black Farming and Land loss</u>

✓ <u>Timeline of Black Land Loss</u>

✓ <u>A Vanishing Breed, Black Farm Owners in the South, 1651-1982</u>

Tell me, what stories about your ancestors relationship to the land have you discovered in your research? If you haven't searched the records fully yet, what has been your biggest obstacle? Figure 11 below shows my 2nd great-grandfather Doss Harbour in Tennessee, standing with his crops

In <u>Part 2 of this blog post</u>, I'll provide some basic definitions and examples of deed types.

FIGURE 11, DOSS HARBOUR IN HIS CROPS

9 JANUARY 2012

FIGURE 12, NELLA HAYES

The picture above is my great-grandmother's first cousin Nella Hayes posing in a crop, umbrella laid to the side. This is part 2 of a series of posts I'm doing on land records. You can read the first post if you missed it before.

My goals here are to outline general types of deeds, show examples, and point the way to some other resources for further study. There are lots of other sites and other blog posts that cover deeds more extensively, but my current interest in them made them a "must-post" anyway.

Land records contain dense and wordy legal language that can be difficult to weed through. I'm going to cut out a lot of the legalese in the examples and just quote the relevant language. Land records are rich records and the patient researcher can be rewarded with information not available anywhere else.

A few basic concepts first: a deed is defined *as a formal document that transfers property from one party to another*. The seller is referred to as the "grantor" and the buyer is referred to as the "grantee." Most land records are indexed by both grantor and grantee and when researching, you'll need to check both indexes. Deeds typically contain:

- ✓ the names of the buyer and seller

- ✓ the date the deed was written and recorded

- ✓ the consideration (fee) paid

- ✓ a description of the land, possibly adjacent landowners and/or purchase history

- ✓ signature or mark of the grantor and if required, any witnesses, acknowledgement or proof, and

- ✓ a dower release (if required)

Some of the most common types of deeds are:

1. Warranty deeds: This deed warrants (i.e., guarantees) clear title to the land. Look for words/phrases like *warrant title* or *guarantee title*.
Most deeds will be of this type.

"This indenture made…between A. Gammel and A.S. Brooks…hath sold…all that parcel or tract of land…and the said A Gammel…will warrant and forever defend the right and title thereof."

Try to find the first deed where your ancestor purchased land; it may be purchased from their former slaveowner. Always trace the origins of the land your family owned. If not former slaveowners, you may find other relatives.

2. Deed of Trust (or Trust Deeds): This type of deed secures a debt. Property is usually transferred to a third party called a *trustee*. If the debt is not repaid, then the property can be sold. Sharecropping agreements can be found in these types of deeds. They also provide a close look of what life was like for the average farmer. Look for phrases referring to a *trustee or third party*, and also discussion of a *debt* and when it is to be repaid (Note: Church deeds were often sold by and to the *trustees* of the church. This is a different use of the word). For many of my Tennessee sharecropping ancestors, the debt was repaid in November, which was when the crop was harvested and sold:

"We, George Holt and wife Leonia…do hereby transfer to Douglas Shull, trustee, the following tracts of land…we are indebted to J.S. Dickey…for $275.40 due November 12, 1928…and this conveyance is made to secure the payment."

FIGURE 13, GEORGE AND LEONIA HOLT

Most deeds also name the property being used as security, and you may find descriptions of animals and crops, as shown here:

"I am indebted to KW Welsh by note $106.10 made June 1, 1909 and J.W. Holt as security, also for merchandise and supplies furnished…I have sold unto trustee JH Joyce, 7 acres of cotton and 1 mare named Roxie."

3. Deed of Gift: This deed conveys property often without a normal purchase price. You'll often find fathers and sometimes mothers conveying land and/or slaves as gifts to their children using this instrument. You will often find the phrase *"for love and affection I do hereby give…"* or similar language.

"Alex English Sr…for love and affection have this day given to my son John's oldest son James, one negro man named Peter, to his second son, Alexander, I give one negro woman named Betsey…"

These are very important for researching enslaved ancestors and finding this kind of deed (or a bill of sale) could be the key to breaking down a brick wall. Look for some of the phrases I mentioned above when unsure about what type of deed you are viewing.

Like anything else, the more deeds you examine, the easier it will become to recognize the language Using a deed extract form when you're just beginning will be of a great help. I also recommend transcribing deeds that are especially relevant to your family.

In these posts, I'm only scratching at the surface on land records. The premier book that every genealogist should have is *"Locating Your Roots: Discover Your Ancestors Using Land Records"* by Patricia Law Hatcher. The National Genealogical Society also offers a wonderful course on land records. Also, remember that there will be differences that exist depending on the state involved and the law in place at that time.

When you're ready, wade into the rich waters of your ancestor's land records. They hold a world of possibilities.

FIGURE 14, PEANUT PATCH, 1900-1905

15 MAY 2011

Recently, I solved a genealogical mystery that I'd had for many, many years. The solution utilized many tools, but newspapers and the ease with which we can now search some of them deserves the biggest praise for solving the puzzle. My friend Tim Pinnick who offers a class in newspapers at Family Tree University and a free e-newsletter, has been preaching and teaching about black newspapers for years. He has even written a book on the topic, which I would highly recommend for your personal library.

The puzzle starts in Hardin County, Tennessee, where one branch of my research is centered. The 1880 census showed two black men named "James Holt" both around the same age. One was living with his brother, one was newly married and living with his wife. For years I thought they were the same man, and the census taker had made an error. To further confuse the issue—both James married two sisters.

One "James Holt" stayed in Hardin County, and I eventually found the 2nd James living in Obion County, Tennessee in 1900. I was pretty sure it was the same man (his kids had odd names like Phlenarie, Ferdinand & Ollie), but he now had a different wife named Alora. At least the presence of her brother in the household tells me the wife's probably maiden name. But James Holt's occupation was listed as a "minister." And that's when the trail ran cold—again. I realized he was probably moving a lot with the church. Shown below is the 1900 entry for him and his family. (Don't you just HATE when the census taker uses initials?)

If I was ever going to solve this mystery, I was going to have dig a little deeper and get a little creative with my analysis.

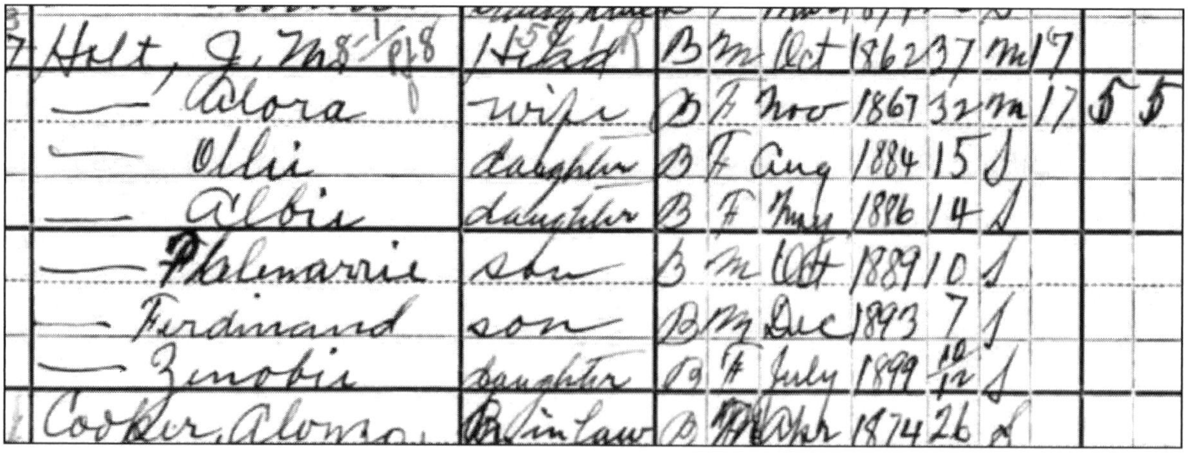

Holt, J. M.	Head	B	M	Oct	1862	37	M	17			
— Alora	wife	B	F	Nov	1867	32	M	17	5	5
— Ollie	daughter	B	F	Aug	1884	15	S			
— Albie	daughter	B	F	May	1886	14	S			
— Phlenarrie	son	B	M	Oct	1889	10	S			
— Ferdinand	son	B	M	Dec	1893	7	S			
— Zenobie	daughter	B	F	July	1899	10/12	S			
Cooker, Alonzo	Br in law	B	M	Apr	1874	26	S			

FIGURE 15, 1900 OBION CTY, TN

A relative had saved oral history, pictures & other memorabilia with regard to this family. One photo (below) showed a well-dressed black couple labeled "Mr. and Mrs. George and Ollie Knucklis."

A postcard was addressed to "Aunt Nannie" and was signed *Ollie*. Perhaps this Ollie was the daughter of James Holt listed in the 1900 census? That hunch

FIGURE 16, MR. AND MRS. KNUCKLIS

turned out to be right. The photographer's studio from the picture was located in Chattanooga, Tennessee (you do search photos for that

information, right?). I found the couple living there in 1930 and 1910. However, in 1920 I found them in Indianapolis, Indiana (Ollie was misspelled as Dollie). Hmm.

I used the Indiana records at Familysearch(marriage and death) to look for Ollie or any of her siblings in Indianapolis & I found a Ferdinand Holt who looked promising as her brother. Searching the *Indianapolis Star* newspaper on Ancestry turned up a court case between George & Ollie Knucklis. The name "James Holt" was listed next to Ollie's name—could that be her father?

A census search found a James Holt, born in TN, living in Indianapolis in 1920 and 1930 but the wife was different (Harriet) and this man was a lawyer.

Well, this couldn't be the man I was looking for—he was a minister after all…right? I decided to search the black newspaper *The Indianapolis Freeman* which is archived on GenealogyBank.com. Searching "James Holt" (and "J.M. Holt") turned up numerous articles on this popular, politically active man.

I learned that he had been a prominent minister—*then he attended law school at and became a lawyer*! His profile was found in the paper:

JAMES M. HOLT, D. D., LL. D.

The Freeman is glad to present to its readers prominent men of the race, especially those who are self-made. We present here the likeness of Mr. Holt, a graduate of the Normal Industrial and Theological Institute of Dixon, Tenn., and also a graduate of the Central Law School of Louisville. For seventeen years Mr. Holt was pastor of some of the leading churches in Tennessee, Kentucky and Florida. In 1906 he was admitted to practice law, and in all of his nearly seven years' experience he only lost two cases in Kentucky and none in Indiana. Mr. Holt is now enjoying a lucrative practice, with a finely appointed suite of offices at 318 Indiana avenue. He is a substantial citizen, owning his own home on Camp street, and is backed by a healthy bank account.

FIGURE 17, JAMES HOLT ARTICLE

Articles described his ministry in other states including his stint in Jacksonville, Florida which is where he was found in the 1910 census. Later, I was able to find his marriage records and also his death certificate. The case was conclusive when his son Ferdinand noted his parents in his marriage record as "**James Holt and Mintha Barnes.**"

I also discovered that apparent 3rd wife Harriet (her first name) and 2nd wife "Alora"(her middle name) were the same person. I simply could not have solved this mystery five years ago.

The story the newspapers outlined about James Holt (Figure 17)—who was the son of an enslaved woman named Judah Holt—was fascinating. Without the *Indianapolis Freemen* newspaper, I don't believe I would have realized this was the same person; there were just too many differences. This case is a great example of how to correlate evidence from different types of records. It also illustrates, once agin, the power of analyzing the evidence we have gathered to tell us the real story.

This is another chapter I have reclaimed from the annals of our precious and often-times lost history. I hope to find some of his descendants one day, and to share his humble Tennessee roots.

FIGURE 18, ALABAMA CONVICTS

Some months ago, an interesting record set appeared on Ancestry: *"Alabama Convict Records, 1886-1952."* I lecture on court records, so these types of records always get extra attention from me. If you watched *"Slavery By Another Name"* which aired on PBS in February, these type of records will come to mind. If you missed it, you can watch the whole episode online, but I highly recommend reading the book itself, which is much richer. I blogged about this book sometime ago. Also, Bill Moyer's interview with the author is quite good.

Alabama was one of the worst perpetrators of convict leasing in the decades after the Civil War. Related to this was also the peonage practices that took hold in the south. All of this was centered around keeping a ready labor force to work the land, if not in slavery, then something *like* slavery. Now that I've traced my Fendricks and Springer ancestors back to Alabama, I'm on the hunt for other records in that state to review.

Ancestry includes some information on the source: these records are state records, ledgers that were filled in by hand with varying degrees of detail, of both whites and blacks. The records detail charges of larceny, grand larceny, assault, attempted murder and a few first degree murders. There were men convicted for running distilleries, which must have been rampant. Most of the ones I viewed were eventually released. The prisoners are also referenced as living in camps."

If you have Alabama ancestors that "disappeared" for a few years, check out these records. There is also a related database on Ancestry called *"Alabama Death Record of State Convicts, 1843-1951."* I haven't found anyone in my family (thankfully), but these were still a valuable part of the social history and landscape of our ancestor's lives.

I've been exploring Southern Claims Commission records and rediscovering how fabulous they are. Fold3 has put up many of the original images. The Southern Claims Commission was established in 1871 to receive and adjudicate claims by loyal Southerners for reimbursement of property damaged or taken (animals, food, housing, etc.) by Union soldiers. The Commission received over 20,000 claims applications. Claims fell into three categories: approved, barred, or disallowed.

The claimant had to present proof of ownership of the items and also had to prove their loyalty to the Union cause. This proof was often in the form of depositions from eyewitnesses. Those depositions include, many times, depositions from former slaves. Content of the files vary. Some have just a few pages and some run 20 or more pages. Here are a few interesting examples of what can be found in these records.

Cupid Hamilton
Beaufort County, SC

My name is Cupid Hamilton. [I am] 45 years old. I live at William Heyward's plantation near Pocotaligo, Beaufort County, SC. I have lived here all my life…I was the slave of Mr. William Heyward. I became free at the end of the war. I carry on farming—plant principally rice. I owned the property charged in this claim before the war. I got the property after Hilton Head was taken by the United States. My master Mr. William Heyward gave me two horses and a wagon to make a living for myself and

family as he could not afford us any longer…He is dead now. He died in Charleston of yellow fever in 1872. His grandson Mr. William Hankel was not present when he gave me the horses and the wagon, but he lives on the plantation now and I believe knows all about it…I was the waiting man of Mr. Wm Heyward

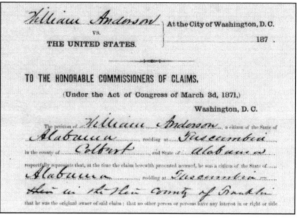

FIGURE 19, CLAIM FORM

on the plantation.. [and he gave] Moses Washington, the driver, also one horse and gave Alleck Wilson [?] the head carpenter one horse also for faithful services.

Coleman Sherrod
Lawrence County, AL

At the beginning of the war, I was a slave and belonged to Mrs. Tabitha Sherrod. *I became free when Lincoln set us free by his Proclamation.* I worked on the farm after I became free. I rented land from Mr. Shackelford. I bought the mule when I was slave. My owner allowed me to own a horse. Mr. Sam Shackelford allowed me the privilege to own a mule. I was with him under his control. I bought the mule from Mr. Gallahan a year or two before the war commenced. I gave him $164 or $165. Mr. Jack Harris and Oakley Bynum went with me to see me righted in the trade…they saw me pay the money. It passed through their hands to him, Mr. Gallahan. I got the money by trading. I was [a] carriage driver and [had] the privilege of trading.I paid $60 in gold which I got from Mr. John Houston for a horse I sold him….

Primus Everett
Halifax County, VA

During the war, I was the slave of William Everett, but lived with Mr. Alex Thompson to whom my wife belonged about seven miles east of the courthouse. For more than six months in the last year of the war I went off to North Carolina for fear of being put to work on the breastworks–I went of my own accord. I said nothing about it to my master…I was always a Union man. *My simple reason was that I wanted to be free all the time and I believed the Yankees would set us free,* and they

did….I was hired to Mr. Thompson–he allowed me to keep all I could make over a certain fixed sum. I bought the horse with the proceeds of my own labor and raised the bacon.

Look at all the details about the lives of enslaved people and their owners that can be gathered from just these few examples. I think one of the most prevalent myths is this image of slavery as a monolithic enterprise. Slavery was differed depending on time and place. Be sure to search all 3 categories–allowed, disallowed, and barred files. Also, Ancestry.com has an index to these records on their website, while Fold3 has many of the original files.

You may not find your ancestor, but you may find other slaves owned by the same person. Research claims by others in the county, especially neighbors. All this can give you important social history for a hard-to-research time period.

FIGURE 20, FORMER SLAVE HENRY ROBINSON

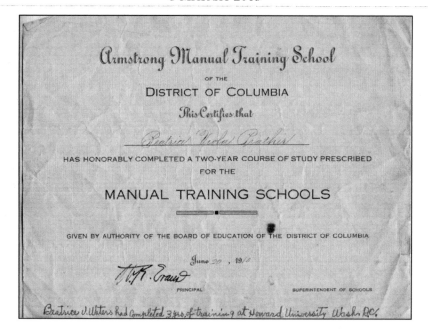

FIGURE 21, ARMSTRONG DEGREE

Artifacts, are items passed down or stored within our families. Pictures are one kind, and family bibles, military papers, marriage and birth certificates, letters, deeds, and even quilts are things commonly found within families. I wanted to post some of the items I have gathered and show how each has expanded my understanding of my family and their communities. The artifacts tell their own stories, and we should use them in the writing of our histories alongside our other records. In many ways these are even more valuable because often they can't be found in public records or archives.

I have a silver necklace my paternal grandmother gave me when I was about 16. It belonged to her mother Beatrice Prather and came with a note that reminded me that it *was pure silver, and don't be too proud when you wear it."* Beatrice was a very well-educated woman to have been a "negro" and born in Maryland in 1888. Her diploma from <u>Armstrong Manual Training School</u> in Washington D.C. is shown above. The Armstrong school tells part of the story of black life in Washington D.C. at the turn of the century. The school is on the National Register of Historic Places and graduated luminaries like Duke Ellington and Billy Eckstine.

FIGURE 22, LUTHER HOLT

In Ohio, my maternal grandfather Luther Holt (above) was a proud Union member and served briefly as leader. I have his lifetime membership card from Local 801 International Union of Electrical, Radio and Machine Workers. Richard Nixon congratulated him on his role in a crucial Union vote.

I recently found a collection of the records of this local union at Wright State University along with a very brief history of the group. My grandfather was a Frigidaire worker, a laborer who later rose to the skilled position of a welder. When he retired he became more involved with the work of the union in Dayton, Ohio. He even served a short time as President of the Union. I thought about granddaddy a lot during the Presidential elections and the debates about collective bargaining. My granddad also was an accomplished carpenter and woodworker who could build or fix *anything*. He made treasured hand-carved gifts for his three daughters and his only granddaughter at the time (me). The image on the next page shows the beautiful sewing box he made for my mom:

The descendants of a cousin, George W. Holt, saved terrific artifacts. These include receipts for paying the poll tax, one of the most pervasive tools in the Southern States used to disenfranchise black.

He also had a copy of a 1953 membership card in the Prince Hall Grand Lodge, (Figure 24) popular in the black community especially in the 20th century.

There was also a receipt indicating payment of tuition for his five children. These records speak to a family (the Holts) that was well-educated, landowning and upwardly mobile. That isn't the case for all my lines; everyone is different.

But they are *all interesting*. I didn't realize how many terrific artifacts I've collected over the years regarding my family. In the meantime, tell me about what artifacts you've found and what did they tell you about your family's life?

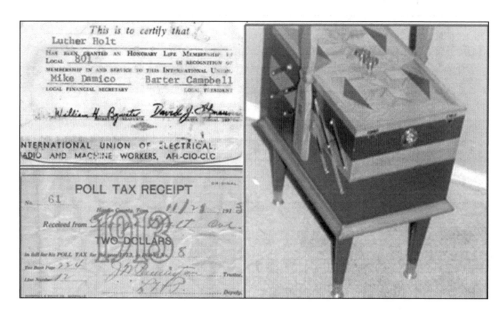

FIGURE 23, ARTIFACTS 1

FIGURE 24, ARTIFACTS 2

I have talked here before about the benefit of researching court records when you get to the intermediate/advanced stage of your research. Divorces, of course, are found within court records. I was amazed when I first started looking at these at how many people actually got divorced. There were more divorces than I would have thought, even back in the 1800s. Divorces can give you unique insight into people and their circumstances. Unfortunately for obvious reasons information about divorces are often not passed down in families. Divorced women, I have found, often represented themselves as "widowed" on documents like the census.

I recently found one for a relative, John Prather. It included his original date of marriage, which I had been unable to find. Sadly, it appears his wife left him. By the time the case was brought, John testified he hadn't seen his wife in three years, and the court eventually granted him a divorce. Part of his testimony is shown at right.

I have a lecture on court records where I talk about my Tennessee ancestor Joseph Harbour. He only appeared on one census record (1880) but when I looked at court records, it looked like he was committing a crime every other week! If I had not looked at court records, much of his life would have remained a mystery to me.

Q: How long have you lived in this county?
A: All my life, except a few months in D.C. about 1912.
Q: You know the defendant Elizabeth Malinda Prather?
A: Yes sir, she is my wife.
Q: When did you and said defendant marry? State where and by whom?
A: About November 29, 1910 here in Rockville by Rev. Holt, minister of AME Zion church here.
Q: Where did you and the defendant then go to live?
A: To her home, near Laytonsville, in this county.
Q: How long did you and she live together in this county as man and wife?
A: About 18 months, when we went to Washington D.C. and lived there several months in the winter of 1911-1912.
Q: Are you and the defendant living together now as man and wife?
A: No, sir. I have not seen her since but once in March 1912 when she was at her mother's house, about 5 miles from where I was then living.
Q: Did she leave you or did you leave her?
A: She left me.
Q: How did she come to leave you?
A: She was running around with other men.

The image below is from a divorce in Hardin County, Tennessee between Felix and Matilda Harbour in 1899. It mentions their place and date of marriage which is valuable information because it occurred in another state and county. This case is sad in that Matilda details physical abuse.

To locate divorce records, find out the name of the court for your research state that handled divorces (considered civil cases). Then you can assess what documents survive. They come in numerous formats, such as dockets, case files and minutes. Most court minutes have indexes in the front of individual volumes. Try to find the case number; that should lead you to the actual case files, if they survive. The case files are the original loose pieces of paper associated with the case. These may include the original bill of complaint and answer, testimony and depositions, letters from lawyers and the final divorce decree among other things. They may be located at the local courthouse or archives, or they may be stored at the state archives. Also, the Family History Library has court records and some case files microfilmed; so check for your county/state.

Although an unpleasant subject, to leave no stone unturned, we've got to look for divorces within our families. They may surprise you.

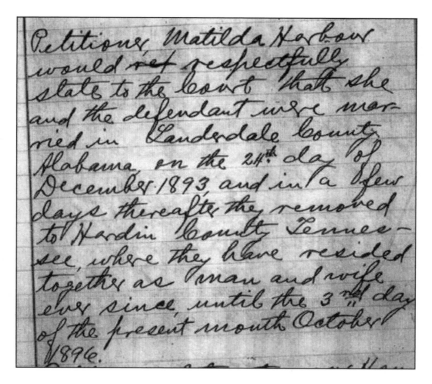

FIGURE 25, HARBOUR DIVORCE

Claire Prechtel-Kluskens gave a lecture on Agriculture Extension Service Reports last year at the NARA Fair. I had never heard of these records before, but after her lecture, I knew I needed to look at them. The photo at center is an ancestor, Hardy Holt with his John Deere in 1963.

Starting around the turn of the century, the Dept. of Agriculture decided to provide a service to "extend" the latest agricultural techniques and processes to farmers. Each state had a state agent and every county (over time) had their own Extension Service Agent. For women of the county, they provided Home Demonstration Agents. They worked with women on everything from canning fruits and vegetables to interior design. "Negro" agents were appointed for some counties to do "Negro Work"; they provided the same services to black farmers, just with less money and fewer resources.

I have always been fascinated with land ownership and farming for our ancestors.

Many of our ancestors lived in rural areas, which can cause a dearth in information vs. those living in large cities. When combined with information from the agricultural censuses and local land records, the extension service records can offer us a closer peek into those rural lives.

The Extension Service Agents helped farmers set up cooperatives and demonstration farms to show the effects of certain fertilizers and farming practices. They distributed information on various crops, seeds, and practices to promote healthy farm animals. The records are grouped into "Annual Reports" and are organized with the Annual Report for the State first, followed by the counties in alphabetical order. What is available for each state varies, but the years covered for each can be found here. NGS Magazine published an article on these records by Mrs. Prechtel-Kluskens and in 1996, Prologue Magazine published another article about these records for Arkansas. Both are excellent.

FIGURE 26, HARDY HOLT

Additionally, many of the agents sent in pictures from county fairs, pictures of farms and crops and animals and living rooms, and every now and then, an individual picture with a name attached. They started Corn Clubs and Canning Clubs. Some sent scrapbooks and newspaper clippings. There are numerous references by the agents about individuals in the county. Here are some examples of interesting items I found:

From the 1911 TN State Report:

"The cotton boll weevil has not made its appearance in Tennessee. The army worm and boll worm did damage. Army worms appeared in late August and stopped whole fields of cotton…we fought to get [farmers to] properly space the cotton and corn. We have induced several farms to do special seed selection."

A 1915 Report said this:

"Tobacco is not grown in this county…The decline in crimson clover acreage was due to high priced seed, and the tangling of crops by wind storm,

which prevented seeding…Soybeans are an entirely new crop to this county… Potatoes are only grown for home consumption. Due to blight, orchard trees did practically no good during the past year… There is no dairy interest or farmers in this county. ..The county was practically free from ticks when demonstration work began…"

Keeping farm animals healthy was always a concern:

"Personally, I have vaccinated no hogs for cholera, but influenced farmers to take up the practice and to consult their local veterinarian…One instance I especially recall was…from Dr. O. Whitlow, of Savannah. He is a cooperator, and he reported that he had 40 or 50 hogs and that he had lost two from cholera. I insisted that he wire at once for serum, which he did, [he] administered the treatment, and only lost 5 hogs."

This is good information to flesh out those write-ups on your family. Check out these unique records if you can; they are located at the National Archives building in College Park, Maryland.

FIGURE 27, ANNIE ORR FARMING

FIGURE 28, EX-SLAVE CLAIMS POSTER

Recently, Ancestry somewhat quietly rolled out the Ex-Slave Pension database which contains Correspondence and Case Files from the National Archives. I was excited because I had always wanted to take a look at these records but hadn't gotten around to it yet over the years. I first heard about these records when Mary Frances Berry wrote a book about them in 2006, called *"My Face is Black Is True: Callie House and the Struggle for Ex-Slave Reparations."*

In short, it is about the movement to secure pensions from the U.S. government for former slaves. The idea for the movement was inspired by the military pensions that were provided to Civil War soldiers; some thought that the government should play a role in also helping ex-slaves, many of whom were old, infirm and destitute. Several groups

were formed that functioned somewhat like other beneficent groups of the era, with their primary purpose being to lobby and influence the government to provide pensions for ex-slaves. The National Archives published an excellent article on these records in their Prologue magazine. Walter Hill at NARA also wrote a story here.

This is one of those topics that wasn't covered in school. We have to educate ourselves, our children and others about these less-known but important chapters in our nation's history..

The records at Ancestry provide a brief historical background, but I encourage those interested to read Ms. Berry's book on the subject. For a small number of very lucky people, you might uncover the name of that elusive slaveowner.

The government received thousands of letters about the pensions. The letter below is from William Brent of Henderson, Kentucky and names his slaveowner.

Isaiah Dickerson was one of the prominent officers who was targeted by the federal government and eventually tried, along with fellow officer Callie House (they are both shown on the flier in Figure 28).

The pensions never happened—former slaves got nothing for their lifetimes of service. However, if you were one of Mr. Dickerson's descendants, wouldn't this deposition be wonderful? Take a look at these records and see what you uncover.

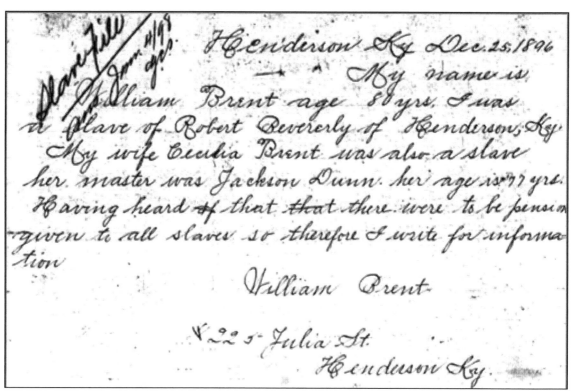

FIGURE 29, WILLIAM BRENT LETTER

In re

The National Ex-slave. M. R. B and P. Association of the United States of America

On this 12th day of May, 1902, at Washington, D.C., before me, A.W. Rooms, a special examiner of the Bureau of Pensions, personally appeared Isaiah H. Dickerson, who, being by me first duly sworn to answer trully all interrogatories propounded to him during this special investigation in the matter of J. C. Bunn, alleged impostor, deposes and says:

Q. What is your full name? A. Isaiah H. Dickerson.

Q. How old a man are you? A. I am 44.

Q. Did you ever go by any other name? A. I did go by another name when I was a small boy. That name was Isaiah Murphy.

Q. Where were you born? A. I was born in Rutherford County, Tenn.

Q. Have you any relatives? A. Yes, sir; brothers and sisters.

Q. What are the names of your brothers? A. One named Ben Murphy - he lives at Fosteyville, Tenn. One is named Robert Murphy - he lives at Hardy Station, Miss.

Q. Name your sisters? A. Jane Lindsey; husband James Lindsey - Chattanooga, Tenn. Other sister is Betty Williams , Raisport, Miss; her husband is dead.

Q. Are you a married man? A. Yes, sir.

Q. Where is your wife? A. She is not with me at present. I last saw her at Union City, Tenn.

Q. What is her first name? A. Her first name was Nannie Bridges.

Q. Are you divorced from her? A. No, sir; simply separated.

Q. When did you see her last? A. Must be near three years since I have seen her.

FIGURE 30, ISAIAH DICKERSON

Church has long been a large part of African-American culture and history. I have had some wonderful bible discoveries in the past year.

I want to share them with you along with some thoughts on evaluating them. We evaluate sources by the following criteria:

- Is it an Original or Derivative Source?

- Does it provide Primary or Secondary Information?

- Is it Direct or Indirect Evidence?

The indefatigable Elizabeth Shown Mills has written extensively on this. I also suggest the book *"Genealogical Proof Standard"* by Christine Rose. I'm going to only talk about the first two in the interest of keeping this post long and not really long.;)

An *Original Source* is the very first—the *original*—record of an event. For example, a birth certicate is the first official record of a birth (or maybe the family bible), a death certificate is the first official record of a death, and so on. A *Derivative Source* has to copy its information from an original source Examples of derivative sources would be book of transcribed vital records or an index to marriage records on Ancestry.com..

This difference is important because *derivatives always introduce the opportunity for errors.* Typically, an original source is regarded as more reliable than a derivative

source, but not always. Also know that original sources may not be accurate. The person who provided the information may have gotten it wrong or even purposely provided in accurate information. A good example of that might be a marriage record where one provides an older age, in order to meet the requirements for marriage.

The second criteria- *Primary or Secondary Information* refer to the quality of the information. Primary information was made by someone in a position to know firsthand usually at or near the time of the event OR made in writing by an officer charged by law, canon or bylaws with creating an accurate record. An example of this would be a court clerk who records county marriages, or a mother who records her children's births into the family bible.

Anything else is secondary information. Typically, primary information is regarded as more reliable than secondary information.

One of our goals in genealogy should always be to locate as many Original Sources and as much Primary Information as possible. A death certificate is an original source, but it can contain both primary (the death dates) and secondary information (the birth dates).

When evaluating evidence, you want to ask yourself WHO wrote this, WHEN and WHY.

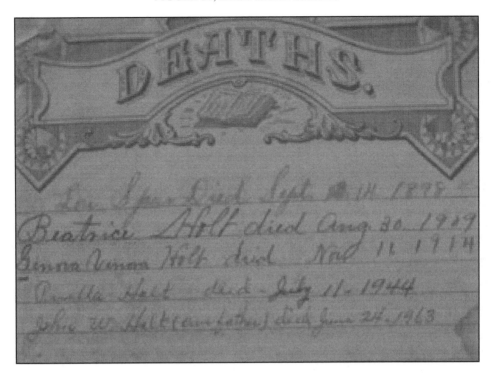

The image above is a page of deaths from a Holt family bible that my newfound cousin Lester Holt shared, which appears to have belonged to his grandfather Samuel.

If you've never taken pictures of a Bible that is falling apart, it works really well. <u>But, be sure to take a picture of the publishing page so you can know what year the Bible was published.</u> If the Bible was published in 1948 and it contained entries from the 1920's, those obviously *could not have been recorded at or near the time they happened*, which would affect how you evaluate the data.

I am fairly sure *who* wrote this:-either the mother Ila Holt or the father Samuel Holt. I know *why*—to record the important dates in their family. But, the copyright/publishing page was disintegrated or missing, so I have no idea what year this bible was published.

This means I don't know *when* the dates were recorded. I don't know if the dates included were copied as they occurred or in bulk entries after the fact— that is an important distinction.

This bible is an original source. But primary information ideally should be written down as the events are occurring or a short time afterwards by someone with firsthand knowledge.

These entries were likely made by parents who were noting births and deaths of their children, which they would have known firsthand.

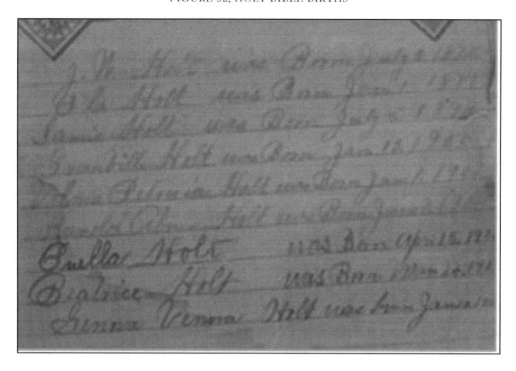

Now notice above a page of births from the same bible. The first six entries appear to have been entered all at once don't they? They probably were.

But, again, because the information in this bible does not conflict with any other data I have on these individuals, and because of the likelihood that a parent recorded it, I can reasonably conclude these dates are accurate. This gives you a sense of all the things you have to think about.

Another family bible (left) was shared with me by my cousin Laverne Prather. It belonged to her mother Sarah. Sarah diligently copied almost everything for all of her kids, and all of the events

happened after the 1903 copyright date. This gives me an added level of assurance.

These Bibles were both filled with information I didn't have. If you come across a family Bible, digitize it so that the data can survive the physical book which is bound to be fragile.

As you can see here, the pictures turn out pretty well. Just don't forget to copy the copyright page so you can properly source the information!

Note: Genealogical standards have been updated since this post! The criteria has been expanded. See the book, "Genealogy Standards" guide by NGS, 2014.

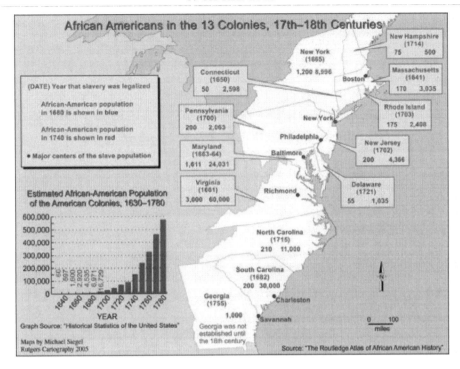

FIGURE 33, AA IN 13 COLONIES

My maternal ancestors lived in Tennessee. How the state was formed was illustrative of the westward movement of white conquerors, as they removed the indigenous populations (notice I do not say white *settlers*). The Schomburg Migrations website is one of the most detailed, fact filled and visually beautifully websites online today and I encourage you to take some time examining it. Here are some of the items I really like.

The map above shows the African-American enslaved population in the original 13 colonies and its rapid change in the late 17th and early 18th century. Not surprisingly, Virginia and Maryland had the highest numbers of slaves.

As this conquest was occurring, slaveowners were bringing slaves they already owned and buying slaves via the domestic slave trade. With the official close of the African Slave Trade in 1808, enslaved families were torn apart as they were sold to the deep south and west, many of these people who were by now 2nd or 3rd generation American born.

Another map shows relative numbers– notice that states in green had net gains while states in red had net losses in numbers of slaves (go to the website to see the map in full color).

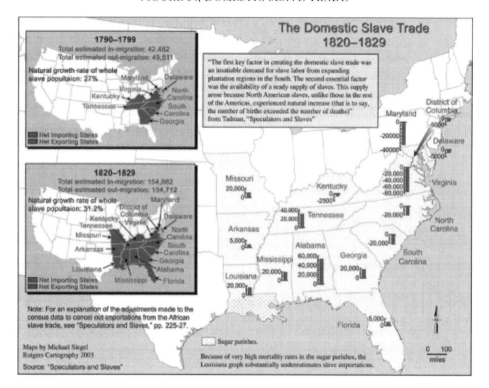

We often focus on the southern states with regard to slavery and forget that it was in the Chesapeake that slavery was born in North America. It was old and tired there by the time of the rise of cotton and the newfound wealth that would later happen in the deeper South in the mid-1800s.

Other maps of interest include the one shown at right illustrating concentrations of freed blacks. There are large numbers of freed blacks in New Orleans, Charleston and also clustered in North Carolina, Boston and Philadelphia. Though they did not have to endure beatings and sales, most freed blacks suffered restrictions on their basic rights and were seen as an anomaly and a threat to the system of race-based slavery in the U.S. Many freed blacks had spouses and children who were enslaved, and many worked alongside slaves.

FIGURE 35, FREED BLACKS

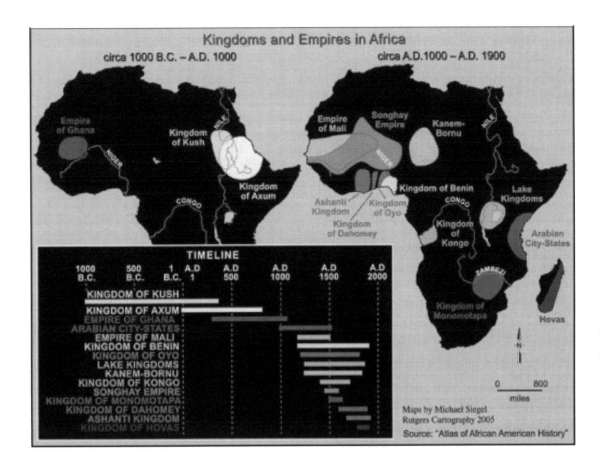

And I really enjoyed seeing the map above of African Kingdoms. It reminds us that African History (and yes, it was recorded) dates back more than 3,000 years and certainly did not begin in Virginia.

Lately, I've been reading books by Frank Snowden, Cheikh Anta Diop, John Henrik Clarke and others to gain a better understanding of Mother Africa herself and the African Diaspora. There are wonderful lectures on You Tube by these and other African scholars.

I think it's important for us as we research our ancestors, to **place them into the broader context of these migratory experiences.** As I mentioned above, many of our ancestors who in 1870 were living in Alabama, Georgia, Louisiana, South Carolina, etc. had their roots in Virginia or Maryland—we can see that by the 1870 census birthdates. We should also understand that the Domestic Slave Trade, which transported over 1 million people deeper south and west wrought devastating separation of families, even more than the African Slave Trade had a century earlier. That means that many of our southern ancestors who ended up in Georgia and Alabama and Mississippi were born in Maryland, Virginia and North Carolina.

Check out the website and (if you can pull yourself away) let me know what you think.

Note: This post was originally about the Chicago Defender, but I changed the subject newspaper to avoid any copyright concerns.

I have posted before about the value of newspapers and the goldmine of information they have. I think newspapers, like Freedmen's Bureau records, are an important resource that haven't yet been made widely accessible and easy to research. However, great strides have been made by various providers, including the Library of Congress, digitizing newspapers.

They are still time-consuming to search, but I suppose anything worthwhile in genealogy is that way. I was even surprised to recently discover that the local newspaper of Montgomery County, MD where my ancestors lived was digitized by the Maryland State Archives. That paper has been on my "to do" list for years. It was not a black newspaper, but I still want to search it for relevant news of the times.

The Chicago Defender was founded in 1905 by Robert Abbott and eventually became the largest and most popular black-owned newspaper in the nation. The paper was famous for detailing lynchings and racial oppression, for referring to blacks as "The Race" and for putting "(white)" after white people's names in the paper the same way white newspapers did to black people. The Defender was a driving force in convincing Southern blacks to migrate to the North. More than 100,000 black people came to Chicago alone between 1916-1918.

Another powerhouse black newspaper, was the *Baltimore Afro-American* newspaper, started in 1892 by former slave John Murphy. Other papers that reached large audiences were the Pittsburgh Courier and the Indianapolis Freeman.

What I didn't realize until I read my friend Tim Pinnick's book ("Finding and Using African-American Newspapers) was that the small, rural towns many of our ancestors migrated from were often covered in these large urban papers.

People wanted news from their towns. Tim's book explains that the papers hired correspondents from those small towns who submitted news. There might be a page called "Tennessee News," and a paragraph for each TN community. The same for North Carolina and other states.

I have recently been searching the *Baltimore Afro-American* newspaper through Proquest Historical Newspapers which is available from my local library (and searched from home!). The tidbits of local history gleaned from these papers is priceless. In addition to marriages, births and deaths, they talked about who was sick, who was moving, black schools and politics, benevolent and lodge organizations, teachers and farmers and of course, black churches and ministers.

REV. WATERS TAKES A BRIDE

Chestertown. Md.. March 5.—
Miss Beatrice V. Prather, one of
the teachers of the public school
here and Rev. Daniel G. Waters of
Stillpond, were quietly married at
Stillpond Saturday at 12 M. Dr.
W. F. Cotton performed the ceremony. Miss Prather comes from
an old distinguished family of
Gaithersburg, Md.,and is a graduate of the Armstrong Manual
Training School at Washington and
Cheney Industrial Institute
Cheney, Pa. She has taught in
Chestertown two years and endear
ed herself to parent and pupil.
Rev. Waters hails from the Eastern
Shore of Maryland, and belongs to
the popular line of Waters. He is
a preacher of wonderful power and
though a young man has easily
forced his way to the front. He
is finishing his first year as pastor
of Mt. Zion, Stillpond, and has
broken all previous records of the
church spiritually and financially.
The church has been repaired,
claims all raised including pastors
support, before Christmas. After
the ceremony toothsome repast was
prepared for them at the parsonage
by the ladies.

FIGURE 37, WATERS MARRIAGE

The articles are filled with visits from out of town relatives and it looked to me like they spent all their free time socializing! I had to remember these were times when television, radios and cars were fairly new.

I really enjoy sort of "taking a walk" into the past through the articles; reading the ads for what kinds of things are on sale and getting a sense of what was important to the community.

The articles often mention the town where people were visiting from, and often named parents, siblings, in-laws, etc. The 1914 article shown at left provided terrific detail on my great-grandparent's marriage.

It's important to mention that most newspapers are not online and are not digitized, but there were in fact hundreds of black newspapers.

It makes me so proud to know that people started these newspapers because they knew what happened in their lives was meaningful and important, even if the larger newspapers did not. It is testament to what people were able to accomplish with very few resources, but with determination and courage.

Note: Tim Pinnickhas a truly wonderful lecture on researching black newspapers on YouTube. It'll teach you everything you need to know to get started. Also, I highly recommend the blog The Ancestor Hunt, at http://www.theancesorhunt.com /blog.

FIGURE 38, CO. E, 4TH USCT

Civil War Pensions remain, in my opinion, the crown jewel of genealogy research for those with enslaved ancestors. The first-hand descriptions of their lives given in the testimonies, both before, during and after the war still take my breath away. I do not have any direct ancestors who served (although I have some collateral), but I have researched soldiers in the counties where my ancestors lived and gotten a rich sense of the times that no other source could come close to describing.

African-Americans from the start of the war clamored to join the Union effort, but were initially repelled in their efforts by the Lincoln administration. Not until the Emancipation Proclamation of January 1863 did formal recruitment of enslaved people begin in earnest. Even that went slowly, as many black men reacted to the blatant discrimination of having unequal pay and no black commissioned officers (a few were later commissioned). Frederick Douglass gave impassioned speeches for black men to join the war effort and demonstrate their manhood; two of his own sons would join. In the end, almost 200,000 black men fought in the Union Army & Navy.

The large numbers of escaping slaves, combined with the Confederate use of slave labor forced Lincoln to eventually have to deal with the issue. However, Lincoln's Republican Party had the destruction of slavery firmly in their party's platform from at least the 1840s on. Lincoln's rejection of the Crittenden Compromise before the war even started, as well as his push to get slave states to abolish slavery on their own are just two of many points that place Lincoln on firm ground in his commitment to ending slavery. He was not, as often portrayed, a reluctant emancipator. James Oakes has written a marvelous book called *"Freedom National: The Destruction of Slavery in the United States, 1861-1865"* if you are interested in reading more about the topic. Ironically, it was the South's secession that removed the legal protection the states had for slavery; the war opened the doors for Lincoln to use "military necessity" as a way to destroy slavery in the states.

FIGURE 39, CHRISTIAN FLEETWOOD

Lincoln had initially tried to avoid freeing and enlisting slaves because he was very afraid that the four border states (Maryland, Delaware, Kentucky & Missouri), all slave states, would abandon the Union and join the Confederate war effort. It's a nod to his political prowess that he read the national mood correctly. He famously stated, "I think to lose Kentucky is nearly the same as to lose the whole game. Kentucky gone, we cannot hold Missouri, nor, as I think, Maryland. These all against us, and the job on our hands is too large for us." I love that quote. Lincoln certainly had a way with words. It goes without saying that as the war pressed on, Lincoln realized the strategic value that slaves brought, not just as soldiers but also because of the crucial intelligence they provided to his officers. It also removed them from use by the Confederate Army.

To research civil war soldiers, the National Archives is ground zero, and the various types of Civil War records they hold can be found here. Of course, the massive Civil War Soldiers and Sailors Database lists soldier's names and regiment(s), but I absolutely recommend reading the three post series on Randy's Genea-Musings blog . My friend Michael Hait also wrote a great post on researching black soldiers. And there is an excellent article on Black Sailors at Prologue Magazine.

I also like the website by Dr. Bronson which explains and describes the various Pension Acts that were passed and the provisions of those Acts.

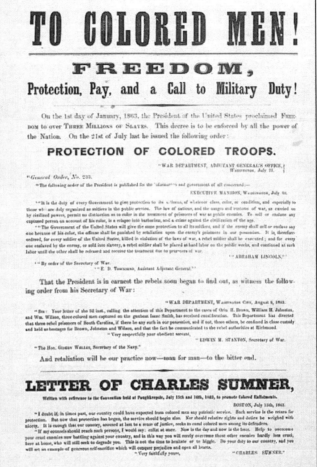

FIGURE 40, RECRUITING BROADSIDE

In the next few posts, I'll discuss some of the amazing stories found in Civil War pension files. Today's excerpts are from the pension file of Cap Ross, a former slave living in Colbert County, Alabama who served in the 101st USCT. Various parts of his deposition give us his background: "I belonged to Walter Sherrod during slavery time… I was born near Courtland in Lawrence County, Alabama and was a farm laborer. I enlisted at Huntsville and the regiment stayed there about 2 weeks then went to Nashville where we were mustered in. Our company was guarding the railroad at Scottsboro when we had that little fight…I was slightly wounded in my right foot in a scrimmage…the ball did not go deep and our doctor…took his knife and picked the ball out."

Cap added this: "I was first a Private and promoted to Corporal while in Huntsville and then to a Sergeant for a short time…they reduced me down to Corporal again because I left camp without permission and went to the correll where there were a lot of women."

Cap, like many former slaves, had no idea exactly how old he was, or exactly when he married, or even exactly the birthdates and ages of his children.

FIGURE 41, BLACK SOLDIER & FAMILY

Most slaves tried to approximate these dates, but since attaining a pension depended on these very things, a large number of black soldiers ended up with a Special Investigator whose role it was to do just that—to investigate the claim. Another common problem with former slaves was their enlistment under one name, and them going by a different surname later.

The investigators had to ferret out false claims (which were rampant). When Cap Ross was asked why he enlisted under the surname "Ross" and not "Sherrod," his answer was telling: "I enlisted under Ross because that was my father's name.

I am generally called Cap Sherrod but I was married under Cap Ross and have voted under the name Ross. A good many people call me Sherrod because I belonged to Sherrod but I calls myself Cap Ross."

That last statement is powerful; it illustrates the desire of former slaves to exercise their newfound rights as freedmen to identify themselves as they pleased.

The constant movement of former slaves to find work, often sharecropping or living as tenant farmers is illustrated in Cap's description of postwar life:

"I was in Mississippi a part of 1892 then I came back here [Alabama] and stayed the balance of that year [1892] and next. I went to Louisiana and lived on Dr. Gillespie's plantation near Panola and lived there 3 years then came back here and lived on the Felton place 1 year with Mr. Stretcher, with Jim Houston 1 year, with Captain Kelly 1 year on the Abernathy place, and 2 years with Albert Eggleston last year."

Cap Ross' Special Investigator, held the same prejudices of most whites of his era. He referred to Cap Ross as "an ignorant negro," but also wrote that Cap had had a "stroke in about July 1902 entirely disabling his right side and he can't get about at all…he owns absolutely nothing and without question suffers for want of food."

When interviewing Cap Ross' wife Edith about their childrens' birthdates, the Special Investigator noted that "she does not seem to be smart enough to know that the younger they are, the more pension they would get." Notwithstanding his prejudices, the Special Investigator did ultimately assist in Cap and later his wife getting a pension.

Research these records for enslaved people from your research county *whether you have an ancestor who served or not.* They provide invaluable insight into the lives of slaves.

FIGURE 42, BLACK TEAMSTERS

In Part 1 of this post, we began looking at examples of the riches that can be found in civil war pension records. We'll continue in this post looking at how the lives of enslaved people are described in these unique records, both before, during and after the war. The name of the ever-important slave-owner is often mentioned. The role of the slave neighborhood is illustrated, as slaves often married slaves living nearby and had neighboring slaves testify on their behalf.

Slave marriages were not legally recognized but were often encouraged by masters. Names of "colored" preachers and church affiliations when given in pensions can provide us with new research avenues. Previous marriages and children hint at the instability caused by slavery.

Rachel Orr testified in 1899 that she and Edward Orr were "...married long years before the war by Ephraim Brighton, a colored preacher, in my master William Orr's house in Danville, Alabama."

George Simpson's widow Annie testified that she "was a slave of the Rev. Anspach who lived at West River, Anne Arundel County, Maryland. [Her husband] George was a slave of John Gale on an adjoining plantation and [they were] married by the Rev. in her cabin on his plantation, him reading the service from a book."

Martha Harbour was married to Isaac Harbour "...in the month of March 1848 by Matthew Broyles, a colored Methodist preacher, at the plantation of his late master Elisha Harbour in slave form by his consent."

Caroline Allen, of Memphis, testified that Betty and Jacob Bradley were married "...in my room in this city. Brother Martin, our pastor in charge of Collins Chapel performed the ceremony." Betty herself added that she "had a husband in slave time in South Carolina. I belonged to Mr. Lewis M. Ayre near Sumpterville, SC and Elias Phoenix, a neighbor's servant was my husband according to slave custom. We had been married only about a year when I was sold to a nigger trader and brought to West Tennessee and bought by Mr. Thomas Kilpatrick (now dead) of Tipton County, TN. I was then given by him to his daughter Mrs. Cornelia Nelson and went to live with her in Bartlett Station."

We can get valuable dates of death from the pension files, sometimes before deaths were recorded by the state. Often there are receipts or letters indicating the death of the pension applicant as well, and sometimes the wife or child of the soldier. Applicants submitted these papers in the hopes of getting reimbursed for the costs. Deaths after the war sometimes reflect the dangerous nature of the jobs freedmen had available to them.

Eliza King testified that her father Edward Hays "…died in July 1879, the year following the yellow fever epidemic."

Eleanor Waters, of Baltimore, testified that her husband William Harrison Waters died "…on or about the 4th day of April 1882 while working on a steam mill at the corner of Pratt & Fremont, the boiler of which exploded killing him instantly."

In Caroline Allen's deposition of Jacob Bradley's death she says, "I know he died because I sat up with the corpse and went with it to the graveyard and saw his body put in the ground.

I think he had consumption, because he had an awful bad cough." Caroline gave the date more specifically as occurring "during the yellow fever epidemic about 1878."

W.C. Woods, the white clerk of the county court, testified that soldier Isaac Bailey "…lived near [me] on a small tract of land he purchased [from me]. [I] furnished Isaac means during his last illness. The servants on my place all quit work to attend the burial of Isaac."

Many pension files include death certificates, marriage licenses and bible pages. The death certificate shown below for Henry Brown of Kentucky, says, " an old slave no one knows exact age:"

Note: The blog contains a 3rd post on this topic with more examples.

FIGURE 43, BROWN DEATH CERT

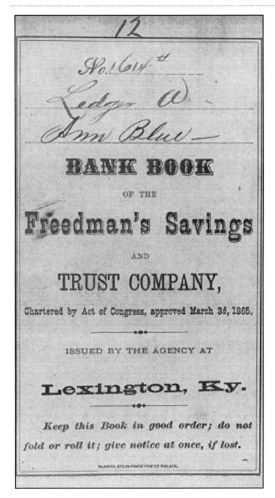

FIGURE 44, BANK BOOK COVER

The records of the Freedman's Savings and Trust Company, better known as the Freedman's Bank, are among the most popular records for those researching African-American roots. Established by Congress in 1865, the Bank was primarily designed to be for the use of the nation's recently freed four and a half million former slaves. It eventually grew to have 37 branches in 17 states and Washington, D.C. While a laudable effort, the Bank closed its doors after nine years due mainly to corruption and fraud.

The National Archives in College Park, MD, holds the original bank records, and their website contains both a general information sheet as well as a lengthier detailed article about their use. The records are comprised of three general types: Administrative Records, Registers of Signatures of Depositors, and Indexes to Deposit Ledgers. The Registers of Signatures of Depositors are the richest collection and have been digitized.

The availability of these records on Ancestry and Heritage Quest has greatly increased the ease of searching these records. However, most researchers type their ancestor's names into the search template, and, finding nothing, move on to other records. I'd like to suggest taking a closer look at these records, whether a direct ancestor has been located or not. I think a lot of us are missing a potential match in this important set of records.

First, after searching for known ancestors (using different spellings), try putting just the county and state in the "birth location" search template; leave everything else blank. What will happen is that you will pull up people born in your target county who were probably sold as slaves and ended up living somewhere else.

FIGURE 45, BECKETT/CALHUME CARDS

Above in Card #1, Lloyd Beckett is currently living in St. Thomas Parish, SC, but was born in Montgomery County, MD.

Other than that specific location search, I want to suggest *browsing* these records instead. Find the bank branch nearest your ancestors. If you have relatives in northern Georgia, browse the Atlanta and August branches. If you have relatives anywhere in Maryland, check the D.C. branch and the Baltimore branch.

Browsing Freedman's Bank records offers a glimpse into the difficult-to-reconstruct life of the enslaved. It also offers insight into other aspects of slavery, like the domestic slave trade and kinship networks. The cards also potentially name other relatives.

The content of the cards was largely determined by the person who was filling out the information. Some bank employees wrote sparse information about the depositor, while others filled every space on the card with as much detail as possible. Some of the cards connect us to the names of family members lost to slavery.

In all cases, substantial information can be drawn about *not just individuals but the entire community*. In the next few posts, I want to highlight information in Freedman's Bank records, and encourage everyone to look again by browsing this valuable resource.

Let's look at examples of enslaved people who were sold away from their families, probably during the Domestic Slave Trade. That trade transported over one million slaves from the North and Upper South to the newly opened Deep South and western territories and states. Leah Calhome of Alabama (previous page), says she was born on the "Easter[n] Shore of Maryland" and laments the siblings she left there.

Henry Somers in Memphis, Tenn. (below) was born in Rappahannock, VA, and "sold from Va when 5 years old." He was "raised" in Fayette County, KY, then "was sold from Fayette Cty to Smith [Cty] when his youngest child was a baby". His card also tells us his wife Rhody died in

Kentucky "5 years before the war". He could not recall the names of his siblings. Also, his parents full names are given– "Phil Shirley" and "Matilda Stencil." Henry is not using either of those surnames.

Mingo Steele of Huntsville, AL was born in North Carolina (Figure 57). He was "removed to Huntsville" when a boy. His mother was "taken away from Huntsville" when he was a child and he had "not heard from her since". He had "not heard from his father since he left North Carolina." His parents names are given as "Ned" and "Hannah":

FIGURE 46, SOMERS/STEELE CARDS

Miller Featherston of Alabama was "took to Miss. ten years ago" and had made her way back to Alabama (Figure 58). She "was parted from her husband ten years ago."

Samuel Edwards of Alabama (Figure 58) was born in West Virginia, and "had 4 brothers but don't know if any of them are living and one sister but can't say whether she is living or not." He names his parents as "Bailey" and "Rachel." He also served as a soldier in the war in the 42nd Regiment, Company E. The bank was originally started for the use the use of soldiers, so you'll find them well represented.

These cards, and thousands of other original sources, illustrate the tragic consequences and frequency of slave sales, especially the fact that young children were often separated from parents at very young ages.

Note: Two follow-up posts on this topic are available on the blog.

JULY 28, 2014

FIGURE 48, PEAKER PETITION

I have posted before about the need to search every step in the probate process, as opposed to just viewing the will and the inventory. One of the first steps in the probate process is that an individual petitions the court for authority to probate the estate. Depending upon whether the deceased had a will, the petitioner will ask the court for either "Letters Testamentary" or in cases where there was no will, "Letters of Administration." The petitioner is usually a family member, but could also be a creditor of the estate. Sometimes these records are mixed in with other probate records, but they can

be also found bound together in a single book. The value of these records is that they *usually state the existing heirs at law of the deceased individual.* Remember: besides the fact that most people did not create a will, when they did, they did not have to name all of their heirs. From my previous post, Leanna Peaker's petition in Kent County, MD (above) named all her deceased husband's siblings; it was especially valuable because it provided his sister's married names and also the cities where they lived.

FIGURE 49, CRAYCROFT PETITION

Earlier versions of this kind of document were handwritten into the court records, while later in time we start to see pre-printed forms. Shown above is Cora Craycroft's 1944 petition in Macon, Illinois.

As with anything, sometimes the hardest part is finding these documents. If they survive, they can be buried inside books called "Administrations," "Probate Records," or any of the other myriad titles given by the various states. They may be loose papers, not bound in a book at all. Also, and this is key: you don't want the **actual** "Letters of Testamentary" or "Letters of Administration." Those documents are the RESULT of the *Petition* that was filed. Those are very often kept

and very often bound together, but they will NOT include heirs.

This is a rarely mentioned record set, so try to search for these where they exist. I've been pretty successful finding them in many cases. This is just one more record that can unlock the doors to the secrets of our ancestors. If we are thorough in our research, we can often reap the reward.

Note: I also really enjoyed the post below from Matt's Genealogy Blog that "walks" through a set of probate papers, including a petition for administration:

http://matthewkmiller.blogspot.com/2014/06/doran-probate-and-property-records-in.html

FIGURE 50, EX-SLAVE VOTING

The challenge to find the last slaveowner for those researching African-American ancestry can be daunting. We need to trace our lines back as close to emancipation as possible and the 1870 population census is a critical document. If you can't locate your ancestors in 1870, you can use other documents to record their presence in a particular time and place. Voter registration records are a widely untapped source, and although incomplete, they should always be searched.

For my friend Carole Hyman, we traced her ancestor Arden Hyman to the 1880 census in Edgecombe County, NC, but could not find him in 1870. However, searching the 1867 voter registration record for Edgecombe County showed us that our Arden was in fact there. It also showed another Hyman—Zion Hyman—noted as living in the same district. Finding those names together uncovered an important link to Arden's enslaved roots. That "Zion" was likely Arden's father Zion who was named in one of Arden's marriage records.

By the end of 1866, Radical Republicans were in control of Congress and wanted to ensure some civil rights for blacks in the defeated south, but the new President Andrew Johnson (who came to power after Lincoln's assassination) wanted to deal with the South more leniently, and firmly believed in white supremacist notions of black people's inferiority. He also wanted little to no retribution for former Confederates, and this clash set the scenes for what would be very familiar to most of us watching Congress today.

Important bills were often vetoed by Johnson (like the Freedmen's Bureau bill and the Civil Rights bill); but Radical Republicans enabled them to override those vetoes. Finally, the Congress decided to impeach Johnson and just get him out of the picture altogether. The House voted to impeach Johnson, but it lost in the Senate by one vote. Congress passed the Civil Rights Act of 1866 (and later 1875) and four Military Reconstruction Acts. This divided the South into 5 Military districts each run by a Union General. Neither Tennessee nor Maryland went through Congressional Reconstruction and had rejoined the Union prior to enactment of these laws.

As a condition of re-joining the Union, the Southern States were required to ratify the 14th amendment, conferring citizenship to former slaves, and after 1870, also the 15th amendment. Reconstruction, the name given to the period between the end of the war in 1865 and about 1877 (although the opinion varies) was a volatile time period that I've discussed here before.

Take a walk around the web and read about the battles between the Congress and President Johnson. There's much more to the story that deserves a post of its own.

The brief taste of voting rights for blacks, which beginning in 1870 ushered in the first wave of blacks to serve in the U.S. Congress would not last. Violence and intimidation increased against blacks who dared to vote. The Ku Klux Klan was born. After 1877, Democrats start to take back state legislatures and later re-wrote their constitutions with laws designed to circumvent the 15th amendment, but designed to strip blacks of the right to vote using grandfather clauses, poll taxes, literacy tests and other tactics. Supreme Court cases like Plessy v. Ferguson in 1896 and the 1883 cases that overturned the Civil Rights Acts of 1875 all closed the door to black voting and led to the resurgence of white dominance over black lives. By 1900, southern blacks were almost completely wiped out of the electorate.

Some of the voting records created during Reconstruction survive. Here are some of the voting records that I am aware of for the various states (not available for all counties):

Tennessee, 1891 Voter's List.
Available on Ancestry, gives election district, name, sometimes race, and age.

Alabama: 1867 Voter Registration.
searchable online at the AL archives. Some of these include length of time in county. Also check Alabama's 1866 state census.

http://www.archives.alabama.gov/voterreg/index.cfm

South Carolina: 1867-68 Voter Registrations available for some counties, Clarendon County is online (also check South Carolina's 1869 state census and militia enrollment)

Georgia: 1867-69 Returns of Qualified Voters and Reconstruction Oath Books. Available on Ancestry.

Texas: 1867-1869 Voter Registration Lists. These record how long a person has been in that county, in the state and what state they migrated from. Available on Ancestry. Someone posted a PDF of these records for Tyler County.

North Carolina: A book entitled "North Carolina Extant Voter Registrations of 1867," by Frances Wynne lists records from 17 counties. This book is what led me to the Hyman discovery. Originals should be at the State Archives in Raleigh.

Louisiana: I found references to records available for New Orleans, but no info for other counties in Louisiana.

Virginia: Search by county in the Library of Virginia's catalog, and search under the heading "Election Records." Some records exist, although many seem to be from the 1880s, 1890s.

Arkansas: The Arkansas Genealogical Society offers a "1867 Voter's List" on CD for 25 counties.

Related to these records are the Poll Taxes that many southern states created to try to disenfranchise blacks. If they are available, they are also an excellent source to locate your ancestor between censuses. In one of my research counties, Hardin County, Tennessee, the tax collector wrote valuable notes beside each name like "dead," too old," or "gone." These were found in county court minutes.

Some of these counties have voter registers through the 1880s and 1890s—be sure to check those as well. In various state archives, voting records are often "hiding" under Secretary of State Records. Also, check the online Family History Catalog for your state and county. They have a category called "Voting Registers." Please post a comment if you can add to the list above or have a story about how a voting record helped your research.

.

Note: Some of the richest records relating to the violence during Reconstruction, other than those found in Freedmens Bureau records, are the Congressional hearings that took place on the Ku Klux Klan.

FIGURE 51, TEACHING FREEDMEN

Freedmen's Bureau records are a good example of "needle in a haystack" records. They are voluminous and rich, but they are notoriously difficult to approach. Most aren't indexed; heck, most aren't even paginated. That they were governed by the military, and arranged as such— is itself another obstacle. The National Archives won a congressional grant years ago to microfilm the originals, but they remain an uphill challenge to navigate.

I don't recommend these records for beginners. They are an important resource, but you will be forced to read each page. I offer here a process for those of you just starting to tiptoe into the murky waters of Freedmen's Bureau records.

1. Start with the Field Office records. You can download a copy of the descriptive pamphlet for your state on the lower right hand column of this page at the National Archives website. Each pamphlet will tell you what each roll of film contains. They also contain excellent condensed histories about the Freedmen's Bureau operations in that state and pointers to other books and articles. Pay attention to the descriptions of what happened in the state. This period of time is important in the lives of our ancestors, so mine this resource for as much information as possible.

2. Next, **print a copy of a map of your research state**—find one that has major cities identified.

Using the Freedmen's Bureau pamphlet for your state, find the sections that identify the locations of the field offices. On the map you printed out, mark each city that had a field office. The tricky part is finding cities that no longer exist today; Google searches will help you find them. Also, realize that the closest Bureau office for your ancestor might be in the next state over if they lived close to the border.

3. Now you can start with the place where your ancestor lived, **and start looking at records in the nearest field offices.** For example, my ancestors lived in Lawrence and Colbert Counties, Alabama—so I have focused first on field office records in Tuscumbia, Athens and Huntsville.

4. Every field office has a different set of records. **Use the descriptive pamphlet and read the descriptions of the type of records available for those field offices.** Look first for any labor contracts. You can see examples of these at the wonderful Freedmen's Bureau online website. Former slaves often had contracts with former slaveowners. Beware that there was no "standard" contract; some were clear and detailed, identifying entire families, while others looked more like chickenscratch on a napkin.

5. After labor contracts, check to see if there are any local marriage records. Many of these records were sent to the headquarters office in Washington D.C. Read this article to find out more details about Freedmen's Bureau marriages. Many of those are starting to pop up online, like this one website indexing marriages in Mississippi.

6. Next, check letters received and/or sent, but only *if* they are indexed by surname. If not, save them for last and instead look for any rations or provisions issued to freedmen or transportation or employment records. Then look for any hospital records, school records, or census records taken. For example, the Huntsville, Alabama office took a census of blacks in 1865 that includes name, age, sex, former residence and former slaveowner of each person!

7. Next, **look through the murders and outrages.** Reading about the horror the freedmen experienced humbles me. Some areas were worse than others, but imagine having to feel the wrath of the white Southerners who had just lost the war. There are so many stories of freedmen who were killed, whipped, raped, those who worked until the crop came in and then were kicked off the farm without pay, those who couldn't get their children out of the slaveowner's house, etc.. An Arkansas record described a slave having his penis cut off by the owner—in fact he made another slave do it! These records detail the widespread violence in the South. The Freedmen's Bureau tried to adjudicate crimes, but many were committed by "persons unknown."

The Freedmen's Bureau online site contains some examples of outrages. Combined with the zeal of the freedmen for education and land ownership, and *I believe these former slaves were truly the Greatest Generation.*

8. If your head is not spinning yet and your eyes are not yet crossed, **go back and search more diligently through the letters.** You can also check the general or special orders, and/ or circulars.

9. Once you've thoroughly examined the relevant field office records, **check any records of interest at the State Level** (i.e., the Office of the Assistant Commissioners, Quartermaster, Disbursement Officer, etc.), **and check the Commissioner records at the**

Washington Headquarters for that state.

Its an exercise in extreme patience. Some of these records are starting to get transcribed and indexed, I do believe Virginia has their entire series of <u>Freedmen's Bureau Field Office records online at Ancestry</u>. Also, read the terrific Powerpoint slides that David Paterson created about searching through Freedmen's Bureau records. You can download them at Afrigeneas, under the heading "Resource Guides."

Also, read some of the monthly reports about the local area from the local military leadership. Although they are summaries and often don't name individuals, they are invaluable in helping us better understand the climate in terms of education, violence, and finding work.

Update: Familysearch.org has digitized several sets of Bureau Field Office Records, so check there! Also, a terrific new website has just come online called "Mapping the Freedmen's Bureau," which makes many of the steps above easier— including mapping field office sites and links to those all important descriptive pamphlets. It is packed with even more tips and guides as well.

http://mappingthefreedmensbureau.com

FIGURE 52, FAMILY IN SAVANNAH, GA

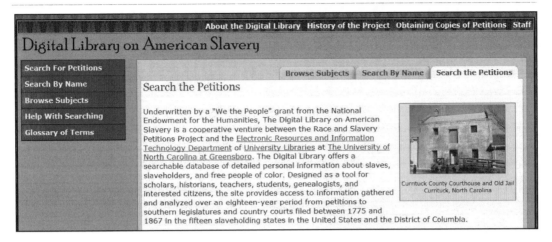

FIGURE 53, DIGITAL SLAVERY WEBSITE

The Digital Library on American Slavery is a web-based database that contains 18 years worth of research from the Race and Slavery Petitions Project. The site has been updated and anyone researching slaves and slavery should take some time to utilize this wonderful resource. Here's a little background from the website:

"The Digital Library on American Slavery offers data on race and slavery extracted from eighteenth and nineteenth-century documents and processed over a period of eighteen years. The Digital Library contains detailed information on about 150,000 individuals, including slaves, free people of color, and whites. These data have been painstakingly extracted from 2,975 legislative petitions and 14,512 county court petitions, and from a wide range of related documents, including wills, inventories, deeds, bills of sale, depositions, court proceedings, amended petitions, among others."

You can search the site from the home screen using the basic search criteria or choose several other searching options. You can also limit the searches using keywords, for example, you could put your research county or state name in to pull up those entries only. I did a search for petitions from Maryland during the period of 1820-1850 and got 533 results.

Each entry is numbered and summarized and the site explains how to order copies of the actual petitions if you find one relevant to your research. Here are two examples:

Claiborne County, TN, 1841
Lewis, "a man of Color," represents that "he was the property of William Graham Esquire … and was by him [directed] in his will to be emancipated." Noting that Graham's executors "have performed the trust confided to them," Lewis laments that "the act of assembly require for them to leave the State." He further submits that "he is now getting old" and that "he has a wife & several children, from whom he feels a great hardship to be separated." The petitioner therefore "prays that your Honorable body would … so modify the Law, that he might be permitted to remain in this State."

TN, 1841
Thirty-one petitioners, lamenting the deplorable condition of people of color and citing rights promised in the

Constitution, seek a gradual end to slavery. The petitioners argue that slaveholders should be permitted to free their slaves on terms that will not involve their estates so long as the emancipated slaves can maintain themselves. They also argue that descendants of slaves born after the passage of an emancipation law should be freed when they reach a certain age. Black people to be freed should be taught a useful occupation and to read the Scriptures. Lastly, a law should be passed prohibiting within the state "the inhuman practice of separating husbands and wives."

The website is easy to use, beautifully organized, and contains a wealth of information. Try browsing through the various subjects as well .

Kudos to Loren Schweninger and his entire research team for making a tool that both historians and genealogists can utilize.

FIGURE 54, A SLAVE COFFLE

2A. DECONFLICTING "THE SAME NAME"

8 NOVEMBER 2009

One of the most common errors for new genealogists is falling into the trap of *"The Names the Same."* What is meant by that is that because we see someone with the same name, living in the same place, we too quickly assume it is our ancestor (or person of interest).

This is one of the reasons we shouldn't jump around sporadically in census records, but rather work methodically back, slowly but surely. The goal should be to recreate *identities*–and a person's identity is far more than just their name. In a previous post, I listed this concept as one of my 10 key genealogical principles.

A person's identity is made up of things like:

✓ who their spouses and children were

✓ who their parents were

✓ what they looked like

✓ their literacy (or lack thereof)

✓ who their neighbors and friends were

✓ their military service (or lack thereof)

✓ what their birthdate, date of marriage and death dates were

✓ where they lived

✓ what their occupation was

✓ what religion they practiced

✓ what their economic/financial standing was

…and lots of other things. I read a quote once that said if you always *assume* there is at least one other person living in the same area with the same name, then you will force yourself to use other criteria to identify that person.

We all use the census and vital records when we begin, but other records like city directories, tax, land and court records are especially good at helping to discern identity.

Focusing on identity and not just matching names is the practice you'll want to master as you continue your research. You may think a name is uncommon today, but it may have been a very common name historically. I thought my ancestor Rezin Prather would be easy, but it turned out that there were lots of black men named Rezin Prather all living in the Maryland/ D.C. area!

FIGURE 55, JOHN SMITH

Everyone who reads this blog knows I believe in using charts in my genealogy, and identity is something that can be analyzed very well with charts. Make a list of the prospects in the first column, using numbers—for example, Jane Johnson #1, Jane Johnson # 2, etc. Then make additional columns where you fill in the distinctive data for that individual: birthdate, marriage date, spouse(s), land, occupation, children, etc. Pretty soon, you'll start to see patterns emerge, and you should be able to have a better sense of who was who. Maps are important during this process—something as simple as seeing where people lived could be enough to help you see it's not your person of interest. Complicating factors

are really common given names and people who lived in the same vicinity, were born around the same time and married around the same time. Believe it or not, two men named Bill could marry two women named Mary. I've seen it!

The more evidence you gather and scrutinize, the more you will be able to distinguish between individuals. My ggrandfather, John Smith (shown left) is one ancestor that has really challenged me to prove identity. There were more than 10 black "John Smiths" living in Jacksonville, Florida in the early 20th century! It has been no simple task.

Take a look back over your research and ask yourself if you have really done due diligence in this area. Especially if you're stuck, have you glossed too quickly over a person, and attached him/her to your tree? I like to say *if the only reason you believe someone is your ancestor is that they have the same name and are living in the same place, then you have more work to do.*

Note: Another helpful resource is the webinar called "*Common Surnames: Finding Your Smiths,*" by Juliana Smith on Ancestry's website. She provides excellent tips. I also recommend reading Elizabeth Shown Mills' archived Quick Lesson #11 titled "Identity Problems and the FAN Principle," which can be found on her website, http://www.evidenceexplained.com.

FIGURE 56, BEATRICE PRATHER

grandparents and great-grandparents—all my direct ancestors only. Opening my eyes to include all siblings in each generation, and understanding the necessity of knowing the informant on sources like death certificates (and their relationship to the decedent) unlocked a world of information.

My great-grandmother, Beatrice Prather (shown at left) had eight siblings. The table below shows the parent's names gathered from Beatrice's death certificate and six of her siblings. I have also included the relationship of the informant.

There's a lot of room for confusion here, and the table makes that point clear. Had I stopped at pulling just my great-grandmother's death certificate, I would have been forever lost, *because Beatrice's son remembered "Eli" instead of the correct name "Levi."* And he didn't remember her mother's name at all.

The chart below is one I like to share with my students to show the importance of collateral research. Like almost everyone, when I began I was focused strictly on my

Sibling	Parents	Informant
Beatrice	Eli Prather & ?	Son
Cornelius	Levi Prather & Martha Simpson	Brother
Hattie	Levi Prather & Martha J. Simpson	Sister
Idella	Levi Prather & Susan Simpson	Husband
Maria	Levi Prather & Margaret Simpson	Sister
Rezion	Levi Prather & Martha Simpson	Hospital records
Mamie	Levi Prather & Martha Simpson	sister

FIGURE 57, INFORMANT COMPARISON OF PARENTS

Beatrice's mother was Martha Simpson (on right, seated) and four of the seven death records got her name right. What's interesting is that Margaret Simpson and Susan Simpson were both in fact family members, but they were *not* the wife of Levi. People gave what they remembered at the time. Margaret was Martha's stepmother, and Susan was Martha's sister.

All of this information was correlated with census, probate, deed and other record types to paint as clear a picture as possible of this family. When you research, don't forget to research **all** the siblings. (Photo below shows Beatrice Prather at the Institute for Colored Youth (later Cheyney University).

FIGURE 58, BEATRICE'S GRADUATION

I read an article a few weeks ago that I think every genealogist should read. It is a special issue of the *National Genealogical Society Quarterly* dated September 2001 (Volume 89, No.3). The issue was completely devoted to discussion of the Thomas Jefferson-Sally Hemings affair that I'm sure everyone has already heard about.

If you are a member of NGS (which I highly recommend) you can log in to their website and download this article from their NGS Quarterly archives immediately.

The esteemed Helen Leary, who is an extraordinary genealogist, tackles the subject in an article entitled, *"Sally Heming's Children: A Genealogical Analysis of the Evidence,"* which starts on page 165. It is a 40-plus page article, long, but well-worth taking the time to print out and read. Helen illustrates use of the Genealogical Proof Standard in one of this country's most enduring mysteries: *Was Thomas Jefferson the father of Sally Heming's children?*

FIGURE 59, THOMAS JEFFERSON

In Helen's gifted hands, the evidence is laid out (truly massive amounts of evidence), every hypothesis tested, each conflict addressed and a clearer conclusion you won't find anywhere else.

Helen is a masterful teacher and a thorough researcher. I feel that I grew as a researcher just seeing how she approached the topic and addressed each and every concern. I will continue to apply these methods to my own research.

DNA testing performed in 1998 matched Sally Hemings' youngest son Eston's DNA to that of a Jefferson male. Along with the other evidence, I particularly enjoyed how Helen illustrated handling of bias on the part of researchers, and how that bias can negatively affect results.

Especially with important historical figures such as Jefferson, there is always a lot of pushback and resistance to findings that upend our traditional views, or what me may have been taught in school. This is certainly true with the hot-button topic of race and slavery. This article also shows how you can't the play the game of "XYZ coulda happened" with research. Genealogy is not about "coulda, woulda, shoulda."

I'll leave you with a clip from the 1870 census that this article discusses (below). In 1870, a census taker in Ross County, Ohio, enumerated Sally's son Madison and wrote the following notation into the census next to his name:

"This man is the son of Thomas Jefferson!"

That has got to make you say *Wow*. I've never seen anything like that in the census and I have to confess it kinda took my breath away. I hope you'll go read this article, come back here and let me know what you thought.

I encourage you to read the entire issue: an article by Thomas Jones dissects the "official" report done by the Thomas Jefferson Scholars Commission (who continue to deny the pairing), and there is an excellent article by Gary B. Mills about proving children of master-slave relationships.

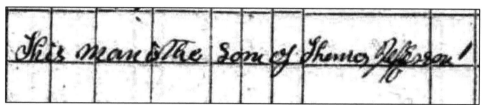

FIGURE 60, HEMINGS NOTE

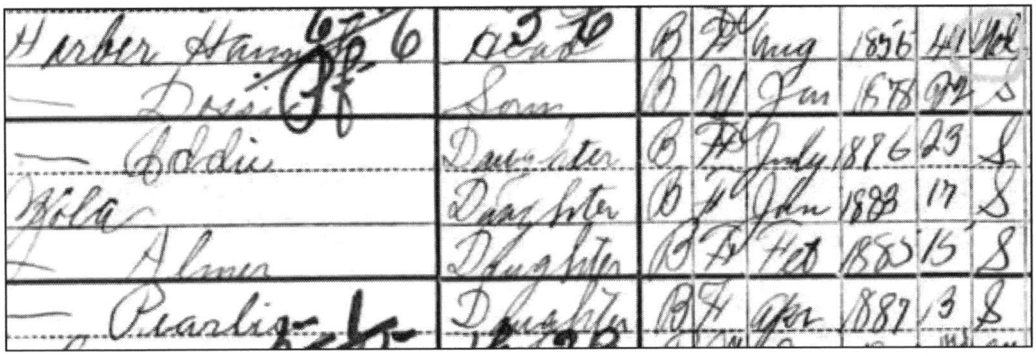

Harber Hannah	Head	B	F	Aug	1856	41	Wd
— Doris	Son	B	M	Jan	1878	22	S
— Addie	Daughter	B	F	July	1876	23	S
Viola	Daughter	B	F	Jan	1883	17	S
— Almer	Daughter	B	F	Feb	1885	15	S
— Pearlie	Daughter	B	F	Apr	1887	13	S

FIGURE 61, 1900 HARBER CENSUS

Records lie to us. The very records we depend upon to reconstruct our families, lie all the time. The 1900 Hardin County, TN census (above) for my 3rd great-grandmother Hannah Harbour stated that she was a widowed woman. But her former husband was alive and well; he had just left her for another woman. I guess I wouldn't want to say that either. The 1920 Hardin County, TN census (below) shows my ancestor Ada Seaman happily ensconced with her family:

.

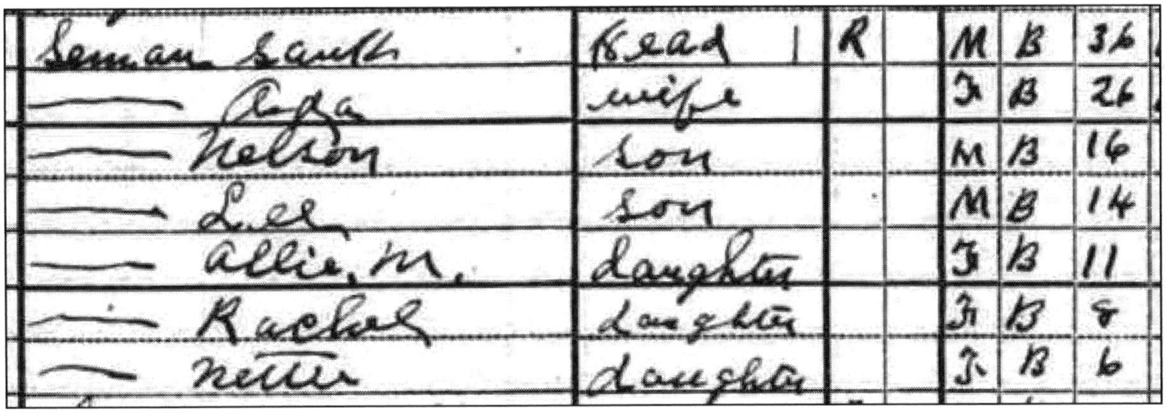

Seman Smith	Head	1	R	M	B	36
— Ada	wife			F	B	26
— Nelson	son			M	B	16
— Lee	son			M	B	14
— Allie M.	daughter			F	B	11
— Rachel	daughter			F	B	8
— Nettie	daughter			F	B	6

FIGURE 62, 1920 CENSUS CLIP

FIGURE 63, SEAMAN DEATH CERT

But Ada died in 1918, as her death certificate above shows. She could not have been in the household in the year 1920, unless they were living with her ghost. Ferdinand Holt migrated to the great city of Indianapolis in the early 20th century. He filled out a World War II Draft card that proclaimed his birthdate, Dec. 6, 1895 (below).

FIGURE 64, HOLT WW2 DRAFT CARD

But Ferdinand wasn't born in 1895. He was born in 1887. His correct birthdate was shown on his World War I draft card. Oddly, the actual day (Dec 6) stayed the same, even though the year changed by eight!

Records lie. Records manipulate and deceive. The only way to be sure that what we are recording is accurate is to closely examine every document, correlate each one with other sources, and rationally explain any conflicts. *Every document has the potential to contain inaccurate information.* Viewing records in isolation

and accepting what they purport as true <u>can't be our practice</u>.

I only show a few examples, but these examples kept me going in the wrong direction for years. It is only by researching many different document types (census, vital records, deed records, court records, military records, bible records, etc.) over a wide geographic area and timeframe that we can we begin to form an accurate picture of our ancestor's lives and flesh out the data that is incorrect.

So, *what documents have been lying to you?*

FIGURE 65, HOLT WW1 DRAFT CARD

7 FEBRUARY 2012

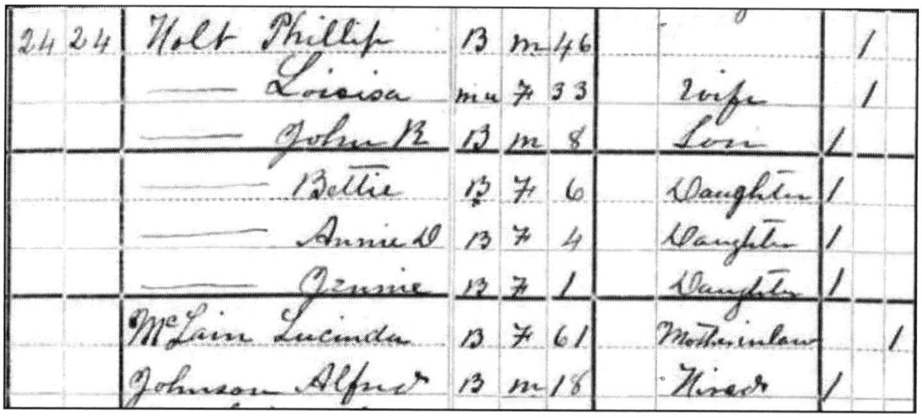

24	24	Holt Phillip	B	m	46		1	
		— Louisa	mu	F	33	Wife	1	
		— John B	B	m	8	Son	1	
		— Bettie	B	F	6	Daughter	1	
		— Annie D	B	F	4	Daughter	1	
		— Jennie	B	F	1	Daughter	1	
		McLain Lucinda	B	F	61	Mother in law		1
		Johnson Alfred	B	m	18	Hired	1	

FIGURE 66, 1880 PHILLIP HOLT CENSUS

It's amazing what can be discovered when you closely analyze and scrutinize your previous research. Sometimes it's the fact that new records have become available that weren't available before, and sometimes it's that your skills are better than they were before. I am quite happy to be my own biggest guinea pig and continue to prove this mantra be true. Phillip was the brother of my 3rd great-grandfather John W. Holt of Hardin County, Tennessee. Earlier in my research, I'd located Phillip and wife Louisa living in neighboring McNairy County, Tennessee in 1880, but never found them again and considered that

they had possibly died. Phillip's wife Louisa who had been enslaved on a neighboring farm; her maiden name was McClain. You can also see Louisa's mother Lucinda living with the couple in the 1880 census.

Ancestors can easily be lost in that dreaded 20-year gap between 1880 and 1900 (I call it the Donut Hole). That's enough time for kids to be born and out of the house and you'd never know they existed at all. Shown below, I later found this 1900 census record in Madison County, Tennessee.

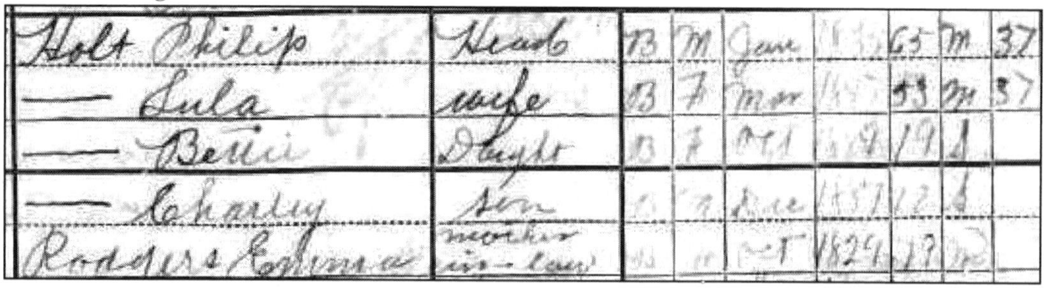

Holt Phillip		Head	B	M	June		65	M	37
— Lula		wife	B	F	Nov		53	M	37
— Bettie		Daught	B	F	Oct		19	1	
— Charley		son		F	Dec		12		
Rodgers Emma		mother in-law				1829			

FIGURE 67, 1900 PHILLIP HOLT

I quickly dismissed this as not being the same Phillip from McNairy County for two reasons: the wife was Lula instead of Louisa (which really shouldn't have thrown me off) but more importantly, the mother-in-law listed was Emma Rodgers, which led me to believe this woman's maiden name was Rodgers.

The fact that Tennessee Death Certificates are now online (through 1959) is what ultimately helped to solve the puzzle: I was able to find a death certificate for *Lula Holt* in 1931, and it confirmed that her mother's name was indeed *Lucinda McClain*. My analysis

before **was too quick to assume that the information I was viewing on the 1900 census was correct;** turns out it was not. Who knows what caused the error, but the fact remains that *Emma Rodgers was not Phillip Holt's mother-in-law*.

I'm really excited that Phillip has "come back from the dead." I was able to isolate the timeframe of his death, and track a few more of his children through 1930. Also, Jackson, Tennessee is a larger city than some of the other places in which the family lived and I'm hoping to eventually find more information on him, or better yet, some descendants.

FIGURE 68, LULA HOLT DEATH CERT

FIGURE 69, VINEY NEALY

I have been having some tremendous breakthroughs in this past year. With every new name, a piece of me and my history slides into place. Into *memory*.

It is a rule of thumb in good genealogy practice to pull every relevant record for an ancestor; to perform "exhaustive research" using the language of the Genealogical Proof Standard. This discovery illustrates the value of that principle and was made even sweeter by the fact that it was so unexpected.

My search for my great-grandmother Matilda's roots has gone full steam ahead this year and last. Matilda married four times but only appears on the census with one husband, and she got married in at least three different cities. I found Matilda's marriage dates in online indexes and databases so, as part of my due diligence, I began the necessary task of *ordering the original marriage and death records* of her husbands from the proper state and county offices. As the records came in, I reviewed and scanned each one and put them in the proper folders. I wasn't expecting to find anything new.

In Matilda's Florida death certificate, "Viney Nealy" was given as her mother's name with no name given for her father:

In Matilda's first marriage record, her surname is given as "Maaly"(Figure 83). Neither of those names (Nealy or Mealy) enabled me to find Matilda as a child in her parent's household in 1880. I found her in the 1900 census, but by then she was already married to husband number two. I also checked the name "Virginia Nealy" thinking "Viney" might be short for that.

FIGURE 70, MATIDA "MEALY" MARRIAGE

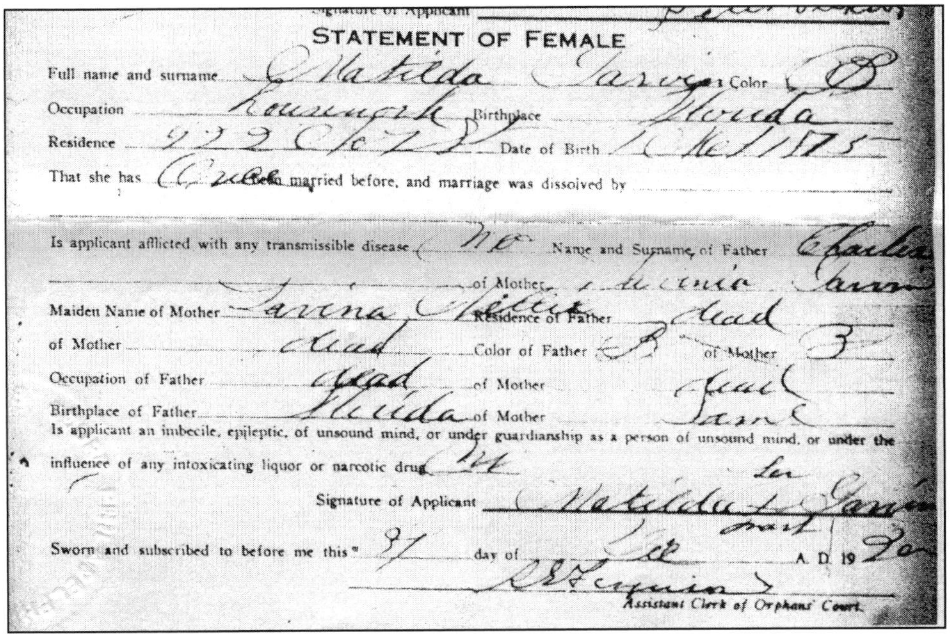

STATEMENT OF FEMALE

Full name and surname Matilda Jarvis Color B
Occupation Housework Birthplace Florida
Residence 922 ... Date of Birth ... 1875
That she has Once married before, and marriage was dissolved by
Is applicant afflicted with any transmissible disease No Name and Surname of Father Charles
of Mother ...
Maiden Name of Mother Lavina Nellie Residence of Father dead
of Mother dead Color of Father B of Mother B
Occupation of Father dead of Mother dead
Birthplace of Father Florida of Mother same
Is applicant an imbecile, epileptic, of unsound mind, or under guardianship as a person of unsound mind, or under the influence of any intoxicating liquor or narcotic drug No
Signature of Applicant Matilda + Jarvis (her mark)
Sworn and subscribed to before me this 27 day of Oct A. D. 19
Assistant Clerk of Orphans' Court.

FIGURE 71, VICKERS MARRIAGE

I recently received a copy of Matilda's marriage record from Philadelphia where she married husband number three, Peter Vickers (Figure 84). Remember, **only her first husband was my actual ancestor.** To my surprise, the record included a copy of the marriage application, and Philadelphia, at that time, *was one of the places that asked people the names of their parents, where they were from, and whether they were alive.* Matilda's father's name was given as "Charles" (no surname given) and her mother's name was given as **"Lavina Nellie."** Viney, turns out was short for Lavina! Now that I had the correct names of her parents, I finally, 15 years later, was able to locate **Matilda Nealy** living in Taylor County, Florida with her father "Charles Nealy" in the 1880 census! Charles' wife's name in 1880 is shown as "Netta" and there is Matilda, at 8 years old, right where she should be:

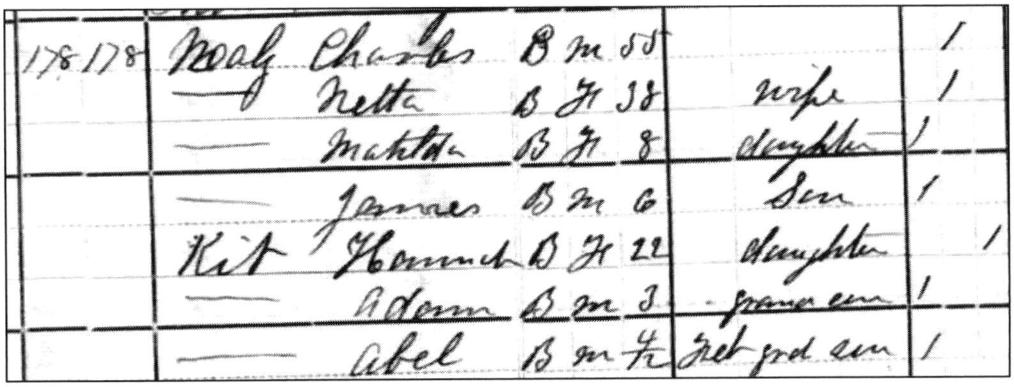

178 178	Nealy	Charles	B	M	55			1
	—	Netta	B	F	38	wife		1
	—	Matilda	B	F	8	daughter	1	
	—	James	B	M	6	Son	1	
	Kit	Hannah	B	F	22	daughter		1
	—	Adam	B	M	3	grand son	1	
	—	Abel	B	M	4/12	grd son	1	

FIGURE 72, 1880 NEALY HOUSEHOLD

Charles "Nelley" is also found in the same county in 1870 before Matilda's birth, and his wife's name in 1870 is a closer match and shown as "Nelvina."

This is so exciting and merits four exclamation points!!!! I now have siblings for Matilda that I can go on a crazy manhunt to find and I can also start the tough work of uncovering the likely enslaved roots of Charles and Lavina. I guess I have just added another 10 years of research to my lifetime. If this doesn't show **why we need to pull every relevant original record, even those for other spouses,** I don't know what would. I am now another branch back on my family tree.

Note: Now I want to know if I am related to the Neelys on the cooking show, so I can get some discount barbeque!

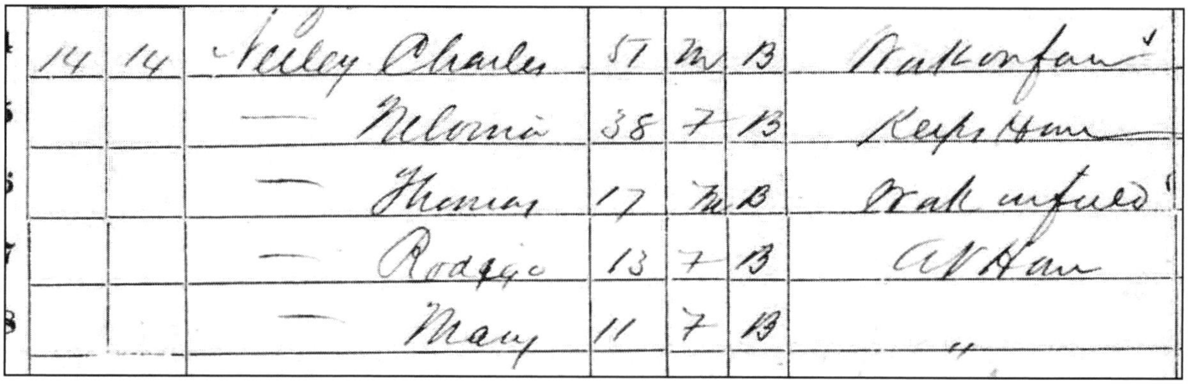

	14	14	Neeley Charles	57	m	B	Walker fan
			— Nelvina	38	f	B	Keeps Hous
			— Thomas	17	m	B	Work on farm
			— Rodger	13	f	B	At Hom
			— Mary	11	f	B	"

FIGURE 73, 1870 NEELEYS

In my class, I try to emphasize the importance of seeking original documents during our research. In this era of Ancestry.com and Familysearch.org, online transcriptions, indexes and databases are becoming accessible at a dizzying rate. While more access is always a good thing, sometimes what can be lost is the need **to always view the original record when we find evidence that appears promising.**

Original documents can be hard to read. Transcribers do their best to interpret words, but we're only human, and mistakes are plenty. My "Holt" ancestors are often transcribed as "Halt." Another thing is context. Someone creating an alphabetized index to a set of records can inadvertently destroy our ability to discover new clues. For example, we can't see who the neighbors are anymore. Sometimes notes made in the margins of the original records aren't included in the index. I've seen original Freedmen's Bureau records that draw a semi-circle around names and indicate "wife and children." I've seen original birth registers that note the child is "illegitimate." We need all the clues we can get.

We *must* to be able to verify that the information we are receiving is accurate, and that can't be done without seeing the original.

To illustrate, I have a book of will abstracts of Montgomery County, Maryland wills. While researching enslaved families, I found an entry for Rachel Magruder. It contains references to her sister and mother-in-law, who were named in the will, as well as the witnesses, and the book and page where the original can be found. A cursory look at the abstract only could prompt one to conclude that Rachel Magruder did not own any slaves, since none are mentioned. But look at phrases from Rachel's *original* will:

"…**my negro man Hercules** to be the property of my sister…"

"…**my servant girl Helen** to be the property of my mother-in-law…"

"…**negroes Aria and Anna** to go to Mira Magruder…"

We see that Rachel Magruder *did* in fact own slaves. However, the book of abstracts does not abstract *any of the slave data for any of the people in the book.* Reviewing the original document revealed important information.

That's a simple example meant to demonstrate the point. Always. Always. Always check the original.

Marriage Records are a key component of genealogical research. However, when it comes to those marriage records, are you sure of what you're actually looking at? Are you viewing:

✓ a marriage register or index?

✓ a marriage certificate?

✓ a marriage bann?

✓ a marriage bond?

✓ a marriage license?

✓ a marriage license application?

✓ a marriage announcement?

✓ a marriage record book?

✓ a marriage intent?

✓ a minister's return?

Depending on laws and customs, the types of documents necessary to legalize a marriage in your research area will likely be one or more of the above types. However, there are subtle differences between them all and you should scrutinize and understand the differences between them. Most professional genealogy books, such as *Evidence Explained*, will discuss them, in addition to all the good genealogy articles and training available.

Many localities had pre-printed forms such as the one shown (above right) from

Hardin County, Tennessee.

FIGURE 74, MARRIAGE RECORD

This page is from the "Marriage Records" book–sort of a catchall term whose contents can vary greatly from location to location.

A prudent researcher who examines the above page closely will notice that it has several different sections:

✓ a bond that requires a surety

✓ a section requiring consent if underage

✓ the actual license to marry, and

✓ a space for the minister to "return" the actual date of marriage.

This represents a common scenario. Most ministers were required to have a county *license* granting him permission to perform the marriage. Sometimes, the county court clerk tracked marriage license applicants in a *register*–or it may be called an *index*. I've seen places where the register survives, but the actual licenses do not. The actual licenses may contain more information, such as parent's names.

The minister was supposed to "return" the information regarding the actual marriage date and place. Some places had entire books of nothing but those *"minister's returns."* Maybe the court clerk's marriage books don't survive, but dusty boxes full of the actual licenses do. Maybe none of the official documents survive and you're left with those marriage *announcements* in the newspapers–in Hardin County, they were published almost every week. Perhaps you were lucky enough that your ancestor saved their marriage *certificate* gently pressed in the middle of the family bible, containing all the details of their nuptials.

So go back and take a look at all your marriage documents, and ask yourself: what exactly are you looking at?

FIGURE 75, PRATHER/DUVAL WEDDING

For those doing African-American research, antebellum estate inventories are a common resource used to find enslaved ancestors. But we should also get into the habit of looking at the *other* items on that inventory list that help us visualize not just the slaveowner's life, but also our ancestors. Even after the emancipation, scrutinizing our ancestor's inventories can often provide those interesting little details to make a family history come alive.

The first thing I realized a few years ago when I started doing this regularly was that I had no idea what many of the items were! Especially all the animals and agricultural items. What's the difference between a bay horse and a sorrel horse? (it's the colors) What's a shoat? (it's a baby pig) What exactly is fodder? (feed for farm animals). Luckily, for most everything, you can just use Google and quickly get a good definition and even pictures. Or you can use a book like *"From A to Zax: A Complete Dictionary for Genealogist and Historians."*

Let's look below at Alfred Reeds estate inventory in 1858, from Russell County, AL.

FIGURE 76, REED INVENTORY

I noticed:

–How the appraisers are "walking through the property" room by room.
–The appraisers have started outside on the farm. There are plenty of animals, 29 head of cattle may imply that he was selling meat.
–Horses and mules were sometimes given names.
–Alfred has not just a buggy and harness, but also a *rockaway* and harness, a much fancier carriage that would imply his higher status, as opposed to the average farmers who may only have buggies or oxcarts.

–The slaves are listed by name, but no ages or statements are given about their relationships.

Let's look at the next set of items (below):

–Now the appraisers are moving through the bedroom or living quarters.
–A piano and accordion are also signs of his status and musical talent.
–The ability to own a gold watch might signal a higher status.
–The number of guns (2 pistols, 3 double-barrel shotguns) is large, even in an era where almost everyone owned guns.

FIGURE 77, REED INVENTORY 2

Now, let's look at the inventory of <u>Caroline Sibley</u> of Richmond County, GA, in 1859 below:

–Her status immediately jumps out—she owned paintings and valuable portraits.
–She owned a bible and hymn book, which tells us she was probably a member of a local church.
–

Her estate is notable for what is missing—no agricultural items or animals. She lived in Augusta, GA, but obviously did not farm. How did she obtain a living?

1 Mahogany Marble Top Table	20 00
1 Large Arm Chair	10 00
3 Paintings or Engravings	6 00
4 Portraits	100 00
Crockery and Glass Ware	50 00
3 Waiters	5 00
2 Glass Girandoles	5 00
1 Mirror	10 00
1 Wardrobe	25 00
1 Cane Rocker	1 00
1 Ditto with arms	2 00
½ doz Cane Seat Chairs	3 00
1 Leather Chair	3 00
1 Work Stand	3 00
1 Small Glass	25
1 Savior's Tomb	50
1 pr. Vases	50
1 " Candlesticks	50
1 " Snuffers &c	50
1 Towel Rack	50
1 Wash Stand	10 00
1 Shovel Stand	50
Bible & Hymn Book	3 00
1 sett small Tables	3 00
1 doz. Chairs	25 00
1 Safe	2 00
3 Candlesticks	1 50

FIGURE 78, SIBLEY INVENTORY

Let's look at the last page of her inventory:

--I spoke too soon: she owned $33,000 in bonds and notes! According to one online value calculator, that would be $940,000,000 today. Ms. Sibley clearly does not need to farm!

–We also see she *owned a pew in the Presbyterian Church*—a great clue of where to go to search more records.

–There's a piano again, as well as jewelry, and silver.

–She has four female slaves, listed without ages or relation, but we can infer that they were likely working in her home as domestics or rented out.

FIGURE 79, SIBLEY INVENTORY 2

Here are a few general tips as you are perusing estate inventories:

1. Compare your ancestor's inventory with his neighbors to assess his or her relative economic standing.

2. Books are typically indicators of literacy, which was less common the further back in time we go. Many homes only owned a bible, or perhaps one of the classics.

3. We can often make generalizations about slave ages from their monetary values. The most highly valued males will be in their late teens and twenties, with many working years ahead of them. The most highly valued women will be in their prime childbearing years, in their twenties, maybe early thirties. Children and elderly people will have lower values.

4. Some inventories enumerate <u>whips and other slave torture</u> (yes, I believe it was torture) tools. These may indicate the relative violence involved in slaveownership.

5. Wealthier people will obviously have more "luxury" items—carriages, silver and gold jewelry, more books and furniture and as we've seen lots of china and large serving platters may indicate lots of socializing which was associated with the planter class.

Tell me—what interesting items have you come across in estate inventories? What do those items tell you about the person's life?

<u>Note:</u> I recommend the book "*Estate Inventories: How to Use Them*" by Kenneth L. Smith.

FIGURE 80, ESTATE INVENTORIES BOOK

For the first time in my research, I have found two death certificates for the same person, filled out by two different people. As if the missing and inaccurate records aren't enough to make me crazy, now this.

I was perusing the Tennessee Death Database when I found this death certificate for Mrs. Mary Ella Copeland:

She was my grandmother's aunt. Mary's parents migrated from Alabama to Tennessee, and I have never been able to find any document that states *where* in Alabama they came from. What struck me is that this death certificate listed "Tuscumbia, Alabama" as the birthplace for Mary's parents. I thought, *Now I know I have this death certificate already. Why didn't I ever notice the town?*

FIGURE 81, COPELAND DEATH CERT 1

Sure enough, when I pulled out the copy shown below that I had in my records, it only listed "North Alabama" for Mary's parents.

Both death certificates are indeed the same woman, Mary Ella Fendricks, who married Abe Copeland. Both list the same death date, February 9, 1930. However, one was completed by her husband, and one was completed by someone named James Casey. He was associated with the family, but I'm unsure of his exact relationship. One certificate lists the "Gant graveyard" as the burial place, while the other lists the "Savannah Colored Cemetery."

FIGURE 82, COPELAND DEATH CERTIFICATE 2

They both illustrate the weaknesses inherent in so many records: the information is only as good as who gave it. The certificates list different ages for Mary Ella (41 and 47). Her husband says her parents were *Mike Fendricks and Kate Sharard*. James Casey says her parents were *Mike Fendricks and Kate Suggs*.

Mary Ella's mother's name (according to her marriage license and census records) was "Jane Eliza." But so many records consistently state "Katie," that I'm starting to believe that she was actually called Katie or Kate as a nickname. Even my grandmother remembered that name. But there is no evidence that Mike Fendricks married any other woman or had children with any other woman.

I wonder what circumstance would cause someone to have multiple death certificates? Have any of you seen this? Sometimes I think the ancestors just like to MESS with us!

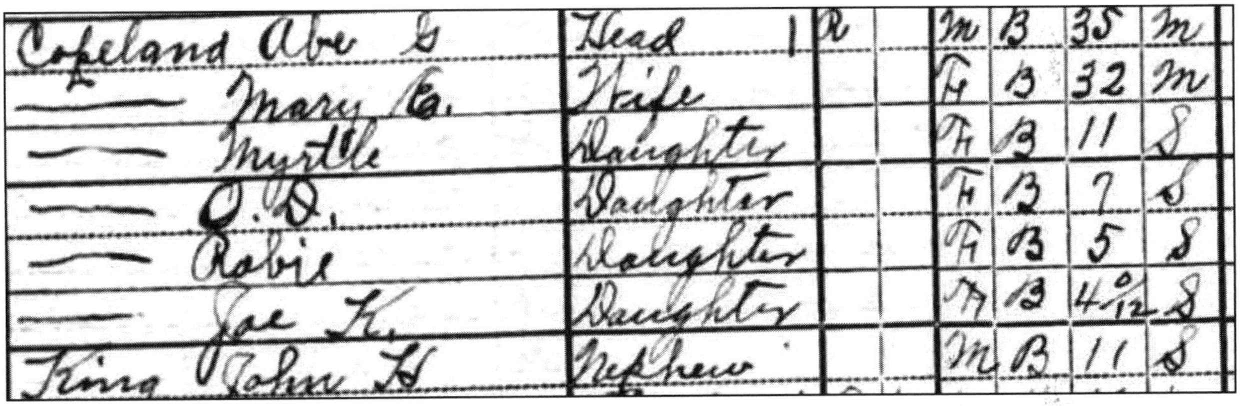

Copeland Abe G	Head	1	R	M	B	35	M
— Mary E.	Wife			F	B	32	M
— Myrtle	Daughter			F	B	11	S
— O. D.	Daughter			F	B	7	S
— Robie	Daughter			F	B	5	S
— Joe K.	Daughter			F	B	4 0/12	S
King John H	Nephew			M	B	11	S

FIGURE 83, 1920 COPELAND HOUSEHOLD

FIGURE 84, RACIAL COVENANT

I ran across a startling deed recently (shown above). In the document, Monroe and Robert B. Warren, of Washington, D.C., are selling land to Harry E. Mockbee in May 1927. After the typical legal language found in many deeds came this ominous phrase:

"...Subject to the further covenant that said land and premises shall never be rented, leased, sold, transferred or conveyed unto or in trust for or occupied by any negro or colored person or any person of negro extraction."

This is the first time I've actually come across a racially restrictive covenant while doing deed research. They are defined as "a legally enforceable contract imposed in a deed upon the buyer of the property." I knew a little about the history, primarily from a few books I've read: "*Not in My Neighborhood,*" by Antero Pietila (focusing on Baltimore) and "*Family Properties,*" by Beryl Satter (focusing on Chicago). Although frequently used against African-Americans, they were also used to keep Jewish people from certain areas in cities like Baltimore.

Many have probably seen the movie "*A Raisin in the Sun*" which portrays a black family attempting to move into a white neighborhood. An even better introduction to the topic can be found in the 2004 National Book Award Winner, "*Arc of Justice: A Saga of Race, Civil Rights, and Murder in the Jazz Age,*" by Kevin Boyle. The book tells the riveting true story of Dr. Ossian Sweet, whose purchase of a home in Detroit in 1925 resulted in attack by a white mob and the death of a white man. If you read any book on this subject, read this one first. You will not put it down, especially since the author does such a beautiful job portraying Ossian's family history.

Initially, covenants became popular in response to the large migration of Southern blacks to Northern cities, essentially forcing racial segregation. On May, 1926, in a case called Corrigan vs. Buckley, the U.S. Supreme Court, by its refusal to hear the case,

tacitly affirmed the legality of these covenants. Their use skyrocketed, and particularly in large cities, the result was that blacks were forced into certain "black" areas, whether they could afford to live elsewhere or not. The Federal Housing Authority institutionalized this racism with their Underwriting Manual which denied mortgages based upon race and by practicing "redlining": deciding which neighborhoods to approve mortgages in.

In 1930, J.D. Shelly, a black man, bought property in St. Louis in a neighborhood covered by a racial covenant. He convinced a white owner to sell to him anyway. A neighbor sued, and the case wound its way up to the U.S. Supreme Court. The resultant ruling, *Shelley vs. Kraemer*, held that the covenants could not be enforced without violating the 14th Amendment. However, it only meant that states could not <u>enforce</u> the covenants; people could and did privately continue to make them and voluntarily follow them.

Still the 1948 Shelly ruling put racial covenants on death row. NAACP lawyers Thurgood Marshall and Charles Hamilton Houston put together a legal strategy to fight these cases all over the country. It wasn't until <u>the 1968 Fair Housing Act</u> that their use was deemed illegal.

There is so much important history that is left out of the "official" story of America.

Huge obstacles awaited black people every step of the way it seems –in education, labor, and housing just to name a few. A generation of people are coming of age who have no knowledge of these obstacles. How would others have fared if after enslavement and Jim Crow, they were prevented from equal education, prevented from many jobs, prevented from equal pay at the jobs they did hold, prevented from living where they wanted, prevented from marrying who they wanted and prevented from partaking in the fruits of society that depended on that labor? People who placed their lives at risk by challenging the system and buying homes in "white" areas should be regarded as civil rights heroes.

What I find interesting is that there were rural Southern communities where blacks lived relatively peacefully alongside whites. One of the beauties of genealogy is the history you learn. Let's keep getting educated and telling others the real story of America.

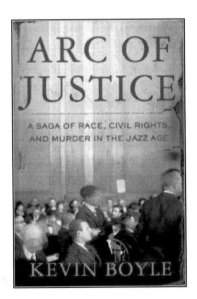

FIGURE 85, ARC OF JUSTICE

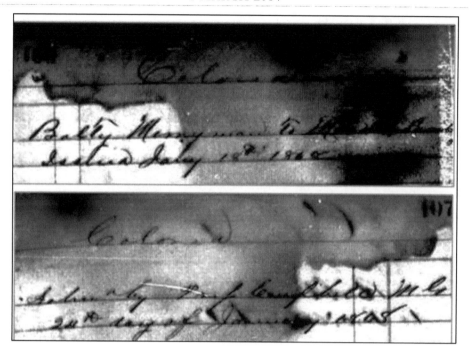

FIGURE 86, MERRIMAN MARRIAGE 1

Sometimes it can seem as if there is a <u>civil war going on in the genealogical community</u>. After we start researching our families, at some point we hear about the necessity of **source citations.** Once we figure out exactly what they are, and we see a few, some of us think, "That looks complicated. I don't have time to do all that." Or we know we need to do them, and just never get around to it. Or we actually don't understand how to create them. Or people disagree on the format. Some think it's just for those "high and mighty" oh-so-serious researchers. When someone asks where we got a piece of information, we think saying "the 1930 census" should be sufficient. We honestly believe we will be able to remember where we got everything. We don't foresee the paper (and now electronic) chaos of five or ten years later down the road.

Then one day, it happens to us: We see a death date we have recorded in Family Tree Maker for Uncle Bob and honestly have NO IDEA where we got it from. We check a record at a library only to realize we've already checked that record. Oh dear.

My first few years of research were indeed spent in the fog of not knowing about and not understanding source citations. Critical pieces of my early research have incomplete or missing sources.

Let me give just one very simple example of how understanding source citations allow for better research analysis and conclusions. I use this example in my class to illustrate the value of citations as well as the importance of examining original sources.

The source citation below is for the marriage of my 3rd great-grandfather, whose full name was Baltimore Merriman:

"Tennessee State Marriages, 1780-2002," database and images, _Ancestry.com_ (http://www.ancestry/search/: accessed 4 May 2011) entry for Batty Merryman, 24 January 1868, Spokane; citing "Tennessee State Marriages, 1780-2002, microfilm, Tennessee State Library and Archives, Nashville."

The citation makes it clear that the document was reviewed from a database on Ancestry (see image on previous page). Ancestry recorded the couple's names as **"Batty Merryman"** and **"Martha Barb."** But I've learned to be a diligent researcher. When inspecting the actual image, the first name "Martha" cannot be seen, nor can any of her surname. You can sort of make out the "M" but not anything else. Clearly there is water damage in the image, but the transcribed marriage date itself appears to be accurate. But I'm certainly not going to use this unknown transcriber's interpretation of Baltimore's wife's name when I can't see it myself.

Now, let's look at another source citation for _the same information_–the marriage of Baltimore Merriman:

Hardin County, Tennessee, Marriage Records, Vol 1: 106, Balty Merryman to Martha Bailey, 24 January 1868; County Clerk's Office, Savannah.

This citation tells me the information came from the Hardin County, Tennessee courthouse.

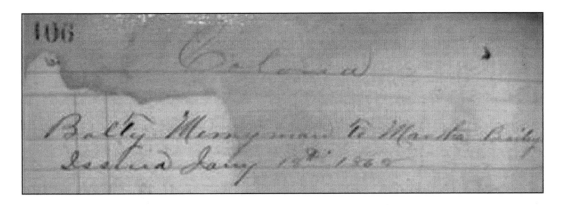

FIGURE 87, ORIGINAL MARRIAGE RECORD

That image is shown on the previous page. Viewing the *original source* now reveals the surname of my 3rd great-grandmother: **Martha <u>Bailey</u>**.

This is one small example of the power of source citations when you understand how to use them accurately. Knowing where the information came from enables you to try to find other sources (or just a clearer copy) for the information.

Here are three of my top reasons to **diligently** cite our sources:

1) We (and others) need to know <u>exactly</u> what sources we are basing our research on, and where we got those sources from.

2) We want to draw the most accurate conclusions, which can only be judged from the breadth, depth and accuracy of our sources.

3) We often invest decades of our lives to this quest; we want our life's work to be considered credible.

Elizabeth Shown Mills is the bible for creating genealogical source citations for good reason. Not only is it organized beautifully into categories of sources, Ms. Mills meticulously and clearly explains the why, what and how for every kind of source. I also highly recommend visiting her companion website; www.evidence explained.com, where she hosts a forum where genealogists answer questions about source citations, which I have used of many times.

My personal process is to record all of the information needed for a proper source

FIGURE 88, BALTIMORE'S GRANDDAU. VANNIE

citation as I am researching. I jot down the microfilm number, page number, book number, and anything else that describes the source I'm using. Then about once a year, I take the time write-up the research on that family line or person or whatever I was researching. I make sure I have Ms. Mills' book beside me. I turn each and every fact I uncovered into a proper source citation. Most of the sources we use turn out to be the same ten or so types—census, vital, deed, court, military, online databases, newspaper articles, etc.—so it's not as difficult as it first seems, although I will admit it is very time consuming.

It takes a lot of time to do citations. But the payoff is incredible, and well-worth it.

FIGURE 89, MATHIES CARD

I once heard a lecturer say that up to 60% of the time, people are researching the wrong woman as mother of the children. This example illustrates the need to prove the father's relationship to a child separately from the mother's relationship to the child. What does that mean? The Freedman's Bank card above is for "London Mathies":

London's bank card dated 8 October 1867 provides the surprise notation that his wife "Martha died in Memphis on Vance St. July 2/67." Most cards don't typically include dates of death, so this is a lucky find. Under the section for children it says "Willy Franklin 1 yr 2 mos" which could be interpreted as one or two children until we compare it with his 1870 census household as London "Matthews." In that document, his wife's name is Amanda. With one year old son "Jackson" in the household, we can probably safely conclude that London remarried and had another son. What these records *together* show is that Amanda is not the mother of the first son "William" or as the bank card calls him, "Willy Franklin." William's mother was probably Martha. If we examined the census record in isolation, we might incorrectly assume this was a man and a wife and their two children.

Of course we'll try to find London's marriage records to confirm our hypothesis. We could also try to find church or burial records that may confirm the death of his wife and perhaps births or baptisms of the children.

We can't assume that the wife in any household is the mother of all of the children in the household. We have to prove that relationship separately.

If you know how to properly pull every clue from census records, you'll notice that the little "M2" in the census shown on the next page means that John Campbell has been married more than once, while this is his wife Harriet's first marriage ("M1").

You'll also see that Harriet has birthed 2 children, and 2 are living. This implies that the last two children are not Harriet's children.

This is where it gets tricky: only the 1910 census requires an "M1" or an "M2"

designator for number of marriages. And, the *"M2" designator means "married more than once."* It could be a 2nd marriage or a 4th marriage, and it should still say "M2".

Additionally:

–the 1900 census <u>provides the number of years married</u> and the number of children born and living for the women. It does not provide the number of marriages as shown in this example.

–the 1930 census <u>provides age at first marriage. That</u> doesn't necessarily mean the person was married *at that time to the current spouse.*

–the 1900-1940 censuses all require a "D" to be written for divorced; if you see that, be sure to search for the divorce record.

As you can see, all of these differences in what information each census provides is critical to understanding and interpreting the document correctly. Incorrectly interpreting the census can lead you astray in your research.

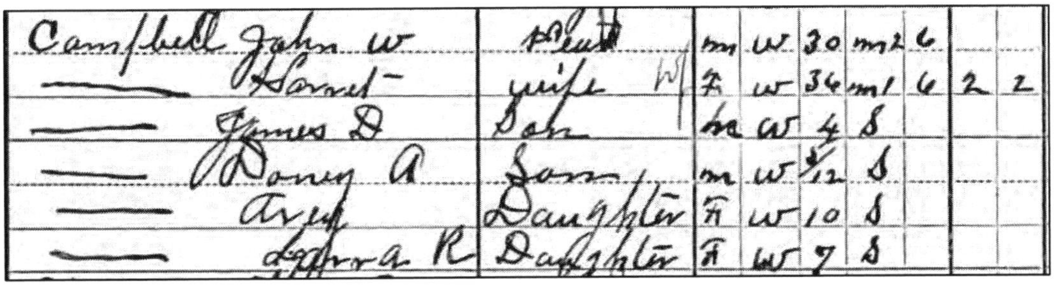

Campbell John W	Head	M	W	30	M2	6		
— Harriet	Wife	F	W	34	M1	6	2	2
— James D	Son	M	W	4	S			
— Doney A	Son	M	W	3/12	S			
— Avey	Daughter	F	W	10	S			
— Laura R	Daughter	F	W	7	S			

FIGURE 91, 1910 JOHN W CAMPBELL

It goes without saying that census records have high degrees of error and should be approached with caution. The censustaker may not have recorded the information correctly or the family member may not have accurately reported the information. I have several examples of women marked "widowed" whose husbands were in fact not dead.

It goes without saying that information in the census records should be correlated with other records that illuminate a family.

It goes without saying that people can and did have children before and outside of marriages.

So how can you prove the relationship to the wife as mother of the children? Here are a few ways:

1. Sometimes simple age deductions can rule out the current wife as mother of the children. (i.e., most women aren't birthing children at age 13).
2. If the husband dies, and the widowed wife heads the census household, the stated relationship of any children in the household will be to her.
3. Marriage and death certificates of the children can name parents.
4. Estate or probate records after the father's death may name children and wives.
5. Bible records, church records, military pensions, obituaries and land records are examples of other types of records that may be used to prove a woman's relationship to children in a household.

Another thing that I frequently do with census records is that I will collect several of them for a particular person, for example, I may collect the census for John W. Holt from 1880-1910. Then I will create a birthdate for him using the ages I found in those censuses, so his birthdate might be 1850-1852.

So go back and pull out some of your census records. Ask yourself, for each family unit: Is the wife really the mother of all of the children? The answer may surprise you.

MAY 31, 2014

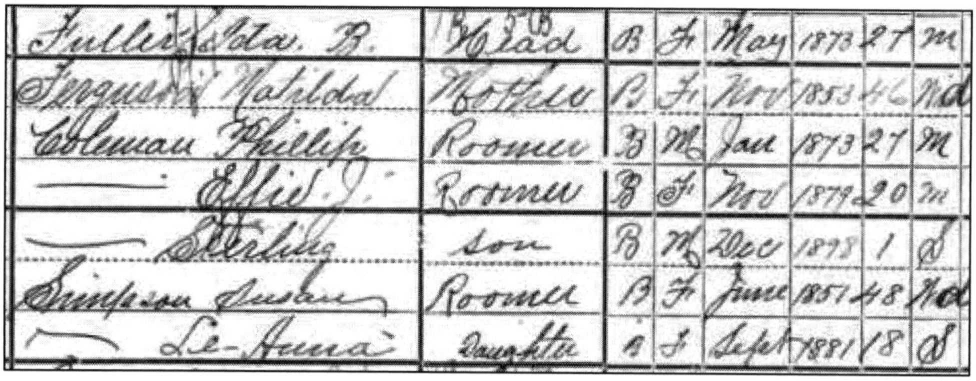

Fuller, Ida B.	Head	B	F	May	1873	27	M
Ferguson, Matilda	Mother	B	F	Nov	1853	46	Wd
Coleman, Phillip	Roomer	B	M	Jan	1873	27	M
— Ellie J.	Roomer	B	F	Nov	1879	20	M
— Sterling	Son	B	M	Dec	1898	1	S
Simpson, Susan	Roomer	B	F	June	1851	48	Wd
— Le-Anna	Daughter	B	F	Sept	1881	18	S

FIGURE 92, 1900 FULLER HOUSE

I have discussed many times in this blog how finding a female ancestor's married name led to breakthroughs on the family line. Most of us automatically think of that when we suddenly "lose" tracking of a woman. What hasn't come naturally for me yet is anticipating multiple marriages. Maybe two marriages is the max my mind thinks of. I am still floored by how many people married and remarried. Even well into their senior years. I found "Le-Anna" Simpson as an 18-year old woman living with her widowed mother Susan in Washington, D.C. in 1900 (above).

However, by 1910 Leanna was gone. She was not found on any 1910 census. A marriage search revealed Leanna's 1912 marriage to "Verbee H. Peaker" in D.C. But the couple didn't appear in 1920 or any subsequent census in that city. Hmm. I thought for sure I'd find them with that unique name.

I searched for a remarriage under the name "Leanna Peaker" and I indeed found another D.C. marriage for her in 1929 to Clarence H. Hackett. That couple was not found on any subsequent census in D.C. Why is she marrying in D.C. but not showing up living in D.C.? I expanded my census search to Maryland, since people flowed pretty freely with work and school between Maryland and D.C., especially Baltimore. To my surprise, I found a "Verb Peaker" and wife "Laura" living all the way on the Eastern Shore of Maryland, in Kent County! They lived near a small town called Galena.

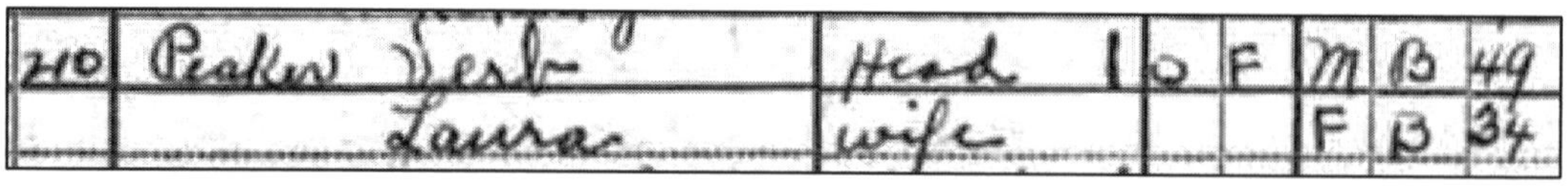

210	Peaker, Verb	Head	1	O	F	M	B	49
	Laura	wife				F	B	34

FIGURE 93, 1920 PEAKER

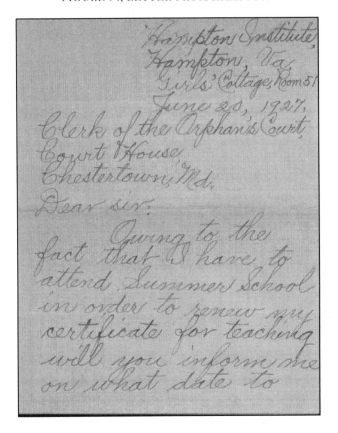

A probate case for Verbee Peaker's death in 1925 confirmed this was my Leanna. That probate file contained a rare gift: a handwritten letter from Leanna, noting that she was away at Hampton Institute getting her teacher's certificate and would need to know the court date to be back for court (shown above).

Leanna was living in Kent County in 1920, and she was still there in 1930 and 1940 with 2nd husband Clarence H. Hackett. Leanna's first husband Verbee left her a small piece of land he inherited and she married Clarence when his 1st wife died. But the story isn't finished yet. Yes, my dear sweet cousin Leanna got married a third time in 1948 to the brother of her first husband Verbee, Robert Morton Peaker. She was 63 years old and he was 67. He was living right next door so I suppose they figured they might as well grow old together;)

My guess about her marriages occurring in D.C. is that the requirements for marriage in D.C. may have been easier or cheaper than those in Kent County. Or perhaps since that was Leanna's hometown, she felt she should marry there. Leanna does not appear to have had any children with any spouse. I continue to research her and her spouses in other records, land, court, military etc. and fleshing out her life as best possible. But this is a great lesson to remind us to keep on searching those marriage records.

The icing on the cake to this story is that all these years I've had a family picture (below) from my dad's childhood in Jacksonville, FL. At the time, the name of the woman seated alone had been lost to history and was given to me as "a cousin, *from Galena, MD"*

FIGURE 95, LEANNA SIMPSON PEAKER HACKETT

3A. WHAT YOU DIDN'T KNOW ABOUT SLAVERY

7 DECEMBER 2011

I confess that blog title is a little sensationalized. Truth be told, much of the following information becomes well-known to researchers within a few years of their African-American genealogical journey. Family research turns many of us into walking, talking, beacons of black history. It is an endlessly fascinating subject, epic, tragic and but often inspiring.

Nevertheless, here are a few thoughts and ideas to keep in mind as you do your research.

1. **Slavery was vastly different at different times, in different places.** A slave's life in 1780 in Virginia would likely not look much like a Georgia slave's life in 1850. A city slave's experience was vastly different than a rural or country slave's experience. Different crops had different labor demands (cotton, rice, tobacco, indigo, sugar). Learn what crop your ancestor farmed.

2. **South America (mainly Brazil) and the Caribbean islands took in most of the slaves from Africa.** Of those who came to the North American colonies, most were imported by 1795. That means many of us have very long histories in this country.

3. **Most slaves had surnames that were known *amongst themselves*,** even though the white

planters did not record those surnames. Check out the WPA narratives, civil war pensions, and the freedman's bank as three types of records where you'll find slaves mentioning their parent's entire names.

4. **There will be many instances where the enslaved father is owned by someone other than the owner of his wife and child.** Don't expect to always find entire family units owned by one owner. Check those neighbors; many slaves found mates on neighboring farms. Very young children, however, were often allowed to stay with their mothers.

5. **Slaves were employed in every conceivable occupation:** they worked in shipyards and wharves, railroads and steamboats, coal mines, iron works, gristmills and sawmills; as maids, seamstresses, tailors, masons, butchers, barbers, and so on. Especially with urban slaves, think of all the ways other than farming they worked.

6. **Understand the dynamics of the interstate slave trade.** The rise of cotton in the early 1800's and waning need for year-round slaves in the North caused hundreds of thousands of slaves to be sold into the deep south and expanding southwest. This had a devastating impact on black families. Note the prevalence of the birthplace of "Virginia" or "Maryland" in the 1870 southern states. Consider

FIGURE 96, VA CONTRABANDS

that your southern slave ancestor may have been sold south at some point.

FIGURE 97, WALTER CALLOWAY

7. **Slaves were often sold or bought through slave traders.** Many of these auction –style purchases will not have any existing records or receipts, as these were private organizations.

8. **Researching slavery will expand your vision of what it meant to be a slave.** Many slaves in cities were allowed to live as virtual freedmen, work for pay and give their owners a monthly fee; others were allowed to earn wages to buy themselves or family members. Many planters worked their slaves on the "task" system, which meant they were responsible for a certain amount of work every day & when they finished they were free to do other things, like work their own garden plot or hunt for more food.

9. **Looking at original sources will broaden your mind as to how the local whites interacted with the enslaved population.** Criminal court records are replete with people being charged with playing cards with slaves and selling them things. This really surprised me. Slaves were plied with liquor by their masters and others. I have a court record detailing the local practice of allowing the slaves to work for pay on their holiday off-days. All these things expanded my view of slave life.

10. **It took me awhile to agree with this idea, but slavery was a *negotiated* relationship.** Yes, the masters had the final and violent upper hand, but I am amazed at how many times the master's actions were altered by a slave's threatening to run away, refusing to do work, refusing to be sold to someone, etc.. They had a measure of bargaining power and they used it. Numerous entries in planter's diaries and other documents make the case:

"Salley won't go without her husband so I'll have to sell him too."

"Joe if you come back home, you may have your choice of master."

"I had to whip Bill today because he would not go with me."

Our ancestors used every tool at their disposal and sometimes were able to influence the master's decisions.

Tell me, what things have you learned during your research about slavery that surprised you?

$50 REWARD.

RANAWAY from the subscriber, living near Upper Marlborough, Prince George's County, Maryland, negro man

I S A A C.

He is about fifty-five years of age; about five feet ten or eleven inches high; very black. One of his legs bend—but which one not recollected. There is one peculiarity about him, and that is, when spoken to, he is apt to raise his hand and scratch his head. He has a wife belonging to Samuel B. Anderson, Esq., living near Tenally Town, Montgomery County, where, I have no doubt, he is lurking. He has also relations belonging to the estate of the late Col. Trueman Cross, on his plantation, near Upper Marlborough.

I will give the above reward for his apprehension,—no matter where taken,—provided he is brought home or secured in jail, so that I get him again.

ROBERT A. CLAGETT.

September 24, 1856—tf

FIGURE 98, RUNAWAY AD CLAGETT

I gave a lecture last Saturday on researching the enslaved at the Montgomery County Historical Society. I had a great time. My Prather relatives are from Montgomery County, Maryland. During the research for the lecture, I found new information as well.

I found Montgomery County Runaway Ads online through the Maryland State Archives' Legacy of Slavery webpage. One night I stayed up until 1 am just looking at Runaway Ads, which I've discussed here before and have a particular fascination with. I'd like to share some of my observations from perusing the various ads.

Slaveowners knew a surprising amount of information about their slaves' families. The ads also speak to the extended kinship communities that slaves formed.

$100 REWARD.

RANAWAY from the farm on Rock creek, belonging to the estate of Thomas Cramplin, deceased, on the 13th instant, the following described negro men, who call themselves Joseph Beall and James Thomas. Joseph is about 40 years of age, six feet high, stammers when spoken to. James is about 25 years of age, 5 feet 10 or 11 inches high, and very black, good teeth, and very stout built. They had on when they absconded, a drab twilled full cloth short coat, and pantaloons of the s me; coarse shoes and burlaps shirts ; but they will no d ubt change their clothing, as they have taken other clo es with them. I will give 100 dollars for the apprehen on of said negroes if taken out of the State, or 50 dolla s if they are taken in the State or District of Columbia, and all reasonable charges paid if delivered to the subscriber living on the Georgetown Turnpike Road, about 5 miles from Rockville, Montgomery County, Maryland.

RICHARD WILLIAMS, Adm'r.

April 17—eotf

Some of the ads demonstrate that slaves had surnames, although many owners didn't print them in the ads(above). I think it's interesting that the ads often say "he calls himself."

There are also common themes of the slaveowner's belief that escaped slaves were headed to Philadelphia (or Canada) and that they were aided by or had free papers from a free negro. Maryland had over 83,000 free blacks by 1860. Evidence abounds of the violence slaveowners exerted to hold slavery in place. The ad on the next page describes the slave's This back as "very much cut for his rogueness"

Runaway Ads all by themselves explode several myths of the slaveowner's mind, such as:

1) the slaveowner's belief that slaves did not form the emotional attachments to their family in the same way that whites did. This was one of the excuses used to defend the buying and selling of human beings. *If that were so, why is it that so many slaves escape and head back to their spouses, parents, children, etc.?*

2) the slaveowner's belief that the natural state for negroes was slavery; they needed white caretakers; they were happiest this way. *If so, why do so many run away again and again, even when the odds were overwhelmingly against them? Why do they run away even when they already wore the marks of painful physical punishment?*

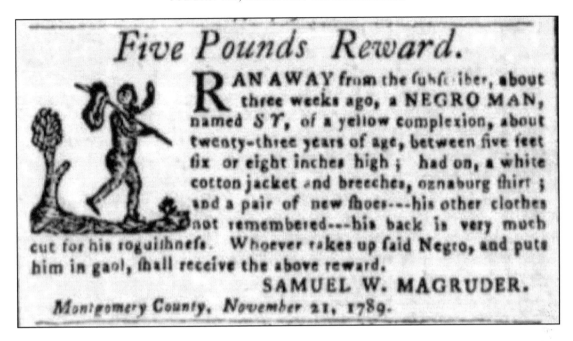

Five Pounds Reward.

RAN AWAY from the subscriber, about three weeks ago, a NEGRO MAN, named SY, of a yellow complexion, about twenty-three years of age, between five feet six or eight inches high; had on, a white cotton jacket and breeches, oznaburg shirt; and a pair of new shoes---his other clothes not remembered---his back is very much cut for his roguishness. Whoever takes up said Negro, and puts him in gaol, shall receive the above reward.

SAMUEL W. MAGRUDER.

Montgomery County, November 21, 1789.

One ad I read describes Susan, a runaway who was "far advanced in pregnancy." (The ad itself is difficult to read so is not included.) But what must have happened to Susan to take off on a journey that would almost certainly fail in her physical state? I imagine it must have been something horrific. This was what slavery was and I never forget that.

FIGURE 101, ESCAPED SLAVES

27 MAY 2013

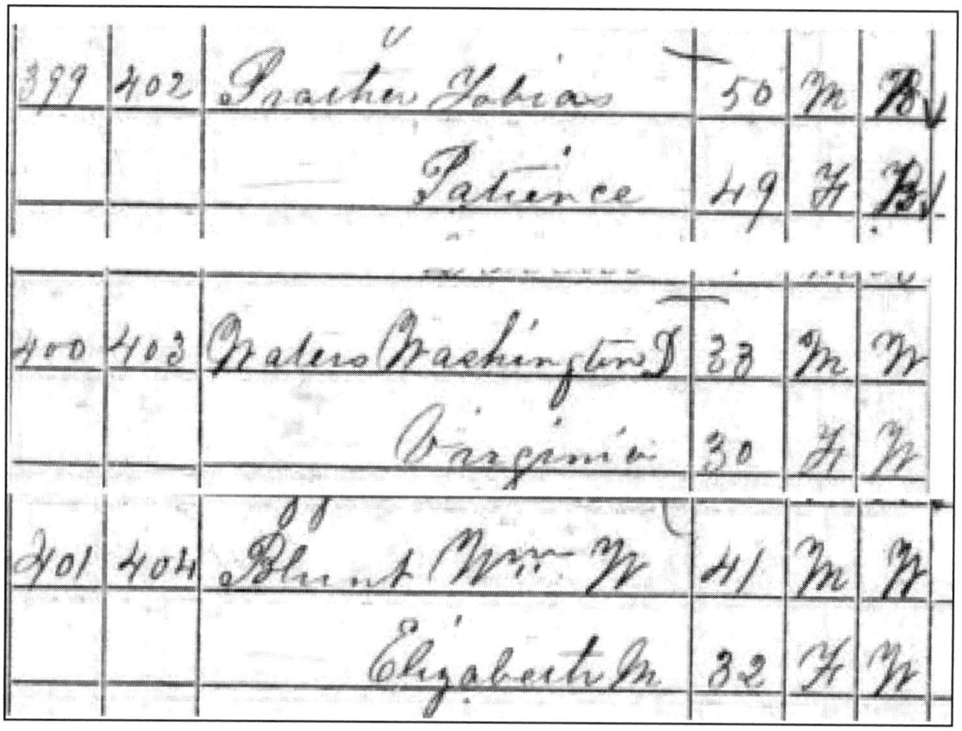

399	402	Prather Tobias	50	M	B
		Patience	49	F	B
400	403	Waters Washington	33	M	W
		Virginia	30	F	W
401	404	Blunt Wm. W	41	M	W
		Elizabeth M	32	F	W

FIGURE 102, 1870 TOBIAS PRATHER

When researching African-Americans, the criticality of the 1870 census cannot be understated. It is called the "Brick Wall" for good reason. Because the vast majority of blacks were enslaved prior to the Civil War, and because most stayed in the area of their enslavement, finding the family in 1870 can be the key that unlocks the door to their enslaved past. As property, slaves were not enumerated by name before 1870 (although freed blacks were).

The upheaval and violence surrounding the Civil War complicates the task. Formerly enslaved blacks varied in the reasons for their surnames and after the war there was still some slaves who chose new surnames as symbols of their new free status. Families can be found in 1870 with one surname and in 1880 with an entirely different surname.

Still, the best tool we have to find the slaveowner is to find the family in 1870. For example, Patience Prather was enslaved by William Blunt in Montgomery County, MD. In 1870, she was reunited with her husband Tobias, and just two houses away was the William Blunt household (above).

It is not uncommon to see several people of differing surnames living together in 1870. Always be curious about others living in the household–researching them can often lead to finding other family members. Remember that former slaves formed kinship ties with one another during slavery and those ties lasted long after emancipation. That was one of the many coping strategies they developed to deal with the frequency of sale.

This is one of the strategies they used to survive in a system where at any moment blood-family members could be sold, never to be seen again.

Elisha Riggs, also in Montgomery County, MD, owned the following slaves along with others:

Tobias Powell
Mary Powell
Candace Boone
Mahala Boone
Anne Boone
Mary Boone
Arianna Boone
Henrietta Boone

The 1870 household of Tobias Powell, who was then living in Washington D.C., is shown below. These people had been enslaved together and those ties continued. Of course, the 1870 census can also cause us to stumble when we forget that *no relationships are given in that census year.* Relationships

are suggested; the census suggests Tobias and Mary were married and had children Lizzie, Lavinia and Willie. But we have to verify those relationships with other records.

There are some family lines that may not yield success for various reasons. While most former slaves stayed in their immediate areas–some were driven out by white violence, others in search of work or family that had been sold. Or they may have stayed in the same place, but the slaveowner may have died or left the area. Some had been forced to move with slaveowners trying to refugee their slaves during the war.

For those who can't find their family in 1870 on the census, **try to get as close to that timeframe as possible.** Be sure to check land and court records, and the tax and voting records that survive in several Southern states. The 1870 census remains, for those researching African-Americans, the most critical census of all.

619	Powell Tobias	37	M	B	Wood Sawyer
	Mary	27	F	B	Washerwoman
	Lizzie	9	F	B	
	Lavinia	7	F	B	
	Willie	1	M	B	
	Boone Candis	39	M	B	Cook
	Mahala	32	F	B	Washerwoman
	Shipley Peter	23	M	B	Drives Carriage
	Boone Ann E	18	F	B	Nurse
	Mary E	12	F	B	At School
	Airy Ann	10	F	B	" "
	Henrietta	7	F	B	

FIGURE 103, 1870 POWELL HOUSEHOLD

FIGURE 104, 1862 HILTON HEAD, SC

One of the things that has contributed greatly to my growth as a genealogist has been reading professional genealogical journals. The tendency when you begin genealogy is to think that if an article isn't specifically about your family or in your research location, that it isn't relevant. I learned later that you read the journals **to learn about new resources and new methodology**. This process teaches you how to become a better researcher by reading how others have solved problems and documented their findings.

I believe that researching enslaved ancestors is some of the most difficult research the field will ever see. I **have a collection of slavery-related journal articles** I've gathered over the years that have helped me over some pretty big stumbling blocks.

In terms of professional journals, I tend to favor *National Genealogical Society (NGS) Quarterly*, but it's not the only game in town. There are also publications like *The American Genealogist, The New England Historical and Genealogical Register* and state journals like *The Virginia Genealogist.* Find one or two that you like.

There are several ways to obtain copies of these articles. If you <u>are a member of NGS,</u> you can download PDF files of *NGS Quarterly* from their website from 2002-present. Your regional National Archives or State Archives is likely to own a collection and you could copy them. You could <u>also download the PERSI form</u> from the Allen County Library and order copies.

I consider these articles to be a part of my arsenal, and these authors have helped me to grow the skills needed to research the landscape of slavery. Here's my list:

Curtis Brasfield, "To My Daughter and the Heirs of her Body: Slave Passages as Illustrated by the Latham-Smithwick Family," *NGS Quarterly 81* (December 1993): 270-282.

Rudena Kramer Mallory, "An African-American Odyssey through Multiple Surnames: Mortons, Tapps, and Englishes of Kansas and Missouri," *NGS Quarterly 85* (March 1997)25-38.

Curtis Brasfield, "Tracing Slave Ancestors: Batchelor, Bradley, Branch and Wright of Desha County, Arkansas," *NGS Quarterly 92* (March 2004): 6-30.

Ruth Randall, "An Interracial Suit for Inheritance: Clues to Probable Paternity for a Georgia Freedmen, Henry Clay Heard Sherman," *NGS Quarterly 89* (June 2001): 85-97.

Ruth Randall, "Family Lore and Effects of Slavery on the Black Psyche: Rosa Grammar's Choice," *NGS Quarterly 97* (June 2009): 85-96.

Gary B. Mills, "Can Researchers 'Prove' the 'Unproveable'? A Selective Bibliography of Efforts to Genealogically Document Children of Master-

Slave Relationships," *NGS Quarterly 89* (September 2001): 234-237.

Douglas Shipley, "Teaming Oral History with Documentary Research: The Enslaved Austins of Missouri's Little Dixie," *NGS Quarterly 90* (June 2002): 111-135.

Del E. Jupiter, "Matilda Madrid: One Woman's Tale of Bondage and Freedom," *NGS Quarterly 91* (March 2003): 41-59.

Christopher A. Nordmann, "Jumping Over the Broomstick: Resources for Documenting Slave Marriages," *NGS Quarterly 91* (September 2003): 196-216.

Gary B. Mills, "Tracing Free People of Color in the Antebellum South: Methods, Sources and Perspectives," *NGS Quarterly 78* (December 1990): 262-278.

Del E. Jupiter, "From Augustina to Ester: Analyzing a Slave Household for Child-Parent Relationships," *NGS Quarterly 85* (December 1997): 245-275.

Elizabeth Shown Mills, "Which Marie Louise is 'Mariotte'? Sorting Slaves with Common Names," *NGS Quarterly 94* (September 2006): 183-204.

C. Bernard Ruffin III, "In Search of the Unappreciated Past: The Ruffin-Cornick Family of Virginia," *NGS Quarterly 81* (June 1993): 126-138.

Katherine E. Flynn, "Jane Johnson, Found! But Is She 'Hannah Crafts'? The Search for the Author of The Bondwoman's Narrative," *NGS Quarterly 90* (September 2002): 165-190.

Donna R. Mills, "Racheal 'Fanny' Devereaux/Martin of Alabama and Florida, A Free Woman of Color," *The American Genealogist 70* (January 1995): 37-41.

Ruth Randall, "A Family for Suzanne," *NGS Quarterly 95* (December 2007): 281-302.

Cameron Allen, "Lucinda Depp and Her Descendants: A Freed Black Family of Virginia and Ohio," *The Genealogist 17* (Spring 2003): 3-36.

Johni Cerny, "From Maria to Bill Cosby: A Case Study in Tracing Black Slave Ancestry," *NGS Quarterly 75* (March 1987): 5-14.

Rachel Mills Lennon, "Mother, Thy Name is Mystery! Finding the Slave Who Bore Philomene Daurat," *NGS Quarterly 88* (September 2000): 201-224.

Elizabeth Shown Mills, "Documenting a Slave's Birth, Parentage and Origins: Marie Therese Coincoin, 1742-1816: A Test of Oral History", NGS Quarterly 96 (December 2008); 245-266.

Daniela Moneta, "Virginia Pughs and North Carolina Wests: A Genetic Link from Slavery in Kentucky," NGS Quarterly 97 (September 2009): 179-194.

The image on left is a famous Thomas Nast drawing of Andrew Johnson's veto of the Freedmens Bureau in 1866. It shows him kicking the "Bureau" and has little black people falling out. The drawing may be a funny caricature, but what black people were experiencing was no laughing matter.

One of the things sometimes overlooked is the absolute terror of the Reconstruction period for many African-Americans. Although they were no longer enslaved, the vast majority of former slaves were still in the South and living amidst a very angry populace that had lost the War. White Southerners lost a war that destroyed slavery, much to their disgust. Most whites (North and South) did not consider black people worthy of anything close to equal treatment. Even minor displays of independence by blacks could and did invite deadly responses. It is no coincidence that the Ku Klux Klan was founded during this period and that former Confederate soldiers were often guilty of much of the violence.

FIGURE 105, ANDREW JOHNSON

Many Freedmens Bureau offices kept records of reported crimes that were committed in their districts, what they termed murders or "outrages." Most take the form of registers or logs or were written as summaries in letters of the reporting officers. Although these records usually captured crimes against everyone, black and white, show the vast majority of crimes were committed against the newly freed black population. The Freedmens Bureau in many places replaced the law enforcement of the local area and had the power to arrest and charge individuals, and to hold trials.

I still remember the first time I read one of these documents. The records detail freedmen and their families working under labor contracts, then being beaten or otherwise forced off the farm without any pay when the crops came in. There were also lots of cases of black men and women being randomly beaten, whipped or raped. Many of the perpetrators in the documents are listed as "parties unknown," which would become a familiar refrain used during the era of lynchings.

These poor people just went from terror to terror. Even filing a charge with the Bureau could expose one to more retribution, so many more crimes likely happened than were reported to the Bureau. Union soldiers, teachers, preachers, landowners and those attempting to vote were especially targeted. Many Southern whites were intent upon keeping blacks in their socially inferior and economically dependent status.

When you read these outrages, what comes across is the widespread level of violence that the newly freed lived under. Surely, some areas were worse than others. But when I think about the joy that freedom gave former slaves, I also remember that joy must have been stunted by the violence and terror that was to come. So many of the people weren't even named, just "colored man" or "colored woman." I wonder how many are our ancestors that seem to "disappear" after the 1870 census?

Freedmens Bureau.com has some transcriptions of these Outrages. Here are some selections from Alabama in the year 1866:

District of Alabama, 1866

March – Bradley killed freedwoman with an axe. Montgomery.

April 3 – Woman taken by three men out of her house in middle of night to swamp & badly whipped – beaten on head with pistol.

April 27 – Freedman shot by Confed. Soldier wantonly [killed] near Livingston, Sumter Co.

May 30 – Mulatto hung by grapevine near roadside between Tuscaloosa and Greensboro.

May 29 – Richard Dick's wife beaten with club by her employer. Richard remonstrated – in the night was taken from his house and whipped nearly to death with a buggy trace by son of the employer and two others.

June 16 – Mr. Alexander, colored preacher, brutally beaten and forced to leave his house at Auburn, Ala.

July – Band of armed men came to house of Eliz. Adams, threatened to kill her & her sister if they did not leave the county, abused & beat them. (illegible) Franklin & (illegible) started to report outrage, not heard from afterward.

Sept. 14 – Black man picking fodder in a field shot dead — & another who had difficulty with a white man abducted & supposed to have been murdered near Tuscaloosa.

Sept. 3 – Murderous assault upon returned black Union soldier in Blount Co.

Dec. 17 – Enoch Hicks & party burned school house in Greenville in Sumner – assaulted Union soldier &c. Judge Bragg & son mercilessly beat wife & daughter of James, freedman & drew pistol on James. Kell Forrest beat wife of colored man George.

July 18 – One Yerby set fire to colored [church] Near Tuscaloosa, threatened to kill black man who saw him do it.

August – Gang of ruffians in Clarke Co. set fire to house & fired on family as they ran from it – one killed, two wounded.

February 1866 – Freedwoman beaten with club by her employer near Selma, head cut in most shocking manner.

June 1866 – Freedman shot while at his usual work by his employer for threatening to report his abusive conduct to the authorities of the Bureau – Mobile.

December 1866 – Freedman killed by parties unknown, brought to hospital in dying condition, shot through brain.

Here are a few reported from **Murfreesboro, TN in 1866:**

July 28th 1865 – Ben (col'd) Plaintiff vs. Beverly Randolph. Ben says " on the 29th of June Randolph beat my wife with his fists then caught her by the chin threw back her head pulled out his knife swore he would cut her throat—His brother-in-law stopped him, he then went to his house got his pistol and swore he would kill some dam nigger——fired of his pistol and went to Mr. Harris's (the woman was large with child at the time)." Defendant admitted the charge——was fined 50 Dolls. Which was paid to plaintiff.

Aug. 1st. Egbert (col'd) vs. J. Irvin. Egbert says "Irvin returned from the Reb. Army & found I had a crop growing (I staid on the place and took care of his family house and stock ever since the war begun). When I began to gather the crop (I was to have the 1/3) he drove me and my family off and would not give us a bit of anything to eat and said he did not care a dam for the Bureau." Got 3 mounted men sent for and brought Irvin who was very penitent under bayonet force and secured by bond. The crop to plaintiff. Since, all paid.

Aug. 2nd. Sam Neal (col'd) vs. Andrew B. Payne. Sam says "Payne hired myself and family 10 altogether to work for the season, he has made several base attempts on my daughter, has ordered me off without pay or share of the crop & because I did not go he got his pistol & threatened to shoot me——he got Miles Ferguson to beat me & the both together beat me badly." Payne came by a summons & on proof of guilt offered to let them go back gather the crop & have their share & I fined him for beating and ordering Ferguson to beat him 25 Dolls. Paid to Sam——

Aug. 4th. Anthony (col'd) vs. Bill Murray. Anthony says "Mr. Murray did on the 1st severely beat my

wife and daughter with a stick because we were singing a union song." Send an order to Murray to appear at this office but was taken with the apoplexy & it is said died from mortal fear of the being put in the Bureau.

These are a sad but informative set of records. Of course, 99.9% of these records are not online, but they can be located by referring to the Freedmens Bureau pamphlets on the National Archives website.

FIGURE 106, 1868, HARPER'S WEEKLY

27 AUGUST 2012

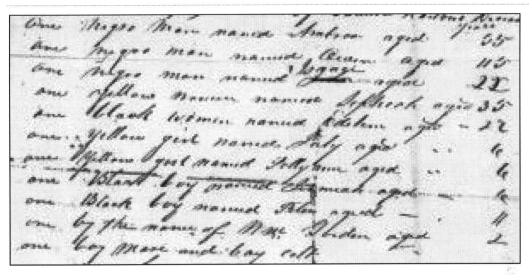

FIGURE 107, HARBOUR INVENTORY

I discuss slave and slaveowner research often in this blog because it's one of my primary areas of interest. For those of us descended from enslaved ancestors, probate records are one of the first record sets we are taught to explore. If we're lucky enough to discover that the slaveowner died before 1865, we may find our ancestors named in the slaveowner's will or listed in their inventories. As we advance in our skills, however, we've got to look even closer at probate records beyond just the will or inventory, not to mention the need to search beyond the slaveowner himself.

I want to show an example of how careful tracing through and understanding of those "other" probate records may provide a more complete picture of our ancestor's path through the slaveowner's family. Familysearch has now posted probate records for many states making this technique possible to do from home in some instances.

I suggest using _Rootsmagic_ (or whatever genealogy software you have) to create a separate family tree for the slaveowner's family. This will be invaluable to your research. Many slaveowners married their first cousins, which makes keeping track of the relationships difficult. **It is imperative that you know at a minimum the parents of the couple, when/where their parents lived and died, all of the couple's children, when and where they died, and especially** _who the daughters married._

As long as the slaveowner died before 1865, start probate tracing with the slaveowner, then trace his wife if she outlived him, then their children if necessary.

2b. Martha Willson, d. 1837.

Item Type	Sourcing	Date	Notes
Will	Vol. V., Pg. 164-167	25 October 1837 (wr) 28 November 1837 (rec) Names Children	Wit: Richard Bowie, Otho Magruder *Slaves Dick & Nelly to sons John W. or Robert P, others sold
Bond	Vol. V, pg. 172	28 November 1837	John W. Mag., Nathan Cooke, Otho Mag. & Wm B. Mag., $20K. John & Nathan, execs.
Inventory	Vol. V, pg. 204-208	16 December 1837	Slaves (9): *Dick, 60, York, 44, Jim, 36, Jerry, 47, William, 30, *Nelly, 64, Milley, 58, Leah, 48, Ann, 10
Sales	Vol. V, pg. 251-257	27 February 1838	Slaves to Her Children: Milley & Jim to Thomas Magruder York, Jerry & Leah to William Magruder Ann to Robert Magruder William to Rebecca D. Cooke
Debts	Vol. V., pg. 292-293	20 March 1838	
1st Acct	Vol. W, 1838-1840	19 November 1839	Value: $2309
2nd Acct	Vol. X, pg. 40-41	25 August 1840	Value: $10293
3rd Acct	Vol. X, pg. 157	26 January 1841	Value: $12166
Final Acct	Vol. Z, pg. 13	5 March 1847	Value: $11098

(Estate Probate spanned 10 years)

In a previous post, I talked about the various steps in the probate process, both for dying with a will (testate) or dying without a will (intestate). Those who follow this blog know I'm a fool for charting. Take a look at the chart above that I made for Martha Willson Magruder, my Prather slaveowner's mother, who died in 1837.

I began the search knowing Martha's date of death. I went to the probate book for that year, and easily found "*Martha Willson, Will*" on Page 164 of Volume V.

Dick and Nelly (from Martha's inventory) were elderly slaves and were probably unable to do much if any work at ages 60

Keep in mind that I am using the term "probate" to refer to these records in general. What they are actually called varies by state and locality—in the case of Maryland, these volumes are actually "Will Books [that also contain] Inventories and Accounts," and are kept by the Register of Wills.

I began my chart above with Martha's will, and extracted any relevant phrases about her slaves. She specified that "*Dick and Nelly*" have their choice of going with either her son Robert or her son John.

and 64. Martha specified that the rest of her slaves be sold at private auction.

The next important document in her estate probate is the bond. Executors (in the case of a will) or Administrators (in the case of no will) must post bond with the State that they will faithfully execute their duties.

It is important to know who is posting bond; they are often family members. For example, Otho Magruder was Martha's son-in-law. Also, a $20K bond infers this was a relatively wealthy estate.

Martha's inventory named 9 slaves. The next step after the inventory was the sales of her estate—**this is where slaves can be missed!** In these pages we find her other 7 slaves were sold, but (because I know Martha's family tree) they were all sold to her children.

The next steps in Martha's estate probate include a listing of Debts and periodic Accounting of the Estate. The number of Accountings (1st Acct, 2nd Acct, 3rd Acct, Final Acct, etc.) depends upon many things, like the size of the estate and whether or not minor children were involved.

Those Accountings can also contain information about slaves, especially slaves being "hired out" for the year, so peruse them carefully. If minor children are involved, guardianship records should also be traced, but may be handled in a different court.

I included in my chart the dates and book and page numbers so I could create proper source citations for each record. Also notice that Martha's estate probate spanned across 10 years. **It is not uncommon to find probates spanning large periods of time, especially if there were minor children involved. I now trace, as a rule, at least 20 years forward after a death.**

Martha was rather well off by the standards of her time. Her final estate value of $11,098 in 1847 was roughly the equivalent of $303,000 today. The actual division of slaves, which would show exactly which of her children individual slaves went to, is not always written in the official probate books.

I have found them in original case files or loose papers (i.e., the papers that are a part of the probate proceedings but not necessary recorded in the official books).

Always try to find the slave division. Martha received 6 slaves from her husband's estate at his death, so we can presume the others were divided among his children, but that division is not recorded in the probate books.

Hopefully I've highlighted a strategy you can use to get the most value out of probate records.

Note: The online blog post also charts Martha's husband's estate probate.

FIGURE 109, 1917 SLAVE REUNION

Lately I have been reading a lot of published slave narratives. These are <u>not to be confused</u> with the <u>WPA slave interviews from the 1930s</u> that many of us are familiar with. I am referring to slave narratives that were written and published from the mid 1800's through about 1900 by former slaves, many of whom had fled slavery. These books were popular during that timeframe, especially as a part of the anti-slavery movement. We probably are familiar with ones like Booker T. Washington's *Up*

From Slavery and Frederick Douglass' autobiography. But I think we forget that this **is primary information out of the mouths of slaves**, and also that there were at least one hundred other narratives published.

The University of North Carolina has an online collection entitled <u>"North American Slave Narratives."</u> It is a part of the collection entitled <u>"Documenting the American South."</u>

"[My master was] coarse and vulgar in his habits, unprincipled and cruel in his general deportment, and especially addicted to the vice of licentiousness. His slaves had little opportunity for relaxation from wearying labor, were supplied with the scantiest means of sustaining their toil by necessary food, and had no security for personal rights... The principal food of those upon my master's plantation consisted of corn meal, and salt herrings; to which was added in summer a little buttermilk, and the few vegetables which each might raise for himself and his family, on the little piece of ground which was assigned to him for the purpose, called a truck patch. The meals were two, daily."

This database contains if not all then certainly most existing slave narratives, including pamphlets and articles through 1920. I had seen this collection many times over the years, but never really explored them. The other day I started reading them, and got so engrossed I stayed for 3 hours. They are very detailed, and I realized that these could be a terrific resource for our research.

At UNC's online collection, I found the story of a man named **Josiah Henson** who was enslaved in Montgomery County (center), where my Prather ancestors lived. He is credited as being the prototype for the lead character in Harriet Beecher Stowe's infamous book *Uncle Tom's Cabin*. The excerpt below is from his 1849 narrative, "*The Life of Josiah Henson, Formerly a Slave, Now an Inhabitant of Canada, as*

FIGURE 110, JOSIAH HENSON

Narrated by Himself." Josiah escaped from slavery and later became an abolitionist and a minister. Doesn't this first-hand account (shown above) make the experiences of my ancestors in that county come alive just a little bit more?

Peruse the UNC website and read through some of the pages of the various narratives. Perhaps you can

find someone who grew up in your ancestor's state, or better yet, the same county.

UNC's entire collection is extraordinarily valuable, and another collection that I also found useful was the one entitled "First Person Narratives of the American South." This collection encompasses all Southerners, white and black, and I found some of the diaries of slaveowners and their wives to be very eye-opening. For example, Elizabeth Pringle, daughter of a prominent planter had a book published about her life growing up on a southern rice plantation called *A Woman Rice Planter*. Here's a tip for this collection: Browse by Subject, and under the heading "African-Americans," you'll find a sorting of the narratives by state. Other standouts in the online UNC DocSouth collections include *The Church in the Southern Black Community* and *Oral Histories of the American South*.

I am always on the lookout for ways to enrich the stories of my ancestor's lives, as well as educate myself on the topic . These narratives are rich reading, even as they relayed horrific realities. Kudos to UNC, and I hope to get there in person to do research one day, as I've heard their library/archives is one of the best in the South.

FIGURE 111, 1870 MALINDA HOLT

My ancestor Malinda Holt was enslaved by Giles Holt of Hardin County, Tennessee. Malinda was enslaved along with another woman, named Judah Holt (sometimes written Judy/Julia). Both women had multiple children of around the same ages. Although I will probably never know whether or not Malinda and Judah were actually sisters, I have decided to track Judah's children as my relatives because it is obvious that their children had close kinship ties and considered each other family. I did a post sometime ago about Judah's son James and his amazing life story.

One of the many wretched things about slavery is that often we trace back to a female ancestor, listed as head of household in 1870 and we find no hint of a man, like the 1870 entry for Malinda above. Our climb through the family tree stops—there is no other branch to trace. Particularly if the children are noted as "mulatto," we wonder whether our

ancestor was one of the millions of children fathered by white men. We all know that slaves often married enslaved neighbors, but this relationship can be difficult to uncover if the couple are not found living together in 1870.

As I tracked Judah Holt's children, a delightful surprise emerged. Judah's son Henry Holt died during the Civil War while he was a member of the 55th US Colored Regiment. His mother Judah's subsequent application for a pensionn in 1887 provided details of her children's names and (approximate) birthdates. One of the depositions, from fellow soldier Richard Kendall, also included this little gem:

> "I was well-acquainted with Henry Holt and knew his family. I do not know whether his father is dead or alive. His name [was] Sam Dixon."

At last I found evidence of Judah's relationship with a (presumably) black man. But where was he? For years I couldn't find him because of my inability to be very creative with name spelling variations.

Looking through Hardin County probate records recently led me to the will of one Elizabeth Dickson (note the spelling). That rang a bell in my mind, and sure enough, among the legacies she left to her daughter Jane in that will was this:

"…and she is to have my black man Samuel while…she lives single"

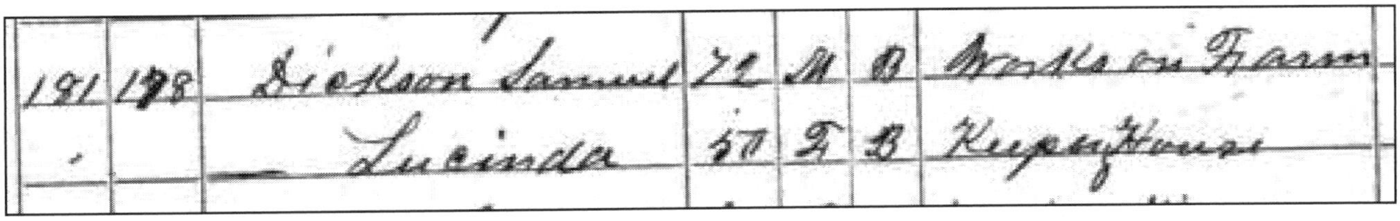

191	198	Dickson Samuel	72	M	B	Works on Farm
		Lucinda	50	F	B	Keeping House

FIGURE 112, 1870 SAMUEL DICKSON

Racing back to Ancestry, there is Samuel Dickson in 1870 (image above), in the town of Savannah, right where he should be, although he appears to be married to Lucinda now. Or perhaps Lucinda is a daughter.

I got even luckier when Judah also included in her pension file the fact that her daughters Sarah and Frances were both now surnamed "Davy." Using that surname, I found Judah's daughter Frances' (nicknamed Fannie) death certificate in 1917. Guess who was listed as her father? Sam Dickson.

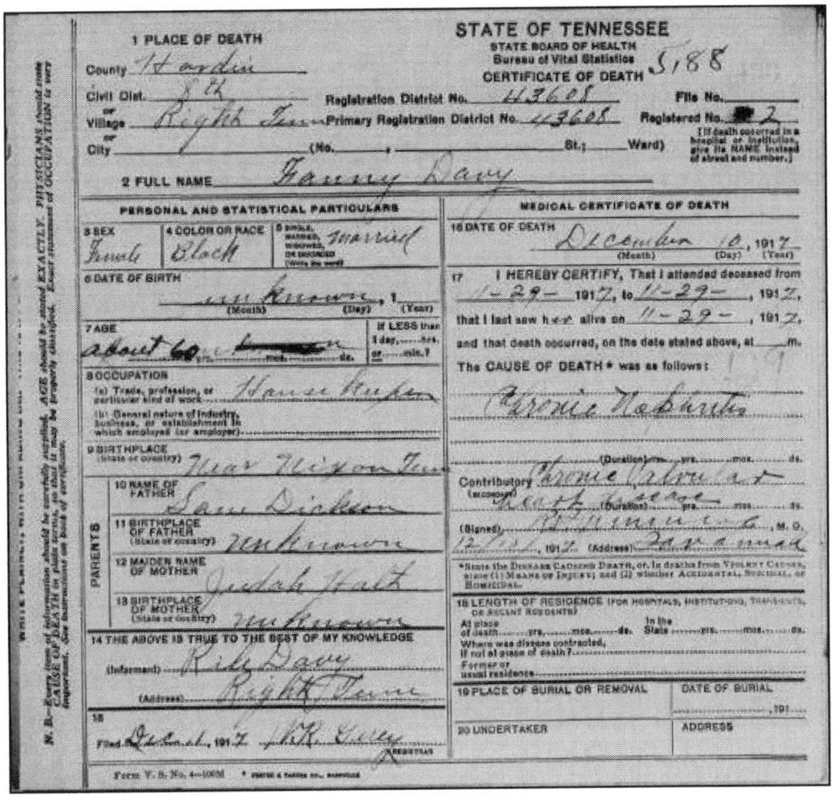

STATE OF TENNESSEE
STATE BOARD OF HEALTH
Bureau of Vital Statistics
CERTIFICATE OF DEATH 5188

1 PLACE OF DEATH
County Hardin
Civil Dist. 8th Registration District No. 43608 File No.
Village Right Tenn Primary Registration District No. 43608 Registered No. 2
City (No. St.; Ward) (If death occurred in a hospital or institution, give its NAME instead of street and number.)

2 FULL NAME Fanny Davy

PERSONAL AND STATISTICAL PARTICULARS

3 SEX Female
4 COLOR OR RACE Black
5 SINGLE, MARRIED, WIDOWED, OR DIVORCED (Write the word) married
6 DATE OF BIRTH unknown (Month) (Day) (Year)
7 AGE about 60 yrs. mos. ds. If LESS than 1 day, hrs. or min.?
8 OCCUPATION (a) Trade, profession, or particular kind of work House Keeper
(b) General nature of industry, business, or establishment in which employed (or employer)
9 BIRTHPLACE (State or country) Near Nixon Tenn

PARENTS
10 NAME OF FATHER Sam Dickson
11 BIRTHPLACE OF FATHER (State or country) unknown
12 MAIDEN NAME OF MOTHER Judah Walk
13 BIRTHPLACE OF MOTHER (State or country) unknown

14 THE ABOVE IS TRUE TO THE BEST OF MY KNOWLEDGE
(Informant) Rile Davy
(Address) Right Tenn

15 Filed Dec 1, 1917 W.R. Curry Registrar

MEDICAL CERTIFICATE OF DEATH

16 DATE OF DEATH December 10, 1917 (Month) (Day) (Year)

17 I HEREBY CERTIFY, That I attended deceased from 11-29-1917, to 11-29-1917, that I last saw her alive on 11-29-1917, and that death occurred, on the date stated above, at m.
The CAUSE OF DEATH* was as follows:
Chronic Nephritis
(Duration) yrs. mos. ds.
Contributory (secondary) Chronic Valvular Heart Disease (Duration) yrs. mos. ds.
(Signed) M.D.
12/1, 1917 (Address) Savannah

*State the DISEASE CAUSING DEATH, or, in deaths from VIOLENT CAUSES, state (1) MEANS OF INJURY; and (2) whether ACCIDENTAL, SUICIDAL, or HOMICIDAL.

18 LENGTH OF RESIDENCE (FOR HOSPITALS, INSTITUTIONS, TRANSIENTS, OR RECENT RESIDENTS)
At place of death yrs. mos. ds. In the State yrs. mos. ds.
Where was disease contracted, if not at place of death?
Former or usual residence

19 PLACE OF BURIAL OR REMOVAL DATE OF BURIAL 191

20 UNDERTAKER ADDRESS

Form V. S. No. 4—10M

FIGURE 113, FANNY DAVY

While there is no way to know exactly how many of Judah's children were fathered by Sam, the fact that I was able to uncover evidence for two of her children is pretty amazing. **This is also a good example of using the technique of using cluster research, to expand your vision and research the group of people surrounding your direct ancestors.** The hunt for those elusive enslaved fathers continues.

As I have researched more and more enslaved ancestors, I have become more immersed in researching slavery itself. I have a friend who is a Ph.D. and professor of African-American studies and he has really helped me understand the history in a different way. We've clocked tens of hours of conversation about the institution of slavery.

Although what genealogists do is similar, it's also quite different from what professional historians do. We are more interested in the individuals and the specific history while historians tend to focus more on larger groups of people. The difference in those perspectives fascinate me.

I wanted to present a short overview of some of the most popular works in the evolution of slavery studies. I highly encourage anyone researching enslaved people to read some (at least one) of these works. I haven't gotten through them all but I'm working on it!

"American Negro Slavery" by Ulrich Phillips, 1918

Typical of the times, Ulrich's racism was front and center. He believed in the

inferiority of blacks and the fantasy of the "Old South." He wrote that slavery was not a financially profitable institution and that it was done mainly to benefit blacks and maintain white supremacy. He wrote that slaveowners treated, fed and clothed their slaves well. Amazingly, this was the prevailing view of slavery for almost 30 years although W.E.B. DuBois vocally challenged his findings.

"The Peculiar Institution" by Kenneth M. Stampp, 1956

Stampp, in this groundbreaking work, was the first to counter Ulrich Phillips' school of thought in several areas. He showed that slavery was not benign but a cruel and brutal system of labor exploitation and control. He argued that slavery was indeed a profitable system. He illustrated the extreme suffering of slaves and he also discussed the many methods of slave resistance. Stampp also discussed how becoming a slaveowner was a part of a social system which allowed whites to enter the upper class and gain status in the community.

"Slavery: A Problem in American Institutional and Intellectual Life" by Stanley Elkins, 1959

Elkins was the first historian to look at the psychological impact of slavery rather than just the economics of it. He compared southern slave plantations to Nazi concentration camps and argued that slavery was so brutal and inhumane that it stripped slaves of their African heritage (i.e., they had a "social death") and transformed them into docile, submissive figures. His most famous thesis was that the system of slavery had **infantilized** slaves, making them "Sambos"—reduced them by brutality to a dependant, child-like status. Although many of his arguments have now been rejected, this single book caused a firestorm and a huge outpouring of responses by other historians.

"The Slave Community" by John Blassingame, 1972

Blassingame wrote one of the first slave studies to be presented from the perspective of the enslaved and contradicted historians like Elkins and his "Sambo" thesis. Through the lens of psychology, Blassingame used 19th century fugitive slave narratives as sources to determine that in fact, a rich and unique culture developed among American slaves, with plenty of evidence that African practices survived. Historians criticized Blassingame's use of slave narratives (which are considered biased) and questioned his neglect of the WPA slave interviews but the book remains an important contribution.

"Roll Jordan Roll: The World the Slaves Made," by Eugene Genovese 1974

Eugene D. Genovese was a Marxist and this book attempts to decipher, from a Marxist perspective, the world of antebellum slavery. Genovese's thesis is that slaves created a rich culture, at once both African-American and uniquely southern. He raised some new arguments and presented a truly dizzying array of footnotes and examples. Sometimes he can lose the reader with his ruminations on social theory, but this is an engaging read nevertheless, from one of the most enigmatic and controversial American historians.

"The Black Family in Slavery and Freedom, 1750-1925" by Herbert Gutman, 1976

In this classic text on black family life, Gutman argues that slavery did not break up the black family, which had become a familiar refrain as a result of the 1970s "Moynihan Report." Gutman was a labor historian who studied workers and social history.

Gutman illustrates that most black families largely remained intact despite slavery and remained that way during the first wave of migration to the North after the Civil War (although he remained open to arguments about black family collapse in the 1930s and 1940s).

Gutman's work was widely praised. I could go on and on, and mention works by **Deborah Gray White** on enslaved women ("Ar'n't I a Woman? Female Slaves in the Plantation South") works by **Ira Berlin** ("Many Thousands Gone") and **John Hope Franklin** ("Runaway Slaves: Rebels on the Plantation"). There are more than I could ever review here, but I hope if you have not yet thought about reading one of these works you will.

The stories of the people we uncover need to be woven with social history, and perhaps nothing looms larger and more complex than slavery. Pick up one of these at the local library or used book store and send me an email and let me know what you're reading.

FIGURE 114, MARY GARRETT

My 2nd great-grandmother Mary Garrett married John W. Holt and they settled in Hardin County,

TN and raised a large family. Mary was from neighboring Decatur County, and *her mother's* death certificate (whose name was also Mary) indentified her parents as Mason and Rachel Garrett (thus, my Mary's grandparents).

Mason and Rachel Garrett were easily found on the 1870 and 1880 Decatur County census but the usual strategies for locating their former slaveowner did not work. I noted Mason's birthplace of Kentucky and his wife's in South Carolina, as well as the fact that Mason and Rachel both were quite old by 1870. His 70-year old age in that year placed his birthdate around 1800, but other documents provide evidence that he was older than that and was likely born in the late 1790s.

FIGURE 115, 1870 GARRETT HOUSE

In 2010, I lucked upon a court case that included testimony from Mason and Rachel. I say luck (or perhaps the spirits guiding?) because I was not looking for them in Hardin County, since they resided in Decatur County, and because the title of the court case was "*NC Davis vs. John A. Smith, et al*" which would not have garnered even a partial glance. An index had been created that named every person in the chancery court records, which is where I first saw their names.

There were over 100 pages of court papers in that chancery court file with documents from at least 3 states. The court case was crucial to my research on this family; it described in detail Mason and Rachel's lives on the property called Bath Springs and the circumstances of its various owners.

The documents identified Mason and Rachel's former owner as Thomas Jeff Johnson who had died about 1854. His enslaved property was then transferred to Thomas' brother, William Johnson, who was killed by "guerillas" in Decatur County in 1863 or 64 during the Civil War. That explained why I could not find any owner in 1870—they were both dead.

There was also the jewel of testimony stating that Thomas Johnson *got the slaves from his wife and stepfather*. The file included a copy of Thomas Johnson's will and inventory which was probated 20 March 1854. The inventory named his slaves(below): **Mason, 80, Rachel, 49, Alexander, 22, Mary, 18, Franklin, 16, George, 14, Anna, 5 and William, 12.**

Recently, I have peeled back another layer of this onion. Researching family trees at Ancestry gave me a prospective family for Thomas Jeff Johnson. He married a woman named Sarah Garrard, whose family was from Kentucky. Now that Kentucky birthplace for Mason made sense.

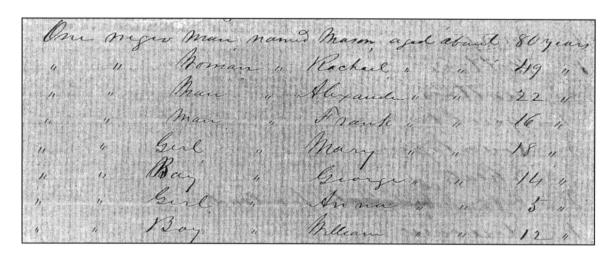

FIGURE 116, JOHNSON INVENTORY

Using Google Books, I discovered a book entitled, *"James Welborn of Muhlenberg County, Kentucky and His Descendants,"* by Gail Jackson Miller. The book described Sarah's family and was footnoted so I could follow where the author got her information. I knew this had to be the genesis of my family—so *"Garrett"* really started out as *"Garrard."* I ordered microfilm reels from the Family History Center. If Thomas Johnson's slaves came from his wife Sarah, it made sense to start the search for Mason and Rachel with William W. Garrard, Sarah's father, who was from Muhlenberg County, KY.

William migrated to Lauderdale County, AL where his family resided for some years. Later, William moved to Hardin County, TN where he died sometime before 1851. His estate inventory, unfortunately, has not been found. However, I found something even more valuable: a June 1838 mortgage in Alabama on slaves by William W. Garrard:

6/1838-William W. Garrard to secure a debt to Arnett and Dillahunty, the following slaves: **Rachel (black), and her children Daniel, Andrew,**

Clayton, and an infant, Mason, age 45, and his wife Rachel, age 30, and her children Lucy, Alexander, Mary & Franklin, and boy Cyrus, age 45, and girl Harriett.

This was valuable because it included the important phrases, *"…and her children"* as well as *"and his wife,"* providing relationships for enslaved people that are almost impossible to find. Notice that even at age 45, Cyrus is still called a "boy."

When William Garrard came to Hardin County, he generated more deed records– two in 1850 again naming his slaves. After his death, tracts of land were sold in order to pay some of his debts, and it appears some of those slaves were sold as well:

5/8/1850-Power of Attorney to Telemachus Jones to recover slaves in possession of Harrison Stephens of Hardin County… they were purchased from Thomas Lassiter as trustee of William W. Garrard: **Rachel, 22 and her son Clayton, Yellow Rachel, abt 22 and her children Alexander, 5, Mary, 8, Franklin, 3, Ellen and Lucy.**

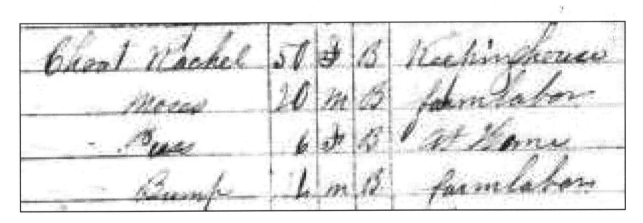

FIGURE 117, 1870 RACHEL CHOAT

5/13/1850-Telemachus Jones of Hardin County, attorney for Henry Dillahunty of Lawrence County, paid $3000 for **Alexander, 15, Franklin, 13, Clayton, 13, George, son of yellow Rachel, 9, William, son of yellow Rachel, 7, Joseph, son of black Rachel, 7, yellow Rachel abt 32 and her child Anna, black Rachel, abt. 32 and her child Felix, Mary, 18, Lucy, 22, and Ellen, 12.**

(Notice one Rachel is described as "black" and the other as "yellow" Rachel). Dillahunty was the party to the mortgage in 1838 which means I've got to research him thoroughly as well. But these three deeds together effectively identify the children of both Rachels. Also notice the widely varying ages for both Rachels and their children, especially on these last two deeds which are both dated in 1850.

By the 1870 census, several of these former slaves are not found living in or near Mason and Rachel's household, which implies some of them may well have been sold or died by that time. Part of their family may still be in Lauderdale County, AL.

I did however, find the "other" Rachel living in Decatur County in 1870 with the surname "Choat." I'm going to search every deed transaction William Garrard made, and along with probate, census and tax records, and I hope to paint a clearer picture of Mason and Rachel and their family while they moved from Kentucky through Alabama and finally to Tennessee.

Some members of their family also show birthplaces in Alabama on the census, which again, matches the path of their slaveowner's movement. Always notice and use those census birthplaces when you see that they are different. I recently gave two lectures on using land records, and this blog post illustrates one way they can be used effectively for slave research. Stay tuned for more on the Garrard family. Photo below shows the children of Mary Garrett and John W. Holt.

FIGURE 118, JOHN AND MARY HOLT CHILDREN

FIGURE 119, DANIEL GARRARD WILL

The Garrett/Garrard saga continues, as I have now extended Mason's history even further back. I discovered that Daniel Garrard was the father of the slaveowner William Garrard, who I discussed in the previous post.

In Daniel's will, written March 1812 in Bourbon County, KY (and images posted on Familysearch), he included the following bequest, shown above.

In that bequest, my 4th great-grandfather Mason was willed first to Daniel's wife then to his son William.

Finding this record made me sadder than usual. I think it was the realization that Mason served 3 generations (so far) of this family—first through Daniel and then to his son and grandson. There's something very powerful and painful about seeing your ancestors named as slaves. The knowledge of slavery as the darkest chapter in our nation's history becomes so very real. It's not just a documentary on PBS or an academic thesis about slavery—it's the tangible reality that these were people, most of whom lived this way their entire lives. I still have deep wells of sadness with all of these documents.

I don't know the name of Mason's mother and father, but perhaps they were enslaved by this family as well. Daniel's inventory is typical of one of the biggest brick walls we hit while researching slaves; there are no family groupings. Most of the time this is where our family research comes to a halt—we can't go any further..

One black man Named Anthony ———— 250

One black boy name Cyrus ———— 500

One Ditto named Mason ———— 500

One girl name Jane ———— 400

One girl named Hannah ———— 333.34

One Girl named Sarah ———— 300

One Ditto name Nancy ———— 300

One Ditto name Grace ———— 300

One Ditto name Esther ———— 250

One Ditto name Ditty ———— 250

FIGURE 120, GARRARD INVENTORY

We can only estimate approximate ages according to their inventory value. At $500 and the highest value, Cyrus and Mason are probably teenagers or in their early 20s. Jane at $400 and the highest valuation for the women, is probably in prime childbearing years. I want to believe that Jane is the mother of Cyrus and Mason, and that at least in going to Daniel's son William there was some attempt to keep her with some of her children. But I have no evidence for that other than heartfelt desire. I see these wills and the breaking up of enslaved families becomes so real; so tangible. I look at the list of names continually, hoping to see an inkling of connection.

FIGURE 121, GOV. GARRARD

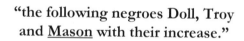

I also discovered that the white Garrards were a famous family, as Daniel's brother James was the 2nd Governor of Kentucky from 1796-1804. He was involved in some of the early political conventions to create the state of Kentucky and interestingly enough, was anti-slavery. He tried unsuccessfully to get gradual emancipation written into Kentucky's constitution. This family's prominence helped me because they are a very well documented family. I easily found Daniel Garrard's father, Col. William Garrard of Stafford County, VA (yes, *maybe not all, but many roads do lead to Virginia*. He left a will written 7 September 1787. In it he bequeathed 24 slaves to his children and grandchildren. Of particular interest is his bequest to his son Robert:

"the following negroes Doll, Troy and <u>Mason</u> with their increase."

The 26 year time span means this is not my Mason, but maybe it was his father? Mason is not a common name. I would love to discover Garrard family bibles or papers that further describe slave relationships. I'm happy to have gotten back this far, although seeing bits and pieces of the reality of enslaved life continues to be a permanent thorn in my soul.

FIGURE 122, HENRY DORSEY

Many enslaved women had children with white men, men whose names are sometimes passed down through oral history in the black family. But many times, only the knowledge of an "unknown white man" survives in the history.

Aaron's ancestor in Texas was a man named Henry Dorsey, and Henry had two brothers named Texas and Richard Dorsey. The oral history gave their white father's name as John Dorsey, and John was living with the three brothers and their wives in the 1880 census for Smith County, Texas (below). The amazing thing is that in John Dorsey's will, probated in 1888, **he named his three black sons** and used strong language describing his close relationship with them:

"It is my will …that whatever may remain [of my estate]…be equally and fairly divided between <u>my beloved sons</u> Henry Dorsey, Richard Dorsey, better known as Dick Dorsey, and Texas Dorsey, better known as Tex, <u>these are three (colored) but bone of my bone and flesh of my flesh and my rightful heirs.</u>"

My friend Aaron has made an incredible find that I wanted to share here because it is such a rarity.

FIGURE 123, 1880 DORSEYS

1. PLACE OF DEATH
STATE OF TEXAS
TEXAS DEPARTMENT OF HEALTH
BUREAU OF VITAL STATISTICS
STANDARD CERTIFICATE OF DEATH
41054
COUNTY OF Kauffman
CITY OR PRECINCT NO. #3
GIVE STREET AND NUMBER OR NAME OF INSTITUTION
2. FULL NAME OF DECEASED Tuck Dorsey
LENGTH OF RESIDENCE WHERE DEATH OCCURRED 25 YEARS MONTHS DAYS (SOCIAL SECURITY NO Dont Know)
RESIDENCE OF THE DECEASED STREET AND NO R. 2 Box 222 CITY Terrell COUNTY Kauffman STATE Texas

PERSONAL AND STATISTICAL PARTICULARS
3. SEX Male
4. COLOR OR RACE negro
5. SINGLE, MARRIED, WIDOWED OR DIVORCED (WRITE THE WORD) widowed
6. DATE OF BIRTH September 21 1854
7. AGE 88 YEARS MONTHS DAYS IF LESS THAN 1 DAY HOURS MIN
8A. TRADE, PROFESSION OR KIND OF WORK DONE farmer
8B. INDUSTRY OR BUSINESS IN WHICH ENGAGED
9. BIRTHPLACE (STATE OR COUNTRY) Smith Co. Texas
10. NAME John Dorsey
11. BIRTHPLACE (STATE OR COUNTRY) Dont Know
12. MAIDEN NAME Dont Know
13. BIRTHPLACE (STATE OR COUNTRY) Dont Know
14. SIGNATURE Harold Dorsey
ADDRESS R. 2 Box 222 Terrell TEXAS
15. PLACE OF BURIAL OR REMOVAL St Mary Cem. Lindale, TEXAS
DATE September 25 1942
16. SIGNATURE McCauley + Son
ADDRESS Gladewater, TEXAS

MEDICAL PARTICULARS
17. DATE OF DEATH Sept 25 1942
18. I HEREBY CERTIFY THAT I ATTENDED THE DECEASED FROM Inquest 194 TO 194
I LAST SAW H ALIVE ON 194
THE DEATH OCCURRED ON THE DATE STATED ABOVE AT M.
THE PRIMARY CAUSE OF DEATH WAS: Senility DURATION
CONTRIBUTORY CAUSES WERE None
DEPARTMENT OF HEALTH RECEIVED OCT 10 1942 TEXAS
IF NOT DUE TO DISEASE, SPECIFY WHETHER:
ACCIDENT, SUICIDE OR HOMICIDE
DATE OF OCCURRENCE
PLACE OF OCCURRENCE x
MANNER OR MEANS x
IF RELATED TO OCCUPATION OF DECEASED, SPECIFY No
SIGNATURE A. L. Scarbro COR
ADDRESS Terrell, Texas TEXAS
20 FILE NUMBER
FILE DATE Sept.25,1942 194
SIGNATURE OF LOCAL REGISTRAR A. L. Scarbro
POSTOFFICE ADDRESS Terrell, TEXAS
NOTE THE INFORMATION CALLED FOR ON THE REVERSE SIDE

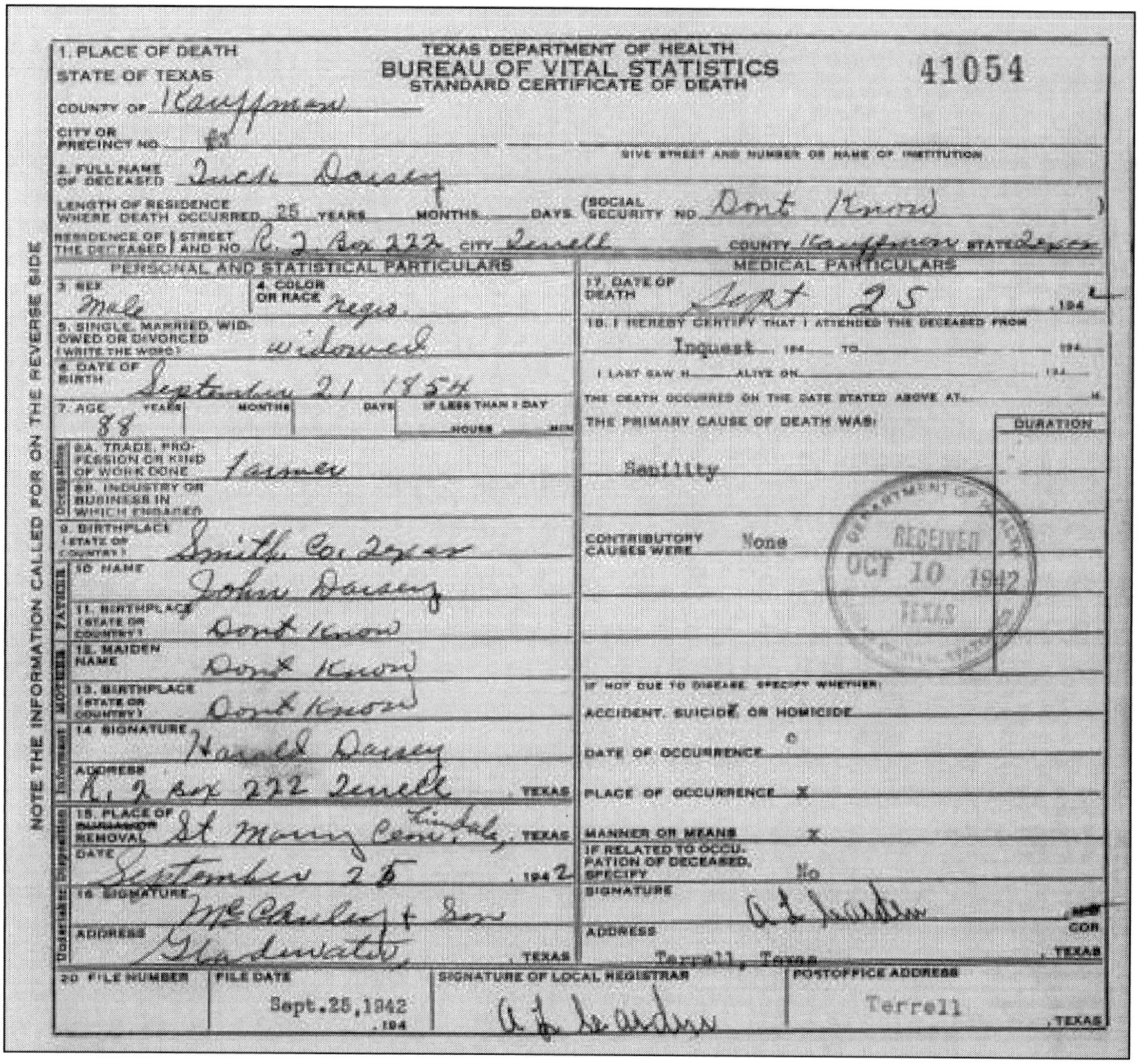

FIGURE 124, DORSEY DEATH CERT

It is rare indeed to find direct evidence of a white man naming and claiming black children, and in Texas no less, in the 1880s! John apparently never married or had any white children, and he named his "best friend" as executor to carry out his wishes. His estate was valued at around $1000, and the fact that the brothers later pay the taxes on his land imply that the land was indeed passed to the three sons. Son Texas' death certificate also directly names his white father (above).

A later examination of the will of John Dorsey's father, Benjamin Dorsey, reveals that the name of the mother of Henry (and his brothers) was an enslaved woman named Ann. Aaron just added a 4th great grandparent to his tree, and is now tracing back through John's roots in Georgia. There are always surprises in store for us in this genealogical journey!

23 JULY 2010

There are great things being digitized and put online by libraries, archives, museums and other repositories. Although as genealogists we are primarily concerned with the details of specific lives, I think it's absolutely worthwhile to expand your vision and look at some of the larger themes that applied to and affected our ancestors: slavery, emancipation, segregation, disenfranchisement, farming and sharecropping and the great migration just to name a few. To that end, I'm sharing some very interesting slave letters I've been reading.

There aren't as many of these available as other sources because so few slaves were able to read and write, or if they did, few letters survived for future generations to read. One good collection is housed by Duke University, Special Collections.

Check out these slave letters. They make for fascinating reading:

Hannah Valentine & Lethe Jackson of Abingdon, VA

Vilet Lester of Randolph County, NC

There are two slave letters on Cornell University's "Abolitionism in America" website: Comfort Jany and Anney McDowell

University of Virginia has many letters from former slaves of James Hunter Terrell who settled in Liberia as well as letters from Samson Ceasar, a former Virginia slave

A letter from fugitive slave John Boston in the Army in Maryland

See also the transcribed Plummer family diary at the Anacostia's Museum website, http://anacostia.si.edu/exhibits/Plummer/Plumm er_Diary.htm

Some excellent books that contain more slave letters and other types of primary source information from African Americans are:

"*Slave Testimony: Two Centuries of Letters, Speeches, Interviews and Autobiographies*" by John Blassingame

"*We Are Your Sisters: Black Women in the Nineteenth Century*" by Dorothy Sterling has a chapter on Slave letters

"*Dear Master: Letters of a Slave Family*" by Randall Miller

Explore these resources, and enter the lives of our enslaved ancestors. I must include probably the most fampus slave letter, written by former slave Jourdan Anderson in responde to his former owner's request for him to come back to Tennessee from Ohio to work for him. The letter is simply amazing.

Dayton, Ohio, August 7, 1865
To My Old Master, Colonel P.H. Anderson, Big Spring, Tennessee

Sir: I got your letter, and was glad to find that you had not forgotten Jourdon, and that you wanted me to come back and live with you again, promising to do better for me than anybody else can. I have often felt uneasy about you. I thought the Yankees would have hung you long before this, for harboring Rebs they found at your house. I suppose they never heard about your going to Colonel Martin's to kill the Union soldier that was left by his company in their stable. Although you shot at me twice before I left you, I did not want to hear of your being hurt, and am glad you are still living. It would do me good to go back to the dear old home again, and see Miss Mary and Miss Martha and Allen, Esther, Green, and Lee. Give my love to them all, and tell them I hope we will meet in the better world, if not in this. I would have gone back to see you all when I was working in the Nashville Hospital, but one of the neighbors told me that Henry intended to shoot me if he ever got a chance.

I want to know particularly what the good chance is you propose to give me. I am doing tolerably well here. I get twenty-five dollars a month, with victuals and clothing; have a comfortable home for Mandy,—the folks call her Mrs. Anderson,—and the children—Milly, Jane, and Grundy—go to school and are learning well. The teacher says Grundy has a head for a preacher. They go to Sunday school, and Mandy and me attend church regularly. We are kindly treated. Sometimes we overhear others saying, "Them colored people were slaves" down in Tennessee. The children feel hurt when they hear such remarks; but I tell them it was no disgrace in Tennessee to belong to Colonel Anderson. Many darkeys would have been proud, as I used to be, to call you master. Now if you will write and say what wages you will give me, I will be better able to decide whether it would be to my advantage to move back again.

As to my freedom, which you say I can have, there is nothing to be gained on that score, as I got my free papers in 1864 from the Provost-Marshal-General of the Department of Nashville. Mandy says she would be afraid to go back without some proof that you were disposed to treat us justly and kindly; and we have concluded to test your sincerity by asking you to send us our wages for the time we served you. This will make us forget and forgive old scores, and rely on your justice and friendship in the future. I served you faithfully for thirty-two years, and Mandy twenty years. At twenty-five dollars a month for me, and two dollars a week for Mandy, our earnings would amount to eleven thousand six hundred and eighty dollars. Add to this the interest for the time our wages have been kept back, and deduct what you paid for our clothing, and three doctor's visits to me, and pulling a tooth for Mandy, and the balance will show what we are in justice entitled to. Please send the money by Adams's Express, in care of V. Winters, Esq., Dayton, Ohio. If you fail to pay us for faithful labors in the past, we can have little faith in your promises in the future. We trust the good Maker has opened your eyes to the wrongs which you and your fathers have done to me and my fathers, in making us toil for you for generations without recompense. Here I draw my wages every Saturday night; but in Tennessee there was never any pay-day for the negroes any more than for the horses and cows. Surely there will be a day of reckoning for those who defraud the laborer of his hire.

In answering this letter, please state if there would be any safety for my Milly and Jane, who are now grown up, and both good-looking girls. You know how it was with poor Matilda and Catherine. I would rather stay here and starve—and die, if it come to that—than have my girls brought to shame by the violence and wickedness of their young masters. You will also please state if there has been any schools opened for the colored children in your neighborhood. The great desire of my life now is to give my children an education, and have them form virtuous habits.

Say howdy to George Carter, and thank him for taking the pistol from you when you were shooting at me. From your old servant,
Jourdon Anderson.

FIGURE 125, SLAVE CABIN, COLUMBIA, MD

I just finished reading an article on slave housing in Montgomery County, Maryland. I've been pondering lately how we need to reconsider how our enslaved ancestors lived; the physical dimensions of that space and what it said about their lives. Not long ago I posted a recommendation for a book called "Back of the Big House" and the book got me thinking about the topic much more deeply.

The slave cabin shown above is from Columbia, Howard County, MD. My mind had been imprinted with the common images attached to the slave experience: large plantations, fields of slaves and slave cabins. My research has shown that slavery was a dynamic institution, ever-changing, and different from time to place to farm to master to crop. There were enslaved people doing mining,

and barbering, working on ships, in factories, and in stores. There were slaves hiring themselves out, and making their own money. The nature of rice farming was very different from tobacco which was different than cotton. Though whipping was common, there were other forms of punishment. We have to challenge all our assumptions about the institution. I know I did.

The slave's physical housing could speak to how much privacy (or lack thereof) they were allowed. Were two large families sharing a space or given separate ones? It could speak to the largess of the owner. Was the housing minimal but not decrepit? How far were they spaced from the overseer's house? Many small farms housed slaves in the master's house, in the loft space above the kitchen or other outbuildings. What did that mean for how much control the master had over their lives? Was the master boastful, setting out rows of slave cabins out front for all to see, or hiding them in back, out of immediate view of visitors?

FIGURE 126, G. WASHINGTON SLAVE HOUSING

I took the picture above of the inside of a slave "dormitory" at Mt. Vernon (George Washington's plantation). It had never occurred to me that slaves ever lived in anything like this. I was equally surprised when I found pictures of stone and brick

FIGURE 127, BOOKER T. WASHINGTON

housing, duplex housing, and the myriad other forms that remove that "log cabin–field slave" image out of my mind. Yes, there were certainly log cabins, but many other types as well. In cities or rural areas with small slaveowners, enslaved people often lived in the attic or some other small space in the slaveowner's home. It was common that those who worked in the kitchen lived in a small space above the kitchen, and house slaves sometimes slept in the room with the small children they were caring for. Many slaves slept on the bare floor, or on top of straw or some other filling made into a pallet.

Have you searched for pictures of surviving slave housing in the area where your ancestors lived? As we tell the story of our enslaved ancestors, let's not forget the physical aspect of their day-to-day lives. Consider this sobering description from Booker T. Washington's *"Up From Slavery"* (his photo above):

"The cabin was not only our living-place, but was also used as the kitchen for the plantation. My mother was the plantation cook. The cabin was without glass windows; it had only openings in the side which let in the light, and also the cold, chilly air of winter. There was a door to the cabin — that is, something that was called a door — but the uncertain hinges by which it was hung, and the large cracks in it, to say nothing of the fact that it was too small, made the room a very uncomfortable one…There was no wooden floor in our cabin, the naked earth being used as a floor. In the centre of the earthen floor there was a large, deep opening covered with boards, which was used as a place in which to store sweet potatoes during the winter…There was no cooking-stove on our plantation, and all the cooking for the whites and slaves my mother had to do over an open fireplace, mostly in pots and "skillets." While the poorly built cabin caused us to suffer with cold in the winter, the heat from the open fireplace in summer was equally trying."

Certainly, we can see that the physical dimensions of the space where Booker T. lived while enslaved made a significant impact on him emotionally.

The era of slavery remains the one of the most difficult periods to research. Recently Family Tree Magazine published a good article on another research tool I use often: Online Books (August 2010 issue). Online Books have proved very useful for researching slaveowners. The article points out 6 major sources:

- ✓ Ancestry.com (Stories, Memories and Histories) (for pay)

- ✓ BYU Family History Archives (free)

- ✓ Google Books (free)

- ✓ HeritageQuest Online (only through subscribing libraries)

- ✓ Internet Archives (free)

- ✓ World Vital Records (pay)

I'll show you a few examples. I was researching possible slaveowners in Lawrence County, Alabama, specifically the Sherrod family. I went to Ancestry, their *Stories, Memories and Histories* Collection which I have marked as a Quick Link. Using their search template and searching on the name 'Ben Sherrod', I quickly pulled up a book called "*Recollections of the Early Settlers of North Alabama*," which was originally published in 1899. Starting on page 233 was a fairly lengthy biographical sketch of the exact family I was researching (below).

This bio gave me valuable clues and starting points; now I knew what dates to search for probate records. I was also able to understand the connections between the Sherrods and the other names I had seen on the 1870 census, especially the wife's maiden name and the father's names which we all know also need to be checked as possible sources for slaves.

FIGURE 128, SHERROD BIO

RECOLLECTIONS OF NORTH ALABAMA.   233

Ward and Joseph F., and seven daughters, Marguerite, Rosa, Willie, Augusta, Delphine, Eugenie, Marie Louise * and Josephine. The boys and girls have been well educated, and those old enough are clerks, or teachers, and earn, in the aggregate, a comfortable living.

Sherrod.

In "*The Memories of Fifty Years*," by Colonel Sparks, he speaks of the exodus from Georgia to Alabama, as threatening the former State with the loss of her best population, and amongst the families emigrating mentions "the Sherrods and Watkinses men of substance and character," and in this, and other numbers, we shall find them closely connected.

Col. Benj. Sherrod, was born in Halifax, North Carolina, 20th January, 1776. His father was Isaac Sherrod, and his mother's maiden name was Mary Ricks. She was the sister of Abram Ricks (who once lived near La Grange, moved to Mississippi and became one of the richest men in that State). She was married twice. First, to Mr. Copeland, who died leaving only one child, a daughter, who married Mr. Long. Sherrod Long, and William Long, were the children of this marriage. Isaac Sherrod married the widow Copeland, and by this marriage they had only one child, Benjamin Sherrod, the subject of this sketch. His father died before his birth and his mother shortly after, and he was reared by the father of Abram Ricks.

In the second example, I used Google Books. I searched for the terms "Hyman" and "North Carolina" as that was the family of interest. This turned up the wonderful book, *"The Southern Debate Over Slavery: Petitions to Southern Legislatures, 1778-1864."* This book contained a petition from one of the slaves of the family I was researching, Ned Hyman. He provided details such as who he was owned by and sold to, when the person died, who the administrator was, and his master's wishes for his freedom.

I searched World Vital Records (their *Social, Regional and General Histories* collection) on Michael Holt from North Carolina and I found a 700+ page book entitled, *"The Descendants of Michael Holt."* Also, know that information for the family you need may be included in the collateral lines of a different family, so be sure to do full-text searches when you can. The title of the book may be *"The Potters and Allied Families"* but the book may include information on the Phillips and Trotman families.

Both BYU and the Internet Archives websites do not have very good search functions, and will take considerably longer to search, however, Internet Archive has a beautiful interface for reading the books online. HeritageQuest, accessible through some libraries, has an excellent search function and downloadable PDF files of the books. Note that Google Books does not always provide the entire book, and does not always allow easy download.

The larger, more prominent slaveowners will often be well-documented, but that doesn't mean there is no useful information on smaller slaveowners. There is. In the difficult quest for the slaveowning family, we've got to make diligent use of all resources at our disposal. Add this tool to your arsenal.

Note: Remember that material in any book needs to be verified!

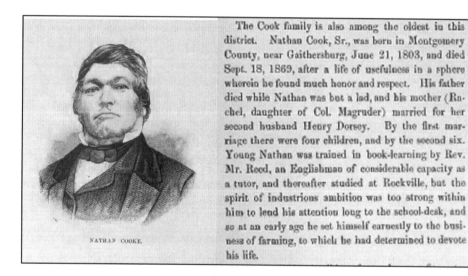

FIGURE 129, NATHAN COOKE PHOTO AND BIO

FIGURE 130, 1862 ESCAPED SLAVES

I recently discovered that one of my Prather ancestors, while enslaved, ran away and was captured and held in Washington DC jail in 1858. That led me to pull out my copy of *"Runaway Slaves: Rebels on the Plantation"* by John Hope Franklin and Loren Schweninger. I also purchased a book recently called *"Blacks Who Stole Themselves"* (what a great title, right?) that I first saw at the Library of Congress. This book features advertisements from the *Pennsylvania Gazette* for runaways from 1728-1790. Many of the runaways were from Maryland, Delaware, New Jersey & Virginia. The photo above is a Library of Congress photo showing enslaved people who had escaped and were with the Union Army during the Civil War.

I keep thinking about what it must have been like to run away and have no idea of where to go. No maps. To risk your life over and over again. To go into the woods with *your baby.* To leave your children. To not be able to read or write, or have anything else than the knowledge that you were born free and have a right to freedom. Could I have done that?

I don't know how they survived. Most runaway ads describe when and who they ran away from, the slave's age and name, a detailed description of their clothing, sometimes comments about their personality, physical looks and perhaps occupation.

The ads are very telling on several levels, in that they reveal the views of the slaveowner and their ideas about black people. Here's a list of specific things in the ads that resonated with me:

- ✓ the large number of runaways who are described as having what are likely African or African-inspired markings: holes in their ears and noses, scars on their faces and foreheads

- ✓ the description of many that are "new to this country," "country-born," "lately arrived from Barbados"(or Angola, or Guinea, or Dominica) and many who do not speak English"

- ✓ many were described as "Spanish negroes" or "Spanish mulattoes"

- ✓ the description of their personalities as: cunning, sly, complaisant, sour, impudent, bold, artful, smooth-tongued, surly, sour, sensible, talkative, shy, well-spoken, lusty (what in the world does that mean?)

- ✓ many are described as having "been much cut" on their backs, by "often whipping"

- ✓ some ran away in groups of 2-5 people, sometimes with white indentured servants

- ✓ several ads discuss the runaway having Indian blood, one even saying "he can talk Indian very well."

- ✓ some of the slaves could read and write, and the ads talked about how they are "pretending to be free,/will pretend to be searching for a master", "is almost white", and could easily "write themselves a pass"

- ✓ the suspicion of the involvement of freed blacks is evident; many ads purport that the runaway is "being hidden by freed blacks

Here are a few interesting excerpts:

- ✓ "'tis' supposed he is being harbored by some base white woman, as he has contracted intimacies with several of that sort"

- ✓ "the said negroe is named Jupiter, but it is thought he may likely call himself by his negroe name, which is Mueyon, or Omtee"

- ✓ "he is a short, thick fellow, limps with his right knee, and one of his buttocks is bigger than the other"(I'm sorry I found this quite funny.)

There are a few websites which have undertaken the goal of documenting runaway slave ads. There's Maryland's Underground Railroad website, which includes runaway ads, and the University of Virginia's project. There's also a site for Baltimore County, MD and The Geography of Virginia website. My friend Michael Hait did a good article on the genealogical value of runaway slave ads awhile ago. I love this short article at Yale University about analyzing runaway slave ads, which was really interesting.

Let me know if you found evidence that any of your enslaved ancestors ran away? I am so proud of the fact that enslaved people constantly resisted the system of slavery. I dedicate this post to a slave who ran away in 1759:

"…a negro man named Caesar, he has both his legs cutoff and walks on his knees."

Caesar demanded his freedom so badly he ran way <u>with no legs.</u> Simply astounding.

100 DOLLARS REWARD!

Runaway from the subscriber on the 27th of July, my Black Woman, named

EMILY,

Seventeen years of age, well grown, black color, has a whining voice. She took with her one dark calico and one blue and white dress, a red corded gingham bonnet; a white striped shawl and slippers. I will pay the above reward if taken near the Ohio river on the Kentucky side, or THREE HUNDRED DOLLARS, if taken in the State of Ohio, and delivered to me near Lewisburg, Mason County, Ky.   THO'S. H. WILLIAMS,

August 4, 1853.

FIGURE 131, RUNAWAY AD FOR EMILY

This is my great-grandmother, Effie Blanche Fendricks, who was born in Hardin County, TN, ca. 1891. She was one of 13 children. Effie married Walter Springer and birthed 9 children, 7 of whom survived to adulthood. She was a homemaker and when I interviewed my grandmother Mattie she shared many fond memories of her mother. Effie's husband Walter farmed, worked on Tennessee steamboats and eventually landed what would have been considered a good "government" job at a factory making munitions for World War II.

My grandmother Mattie eventually migrated to Dayton, Ohio when she married in the early 1940s. Later, her widowed mother Effie joined them as well as other relatives. Sadly, Effie suffered a stroke and died in 1959, at 58 years old.

I got some traction this year on Effie's family after a 12 year brick wall. Effie's "Fendricks" line has been a challenge. The surname has been rendered in every way imaginable (and unimaginable). Her parents, Mike Fendricks and Jane Eliza Sherrill, migrated to Hardin County, Tennessee by 1880 and all I knew was that they were from Alabama. My journey to find out what county in Alabama was finally successful because I am better at analysis.

I've traced back to who I believe is Effie's grandfather, John M. Fendricks living in Lawrence Cty, Alabama in 1870. Once there, I put together a chart of neighbors and potential slaveowners. It's slow work as I'm tracking 3 families (Sherrod, Shackelford and Bynum) who intermarried and had large land and slaveholdings. I'm putting each probate entry into a table for analysis.

FIGURE 132, EFFIE FENDRICKS

I'm hot on the trail, but I realize that "smoking gun" we always want won't always be found. What are some of the ways that we can make the case connecting our ancestors to a slaveowner when we are missing some of those critical documents (ie, using indirect evidence)?.Here are a few thoughts:

✓ **Proximity is always a clue.** Most slaves in 1870 still lived near their former slaveowner. This is not always the case, but proximity is a good clue. Some may be living on a former slaveowner's land.

- ✓ **Use of slaveowner's surname.** We all know all slaves did not take the surname of the most recent slaveowner, but many did. Check those slaveowner's wives maiden names, because slaves may carry *that* surname if they came from her family.

- ✓ **First names for the enslaved people** matching first names in the slaveowner's family. I've seen alot of that.

- ✓ **Interactions with the slaveowner's family.** I've seen slaveowners act as witnesses for marriages as well as posting bond/acting as sureties. Some slaves purchased their first land from a former slaveowner so always look for that first land record. Check the slaveowner's probate records even if they died after 1865–your ancestor may be purchasing items from the estate indicating a connection.

- ✓ **Interactions of generations of both families** into the early 20th century. It is not uncommon to have descendants of the slave/slaveowner still interacting or living in close proximity even in the 1900, 1910, 1920 census.

- ✓ **Freedmen's Bureau labor contracts** between your ancestor and an individual is another good clue. Most of these aren't indexed and don't exist for every locality, but these records should be checked.

Remember, I am talking about <u>when you can't</u> find document(s) that actually names your ancestor (i.e., direct evidence). None of these things *in isolation* would be a good basis for making the claim of a particular slaveowner. But, there are still ways to build a strong case from indirect evidence that your ancestor was owned by an individual. To be safe, you should still add a caveat to your written family history by using words like "likely" or "probable," and then presenting your reasoning.

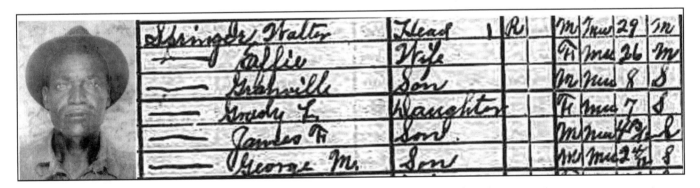

FIGURE 133, WALTER SPRINGER

FIGURE 134, BROWN UNIVERSITY

Brown University released a report back in 2006 entitled "Slavery and Justice." I just read it and found it well worth the time–I encourage you to read it. A steering committee was formed at Brown whose purpose was twofold:

"Our primary task was to examine the University's historical entanglement with slavery and the slave trade and to report our findings openly and truthfully. But we were also asked to reflect on the meaning of this history in the present, on the complex historical, political, legal, and moral questions posed by any present day confrontation with past injustice."

The little tiny state of Rhode Island had a central role in the slave trade and the Brown brothers, for whom the school is named after, all played roles in

the institution. The report goes into great detail using the school's archives.

It provides a good overview of slavery in New England, and the website includes a database of all the historical documents used in the report. The report ends with several recommendations for the University in terms of moving forward, and the school responded by endorsing a set of initiatives based on the report. Earlier this year, they recommended building a memorial to acknowledge the slaves ties of the University.

I think this is a good thing. Too many institutions today want to forget their historical ties to slaverywhen the exact opposite is what should be happening: *acknowledging the truth and continuing to educate the public.* This is true moral leadership and I applaud Brown. The report stops short of offering apologies, but this was a bold and courageous move. We are still, as a society, struggling with the effects of slavery–all of us. I hope other universities and institutions take heed.

Note: See the new book on this subject, *"Ebony and Ivy: Race, Slavery and the Troubled History of America's Universities,"* by Steven Wilder, 2013. Also, University of Maryland has since done a similar study.

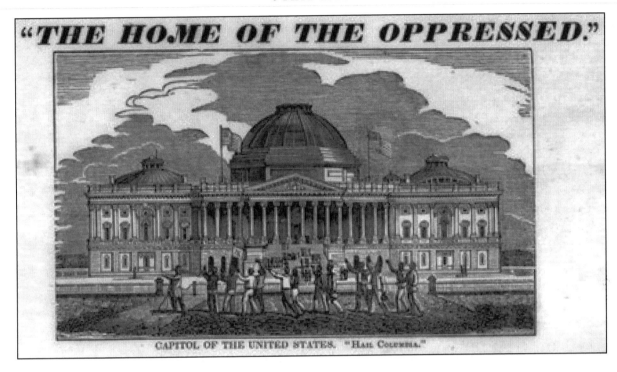

FIGURE 135, SLAVE TRADE BROADSIDE

Many states have unique records that can assist those doing slave research. For example, slave births in Virginia are recorded from the year 1853, and Maryland's 1867 slave statistics name the last slaveowner as well as surnames for most slaves. These records may not survive for every county within a state, but if they do, you're in for a treat.

For those who had enslaved ancestors in Washington, D.C., the National Archives have:

1. Records of the U.S. Circuit Court for the District of Columbia Relating to Slaves, 1851-1863 (M433)

2. Habeas Corpus Case Records of the U.S. Circuit Court for the District of Columbia, 1820-1863 (M434)

These both have good information for those researching slaves. Christine's Genealogy website has indexed parts of several of these records on her website. Even richer records were created when D.C. enacted the Emancipation Act in 1862 allowing the federal government to pay slaveowners up to $300 for each slave freed by the Act. Slaveowners applied in droves. This created the 3rd record set:

3. Records of the Board of Commissioners for the Emancipation of Slaves in the District of Columbia (M520)

These records include the petitions of each slaveowner to qualify under the terms of the Act. In most cases, they provided very detailed physical descriptions of the slaves, what kind of work they did, and amazingly enough, the circumstances of where and how they acquired each slave. Sometimes, that information can take years to discover, if we are ever able to discover it! The records often reveal those precious slave relationships that are so hard to come by. Even luckier for us, Dorothy Provine has published all of these records in a book I just purchased, *"Compensated Emancipation in the District of Columbia."* The book is available for purchase from Heritage Books. A few examples will illustrate the richness of the records (these are abstracted, the originals are more detailed):

✓ **Petition of Alfred Y. Robinson**, of PG County, MD for Edward Humphrey, age 35 or 40, mulatto….Robinson inherited him from his mother Elizabeth Robinson and has held him for over 30 years.

✓ **Petition of William Gunton**, administrator for William A. Gunton, for two slaves, Joshua and Hennie. The late William A. Gunton purchased Joshua from William Tolson, Hennie was a gift from John B. Mullihan of PG County to his daughter upon her marriage to his son, William A. Gunton on June 20, 1848.

✓ **Petition of Mary A. Smoot,** for two persons, Henry and Margaret. Smoot's grandmother, the late Mrs. Mary B. Smoot, left these persons to her by a will that was recorded in D.C. in June 1857

✓ **Petition of Matthew McLeod,** for Ellen Cole, age 51 or 52. He acquired title from the will of his mother-in-law, Mrs. Mary Manning of St. Mary's County, and later the will of his deceased wife.

✓ **Petition of Anna Bradley** for William and James (brothers). Bradley acquired title from her mother. William and James' great-grandmother. Patty was a slave of Bradley's mother, Elizabeth Ann King, long since deceased. Her mother acquired Patty from John Hammond, her father, late of Annapolis, MD. Bradley states she also became the owner of Jenny, the daughter, and Mary, the granddaughter of Patty. Mary was the mother of William and James and they have belonged to Bradley since their birth."

✓ Many slaves were employed in D.C. but were owned by people living in Maryland and Virginia as well as a few other states. Christine's Genealogy Website also has an name index to these petitions on her website.

There are an endless array of records in that uncover the lives of our ancestors. Many are little known and uncommon, but still filled with possibilities. What I'm discussing today are the private records of local citizens. These are usually stored in university, state archive, genealogical or historical society collections. I did another post sometime ago on a subset of these records, referred to as Plantation Papers. However, I want to expand on that concept, so I'll refer to these records as Community Papers: these are records such as **Account Books, Ledgers, Diaries, Receipts, Scrapbooks and Letters.**

They are often found in Special Collections (like this one at the University of Delaware) or Manuscript divisions and can open up a whole new window into our research. These are important records for everyone, but especially for those of us researching enslaved ancestors. This is when it is crucial that you know the community in which your ancestor lived. Who were the prominent people? Who were the merchants, plantation owners, doctors, blacksmiths, lawyers, sawmill owners, etc.? The concept is that *you may find your ancestor mentioned in the records of someone in his/her community.*

As an example, I have been researching the roots of my freed black ancestor Louisa Simpson who in 1850 lived in the Howard District of Anne Arundel County. I researched her neighborhood and I know exactly who her neighbors were—other free blacks but also slaveowners. Louisa's family was long associated with the Warfield family. She married and had children with Perry Simpson, who was a slave of Beale Warfield.

When I visited the Maryland Genealogical Society in Baltimore some months ago, I searched through their catalog for the types of records above, especially for the Warfield family. I found an Account book for Dr. Gustavus Warfield, with records dated 1816-1830. Obviously, doctors, as well as merchants, had to keep records of their customers. He saw whites and blacks, and made notations in many of the entries. Look at some of what I uncovered in his book:

- Joe Anderson, freed by Charles Hammon, 1823, 1824.
- Isaac Baker, free negro on R. Shipley's place, 1821
- Billy Carpenter, free negro, 1823, 1824, 1826.
- Caty, free negro at R. Shipley's, 1829
- Samuel Clark, free negro at Joshua Warfields, 1824, 1827.
- John Cook, free negro at Allen Dorsey's, 1821, 1824 (wife)
- Frank Snowden, freed by Levin Warfield, 1825.
- Dennie, freed by R. Riggs, May 31, 1824
- Dick Dorsey, freedmen at H. Hobbs, 1826
- James Fossett, freedman at Lisbon, 1821, 1822 (vaccination)
- Frank, freed by Levin Warfield, 1820, 1821
- Isaac Dorsey, free negro living by Beckley, 1823
- James Waters, free negro at Lisbon, wife and delivery, Feb. 5, 1819
- Charles Wells, freedman, son of Daniel, 1821.
- Billy Williams, free negro, son of Caspar, 1824.

This account book provides important information about Dr. Warfield's neighborhood, and included entries about slaves and freed blacks. It provides the ever critical association of surnames with some of the freedmen, and sometimes the entries identified who they were freed by or where they were living. We can also see that he was called on to deliver babies as well as perform vaccinations.

I have read many slaveowner diaries, and also the diaries of their wives. I found the diary of George Cooke, a plantation owner who lived in the mid-1800s. He mentioned his slaves and free blacks who worked for him, and his diary gave me a great view of what life was like in the county where my ancestors lived.

Some of the papers and letters you may find will include bills of sale and lists of slaves. At the Library of Virginia some years ago, I viewed the ledger of a man named Joshua Chaffin. He was the sheriff in Amelia County during the early 1800s, and thus tasked many times with administering the estates of people who died. I knew who he was because he oversaw the distribution of one of my slaveowning families' estates. The book was important because he kept records of enslaved people, some I assume he owned, but others who may have belonged to the various estates. I transcribed his records and posted them on my sister blog, Giving Back to Kin.

Just when you think you've researched everything possible—here I go giving you something else to look at! So go back to your county level research, and find out who the "key people" were. I'll be heading back the Maryland Historical Society soon to view some scrapbooks and other ledgers I found in the catalog. And while yes, it's true that many of the papers and records that eventually are housed at institutions are those of wealthier or more prominent people, you just never know until you look. The image is a page from the slave sale ledger of the slave trading firm of Austin and Laurens in Charleston.

FIGURE 136, SLAVE SALES LEDGER

162	Ricks William	52	M	W	Farmer	10930	1500
	— Melville	30	F	W	Keeping house		
	— Willie	6	M	W			
	— Irene	2/12	F	W			
	Fields Laura	18	F	W	At Home		
	Rand Ellen	24	F	B	Domestic Servant		

FIGURE 137, 1870 WM HICKS

Familysearch is rolling with Freedmen's Bureau Records. They now have Field Office Records digitized for **Alabama, Arkansas, District of Columbia, Maryland, Delaware, Mississippi, Missouri, North Carolina, South Carolina, Texas and Virginia!** I have been looking at Alabama, which is one of my research states, and I am struck by several things. The 1870 census entry above shows a man with $10,900 worth of real estate; that much land suggests he had been a slaveowner. This might prompt a search for labor contracts.

Labor Contracts are one of the first categories of records that researchers should browse within Freedmen's Bureau records, if they exist for that particular location. I posted awhile ago a suggested process to follow while searching these exasperating records. I have been searching through contracts in the city of Tuscumbia, Alabama. Most were for the calendar year of 1866. Contracts are very valuable because they were often made between slaveowners and their former enslaved laborers. After reviewing about a hundred of these agreements, I realize they tell us something more about the experiences of our enslaved ancestors.

There was no standard labor agreement; some were short where others went into great detail. What is apparent is that white planters were *most interested in returning if not to slavery, than as close to slavery as possible.* These agreements illuminate why it was so difficult for former slaves to achieve anything close to economic independence. Social equality was off the table. What's also clear is the devastation of freeing four million slaves who for the most part had no property of their own, were illiterate, and had no land when farming was the only skill most of them had.

Freedmen wanted to get their wives out of the fields and refused to work as long and hard as they did during slavery. Most agreements spell out that planters would provide the land, tools, animals, and seed, while freedmen would cultivate and gin the crops. Most paid freedmen by giving them ½ or 1/3 of the crop. Agreements vary on who would provide clothing, medicine, and food. The restrictions on their behavior struck me most, as well as the ability of the planter to unilaterally cancel the agreement for supposed bad behavior.

Most added that freedmen *were not allowed to either leave the plantation or have visitors without consent of their employer*. What kind of freedom was that? While freedmen tried to get more flexibility, planters all but forced them into year-long agreements. The language used in the agreements show the lengths some planters went to maintain not only their workforce but their absolute power and supremacy over that workforce:

- **Fred Sherrod**, in addition to providing land, tools, animals, feed, cabins, meat and meal required the freedmen to "commence work at daylight and work the entire day except for half hour for breakfast and dinner, to work six days out the week, and to work at night if necessary."

- **D.W. Hicks** added that freedmen would "abstain from all impudence, swearing or indecent and profane language to or in the presence of employer or his family." Other planters added that freedmen had to be "respectful, obedient and *submissive* at all times." That is a very interesting word choice…..submissive.

- **Kirk and Drake** demanded in their contracts that there be "no general conversation to be carried on during work hours."

- **Joseph Thompson** wasn't leaving any detail to chance. His lengthy agreements spelled out that freedmen would "do fair and faithful mowing, patching, hauling, plowing, howing, reaping, chopping, making rails, & boards, making and repairing fences, gates, houses, cribs, barns, shops, sheds, gin houses and all labor necessary for successful cultivation & management of plantation…Commence work at sunrise and stop at sunset reserving one hour in spring, fall and winter months and one and a half hours in summer for dinner…freedmen are not to leave the plantation w/o permission and they labor for Thompson at all times except the afternoon of Saturday which is reserved to them for working their own patches…but…when the crop is behind or when any extraordinary occasions occur which requires their services on the afternoon of Saturdays it is to be rendered *faithfully and cheerfully.*" Thompson's view of the freedmen is evident when he further states "anyone failing to work for any cause will be charged 50 cents/day and if any freedmen shall become habitually *idle, worthless and troublesome* then he or she will be discharged and sent from the plantation never to return." He also noted that a journal would be kept of all start and finish times, quality and quality of work.

- **William Hooks** sounded more progressive as he added in his agreements that he would see to it that "peace, harmony and good feelings prevail and equal rights are given." That was a rarity.

By 1870, many of these former slaves would be still living near their former owners. They had few choices. This was about the control of labor, plain and simple. It was also about trying to enforce dependence, and continued racial subjugation. Let's not forget that many of the planters broke these agreements: Bureau Complaints are filled with refusals to pay the freedmen, violence against them, or just plain kicking them off the plantation after the crops were in.

Take a look at these valuable records. Seeing original historical documents still has a powerful impact on me, a strong emotional impact. They tell us much about our ancestor's plight and the hardships that "freedom" brought.

78

State of Alabama

Franklin County } Know all men by these that I William F. Ricks

the County of Franklin and State of Alabama of the first part held & firmly bo

to the United States of America in the sum of five hundred dollars for t

payment of which I bind my heirs executors and administrators firmly by th

presents in this contract. I promise to furnish the freedmen whose nam

are subjoined of the second part with fifteen acres of land to each

grown hand, house & fuel for each family. cotton seed as I may determi

plough & one set of good gear for each horse & mule. and am to lend eac

head of family ten barrels of corn for bread & feeding of work stock. w

they are to return me eight barrels of corn each head of family at new

corn gathering when matured. I am to have one half of cotton & one

half of corn crop besides the eight barrels of corn each head of family is t

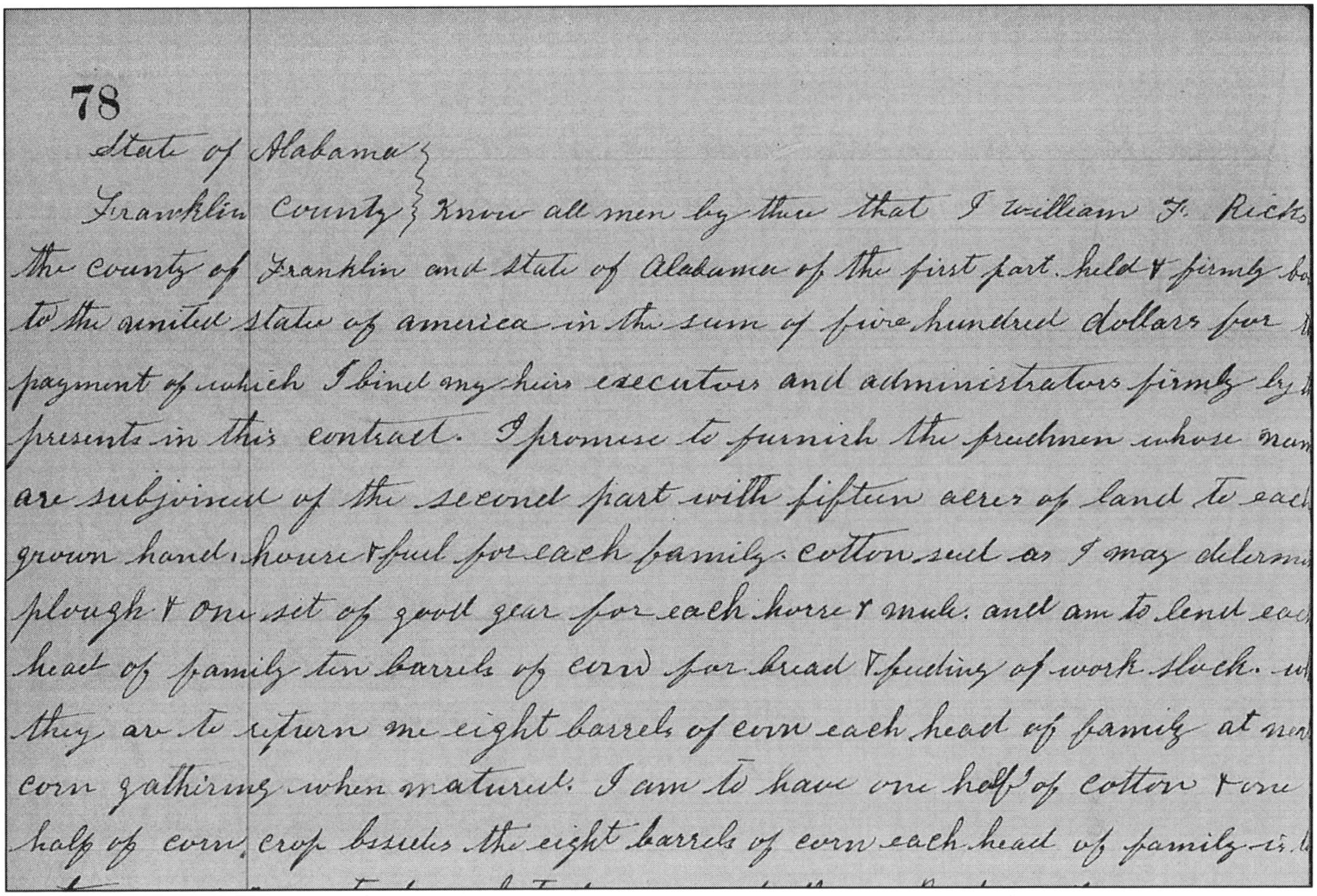

FIGURE 138, FREEDMAN CONTRACT

> *"I served in the War as Henry Lock, the Lock being my old Massa's name, but since the War I've taken my father's name of Rollie."*

> *"...My mammy was called Cassie Hawkins and my pappy was Alfred Jolly..."*
> *Emma Crockett, Alabama*

I've been having a wonderfully lively debate in recent weeks with another genealogist about slave surnames and how many slaves used:

the name of the last slaveowner

the name of a previous/former slaveowner, or

surname origins undetermined

Most books and classes that teach how to discover the slaveowner (once you're back to the 1870 census) teach the *strategy* of starting by looking for white slaveowners in the area with that surname. If that doesn't work, then you move on to other research strategies.

Many researchers who have spent time with this subject have opinions one way or the other about which naming convention was more prevalent or which strategy is more likely to work, You can see well written points of view at my friend Michael's site and Dr. Barnetta McGee discussed this in her blog some time ago. I simply say this: some slaves took the name of the last slaveowner.

Some used a surname from a previous slaveowner. Some picked a completely new name. Most of the names came from their mother or father. And some we'll never know where the name came from. I have seen all outcomes, so I don't believe in ruling anything out. In my own family, out of 5 known slaveowners discovered, 4 of my ancestors took the last slaveowner's surname and 1 did not.

If you peruse the tabs of my family history above, you can find more details on those individuals if you are interested. One thing I know for sure—***most slaves had surnames they knew and were known by amongst other slaves.*** They were not names the larger white culture respected enough to record for the most part—but that does not mean that the use of surnames "started" when they were emancipated. When you read the Slave Narratives, you really get a sense that the slaves had coherent family structures, surnames and all, even in the midst of slavery's frantic desire to stomp them out. Boy, our ancestors were **strong**.

I was curious about what my fellow genealogists have experienced on this subject, so I put a call out on the Afrigeneas_mailing list asking about . Here are the results: Out of 20 respondents quoting 65 enslaved ancestors:

57.0% took the name of the most recent slaveowner

26.1% took the name of a previous slaveowner

16.9% had a surname of unknown origin

This is an area where I'd like to see more specific studies done by slavery scholars.

FIGURE 139, CONTRABANDS IN VA

FIGURE 140, FREDERICK DOUGLASS

There is a good probability that many of us researching our African-American lines will find at least one family line that was freed before 1865. In 1860, there were over 400,000 freed blacks in the U.S.

Although Northern cities like Philadelphia and Boston had relatively large freed black populations, over half of all freed blacks lived in the South in cities like Charleston, New Orleans, Savannah, Baltimore and Petersburg. Escaping blacks would often aim for these cities, as they'd have a better chance of blending in with other freed blacks.

I had freed black ancestors living on the Eastern Shore of Maryland which was not surprising since Maryland had over 60,000 freed blacks by the time the Civil War began—the most of any slave state. More surprising was that I discovered a freed black ancestor living in southwest Tennessee in Hardin County. She was one of only 37 freed blacks living there in 1860. That was truly unexpected.

One of the best books about freed blacks is "*Slaves Without Masters: the Free Negro in the Antebellum South*" by Ira Berlin. He describes how free blacks worked alongside and many times married enslaved people, and that their station in life was always tenuous. They were widely perceived by the white community with suspicion and regarded as an enticement to insurrection among slaves. Some of the most famous slave revolts *were* planned by freed blacks such as Denmark Vesey and Nat Turner. There have also been several books written about freed blacks who attained great success and wealth, such as in *"Black Masters: A Free Family of Color in the South"*

As the number of freed blacks grew in states like Virginia and Maryland, state laws also increased drastically limiting their movement and actions. Examples of some of the laws against freed blacks in various states include the inability to vote or testify against whites in court, the need to register movements in and out of state, the inability to own a dog or gun, and the inability to assemble in groups without a white person present.

281	285	Elizabeth H Barnes	51	F		Farming
		Nancy A	25	F		House Laborer
		Andrew J	16	M		
		Margarett Barnes	30	F	M	Servant
		Louisa	11	F	M	
		Green	9	M	M	
		Sam	7	M	B	

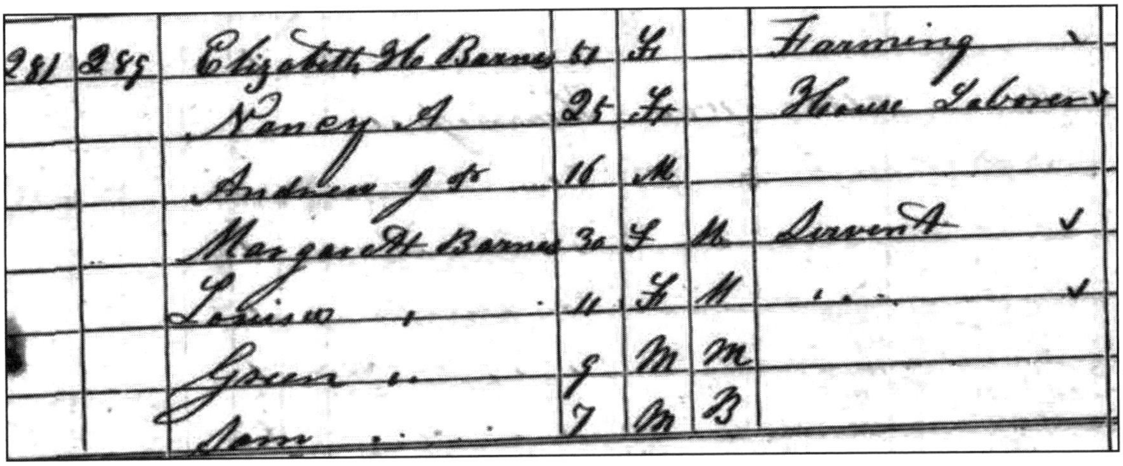

FIGURE 141, 1860 BARNES HOUSEHOLD

Eventually, several states simply legislated that if a black was freed, he or she had to leave the state.

How do you research freed blacks? First, look for your ancestors on census records before 1870. Before that year, only freed blacks would have been included. Sometimes, we *assume* our ancestors were enslaved before 1870 *without first actually checking.*

If you discover an ancestor who was freed before 1865, next you'll want to attempt to discover how they gained their freedom. Slaves could be freed in five general ways:

- ✓ Born Free (legal status came from the mother, so a freedwoman's children would be free)
- ✓ Manumitted (i.e., freed by their slaveowner)
- ✓ Purchased their freedom (slaveowner must allow this)
- ✓ Runaway
- ✓ Military Service

It's not always easy ascertaining the method by which an ancestor became free. Many states required freed blacks to register their freedom with the county court to prevent escaping slaves from claiming they were free. The Maryland Assembly put it this way in 1805:

"great mischiefs have arisen from slaves coming into possession of certificates of free Negroes, by running away and passing as free under the faith of such certificates."

So county court minutes are a good place in general to search. The court would grant the person a "freedom certificate" that he/she was expected to carry on their person at all times and present to any white person when questioned. Some localities with large freed populations kept separate sets of these "Freedom Certificates."

If you're lucky, the record will state how the person became free. **Depending on the state and county, there may also be separate books of Manumissions** (the legal document through which a master frees a slave). According to law, the manumission may also be mixed in with the land records, or it could have been done through the owner's will, both records that can be harder to search because they are typically indexed by the name of the slaveowner, which means you'd need to know that information first. I suggest first checking if there are any whites in the community using the same surname.

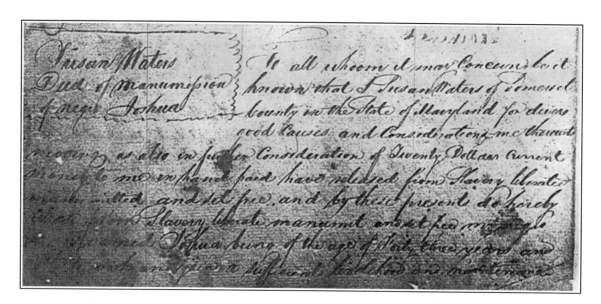

FIGURE 142, WATERS MANUMISSION

In many of the records, there will just be a first name, such as "Negro Sarah." That complicates the process by forcing us to make sure we are connecting the right "Sarah" with the "Sarah" that we've found in the census *with a surname attached.*

If you have no luck in finding Freedom Certificates or Manumissions, check to see if your ancestor owned land and if so, from whom did he or she purchase that land?

Check Indentures, as many freed black children were indentured to whites. They also may be living near the person who freed them, so use Cluster Research principles. Freed blacks often had a white person who served as "protector," someone to vouch for and support them when they were challenged or cheated by whites.

You may be able to identify that person by evaluating enough documents. Also, try to find out what the laws were regarding freed blacks, for example, this book about the black laws in Virginia. and this blog that discusses laws regarding freed blacks in North Carolina.

This is only the briefest introduction to yet another endlessly fascinating topic. There's a good discussion of researching freed blacks on the University of South Florida's website and I also recommend this more scholarly discussion of the topic by James Horton who is one of my favorite historians.

(Shown above is an image of the manumission of my 4th great-grandfather, Joshua Waters of Somerset County, Maryland

4A. WRITE UP YOUR FAMILY HISTORY

15 JUNE 2010

FIGURE 143, MARION SIMMONS BOOK

We love genealogy. We spend years and years researching in every direction. We go to conferences and lectures, we read books, and we develop a network of genealogy buddies to discuss every tidbit of information. We collect marriage licenses and deeds, wills and inventories, pictures and other data. So the question is—when you're gone, what is going to happen to all that valuable research? Will anybody else know about it? Not if you don't take some time out to focus on the importance of writing up your research and sharing it.

I know how hard it is to break out of the "research" addiction to spend time actually writing. Many people are intimidated, and feel that they can't write, or simply don't know where to start. I think the first step is to truly understand the monumental importance of doing it. I'm sure most of us are doing genealogy because we have deep-rooted beliefs about why families need to know from whence they came. However, your research will only be able to achieve that purpose if it *survives* outside of your mind and file cabinets. We want the fruits of our research to survive us, and the best way to accomplish that is to write up and disseminate your research.

The hard part is knowing just where to stop—we often feel like we don't have enough information yet. We're always looking for just *a little bit more*. But if we stick to that, we may never get started writing. As a general rule, I like to tell people after two years of research to stop and write up what you have. You can always publish addendums later.

What form should your write-up take? **You can do an article.** This is one of my favorite formats because it can be submitted for publication in a genealogy newsletter, and it then has another chance of surviving you. Also, I have found family members really respond well to articles. You can add pictures to the narrative, and they work well as hand-outs for family reunions. You can choose one aspect of your history, like my friend Marion's book above, about her ancestor's segregated high school. **You could also plan to do an entire book about all of your research.** Many have taken this route, and in the age of the Internet, it's easier than ever. Websites such as Lulu.com and Scribd.com make it easy to self-publish.

How do you get started? Several good books have been published on how to write-up your family history and make it interesting and I include a few titles at the end of this article. There is also software available, such as Personal Historian, if you think you'll need a bit more guidance. I like to study how others have written up their narratives, and take hints and clues from them. For example, the *National Genealogical Society* (NGS) holds a Family History Writing contest every year. I like to make copies of the winning articles and study them for ideas. Also, getting together on a regular basis with others with the goal of writing is a terrific way to stay motivated.

By God's Grace

A Personal Testimony by Pauline Waters

FIGURE 144, PAULINE WATERS SMITH

Whatever your method, the critical thing to do is just get started. You don't need to be Toni

Morrison or Richard Wright; you're trying to share all the hard work you've put into this research. Another huge benefit to writing up your research is that it reveals gaps and missing information. This has pointed me to new research avenues many times. Be sure to include full source citations to all of your information. If you don't include where you got the information, it's virtually useless. Elizabeth Shown Mill's book "*Evidence Explained*" is the bible for genealogy source citations and should be right by your side as you write.

Once you have it written, be sure to get it out there to the public. I suggest submitting a copy to: the library system of your research county, the State Archives, the local historical society, and the Library of Congress' Genealogy and Local History Division. All of these places take genealogies from the public. This will all lead to the greater likelihood that long after your time here has passed, your descendants will find your research and send up thanks to great-great grandmother/father so-and-so for caring enough to preserve and write the family history!

Book Suggestions:

- ✓ "*You Can Write Your Family History*," by Sharon Carmack

- ✓ "*Writing Family History and Memoirs*," by Kirk Polking

- ✓ "*Writing Your Family History: A Practical Guide*," by Deborah Cass

- ✓ "*The Complete Idiot's Guide to Writing Your Family History*," by Lynda Stephenson

7 JANUARY 2010

I was reading the latest issue of *Prologue* magazine trying to figure out what to blog about, when I realized I was holding it in my hands.

Prologue is NARA's official magazine, and it highlights how to utilize the rich and vast resources of the Archives. It's $24/year (4 issues). The magazine will expand your mind, introduce you to little known record groups, explain various finding aids, and help you navigate through the more expansive collections. The articles provide terrific historical detail on NARA's records and agencies and America's people. It also highlights the extraordinarily talented and brilliant professionals that work at NARA and are the experts in their areas. I have obtained numerous genealogical leads over the years from being a faithful *Prologue* subscriber. I want to highlight some Prologue links on NARA's website that deserve a look.

1) In Summer 1997, a special edition of Prologue was dedicated to African-American research.

Although the original is out of print, you can read all the articles online. Some titles include:

"Freedmen's Bureau Records: An Overview"

"Preserving the Legacy of the US Colored Troops"

"The Panama Canal: The African-American Experience"

FIGURE 145, PROLOGUE
MAGAZINE

"Documenting the Struggle for Racial Equality in the Decade of the Sixties"

2) NARA has taken some of the genealogy articles out of *Prologue* and made them available online. Of course, all of the ones under the African-American section (different from those in the special issue) are worth gold. Some of my favorites in other categories include:

"Native-Americans in the Census, 1860-1890"

"First in the Path of the Firemen: The Fate of the 1890 Population Census"

"Enhancing your Family Tree with Civil War Maps"

"Income Tax Records of the Civil War Years"

3) The Fall 2009 issue of Prologue featured an article called "Face to Face with History." It discussed the rare finding of a photograph of an African American doctor in pension files.

4) One other thing I'd like to mention that is available on NARA's website: their "Researchers News" newsletter is a downloadable PDF file that is created quarterly and includes all the data about what books, microfilms, databases and other records have been recently purchased or accessioned, as well as all the classes and seminars available at NARA. Enjoy!

You want to take all the joy out of a genealogist's day, just bring up the subject of source citations. I have seen faces go from glitter to gloom when you bring it up. Nevertheless, doing them religiously is one of my 10 Key Genealogical Principles, and if you want your research to be taken seriously, you'll have to get around to doing it.

I speak from experience, as I spent the first few years of my genealogical journey happily having no knowledge or understanding of this concept. I have sources today that I have **no idea** where I got them from. You think that's never gonna happen to you. Ahh, such sweet deception.

The uptick is, it's not as difficult as it appears and once you get the swing of it, it becomes 2nd nature. *You become a stronger researcher because you tend to zoom in on source citations for everything you read.* Here are a few resources online about this subject you don't want to miss:

1. Elizabeth Shown Mills' colossal book *Evidence Explained!* is a must have for all genealogists. I also recommend purchasing the PDF file of this book – it is useful when you are on the road and trying to reduce weight. Let me note that Ms. Mills has excellent discussions for each type of source and you should take some time to actually read the sections of this book (over time of course!).

2. The Board for Certification of Genealogists website has some of Ms. Mills' articles which succinctly explain why we need to all be correctly and diligently citing our sources. No one explains it better than she does. Click on the left link marked "Skillbuilding" to access the other articles.

3. All of the major genealogy software packages do source citations (I use Rootsmagic). They incorporate all of the templates from *Evidence Explained!*

4. My favorite free online citation guide is the *Quick Reference Card* Thomas MacEntee created at Geneabloggers and the website over at Progenealogists.

5. Other stuff: I like the "Cite Your Sources" sticky notes available from *Fun Stuff for Genealogists*. You slap one on a copy you've made, and it's got all the information you need to remember to fill in for the citation. They also have "Cite Your Sources" stamps.

I pick a day and devote a few hours to updating my source citations, either in my genealogy software or in my notebooks. I have white 3-ring binders for each family & most of my sources (census, vitals, deeds, etc.) are printed out in each binder. Then I buy neon-colored envelope labels, and put a colored label on each source in the binder containing the correct source citation. It may sound like a lot of work, but consider that the great bulk of your citations are for the same types of records, be it census, vitals, deeds, probate, social security, World War I drafts, etc. You can just 'cut and paste' and change the specifics.

Here's hoping you all learn and remember to cite your sources!

9 JANUARY 2010

Recently, I was perusing the Library of Congress' genealogy reading room website. I clicked on the link to Bibliographies and Guides and the first PDF file in the list is the guide to *African-American Family Histories and Related Works.* I hadn't looked at this list in years so I printed it out and read through the document.

I discovered a potential ancestral family on that list. Not a direct ancestor, but a family that may be connected to one of my ancestors: the Crowders of Decatur County, TN.

If you haven't looked at this list lately (or haven't ever looked at the list) take a look and see what you found. Many of the items I noticed were programs from family reunions that people submitted. Even that is a great find.

Those of us who have been researching 10 years or more (or just those of us who have researched enough to have a good collection of material) need to submit copies of our work for inclusion on this list. That means me too.

And while you're at it, check the published family histories at your State Archives, local historical societies and libraries. You never know what might turn up.

African American Family Histories and Related Works in the Library of Congress
Compiled by Paul Connor, updated by Ahmed Johnson
Local History and Genealogy Reading Room
Humanities and Social Sciences Division
Library of Congress
Washington 2009

Introduction

Revised in 2009, this edition of *African American Family Histories and Related Works in the Library of Congress* incorporates all the past efforts of Sandra Lawson and Paul Connor, supplemented by the edition of 84 family histories and genealogical handbooks. Because of the changing technological environment since the first publication of this guide, links to the Library of Congress vast collection of digitized records and resources related to the African American experience in America have been included covering African American culture and society, places, slave narratives, military records, and resource guides. These electronic resources include digitized oral histories, newspapers, maps, and photographs. The addition of these digital resources and books published after 1997 enriches the availability of resources pertaining to African American family histories at the Library of Congress.

FIGURE 146, LOC AA HISTORIES

FIGURE 147, COLLEGE APPLICATION

My grandmother, Pauline, attended Bennett College. She loved Bennett and talked about it all the time. Her father was a Methodist minister and Methodism shaped much of her life, so a Methodist College was completely in order. Years ago, I wrote to Bennett to see if they had any of her records. They sent me her original application from 1931!

How wonderful is that? One page listed her hobbies and extracurricular activities. I would have never guessed my grandmother played soccer. If your ancestor went to college, write to the school to see if they still have any records left. This worked even better for my grandfather who attended a year at Howard University. They sent me his entire file.

My favorite part of the application was a picture from her senior year, that no one in my family had ever seen (below).I can almost see her walking across that campus, taking her classes, making friends.

Pauline was a teacher and her first job out of Bennett was at the Boylan School in Jacksonville, Florida. Boylan was a Methodist private school for "negro" girls. I found a website called the Florida Memory Project and downloaded a brochure from the 1932-33 year at Boylan School; just a few years before Pauline would have taught there. It had all sorts of details like what classes the girls would take, how much it cost, and what kinds of clothes they had to bring. That was a nice find. Of course the best thing for Pauline was that she met her husband at while she worked at Boylan. They spent the next 30+ plus years together raising a family in Jacksonville. This is just one more way to bring your family history to life.

FIGURE 148, PAULINE WATERS

I talked about the <u>importance of writing up your family history</u> sometime ago. It's easy to get addicted to the "search," but if we never stop to put our research into some organized format, we run the risk of all that research being wasted. My friend Andrea sent me a terrific quote a few weeks ago that is very appropriate: "*Better to write something now, than everything never.*"

Here are a few ideas for jump starting the writing of your family history and some topics to add meat to the bones of just boring old names and dates:

1. **History of the city or area**
   Example: The city of Tifton, GA (and the county) was named for Captain Henry Tift, who built large sawmills to harvest the lumber that would be central to this community. My great-great grandfather John Smith was possibly born in Tifton. Many rural areas were named for large slaveowners.

2. **Geography-what was the landscape like?**
   Example: Many of my ancestors from Hardin County lived along the Tennessee River, so that was a major influence on

people's lives. At the turn of the century, steamboat travel was frequent as were, according to the local paper, drownings of local citizens.

3. **Migration patterns: where did most of the people that settled here come from? Where did many go to?**
   Examples: Most of the people in early Tennessee were a part of the westward migration from Virginia and North Carolina. This matches exactly the path of the slaveowner of my Tennessee ancestor, Malinda Holt. I also mapped the migration of African-Americans from this county to Northern industries in the 1940s.

4. **Events from U.S. national history, state history, and/or county history**
   Example: My friend Marion's family is from Caroline County,

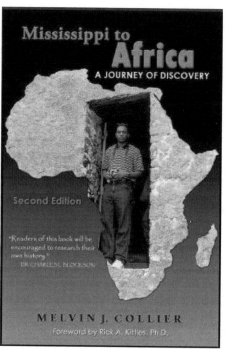

FIGURE 149, COLLIER BOOK COVER

VA, and I think the fact that <u>the Lovings story</u> happened there is very interesting (the couple that won a Supreme Court ruling against laws forbidding interracial marriages). Hardin County, TN was the site of a large Civil War battle and in many ways that informed the experiences of many slaves who ran away and joined the war effort.

5. **Use slave narratives and autobiographies from that area to document the slave experience.**
Example: For my ancestors from Montgomery County, MD, I include excerpts from the autobiography of Josiah Henson who was enslaved in that county.

6. **Laws relating to slaves and freedmen**
Example: After the Civil War, Maryland's Eastern Shore utilized the apprenticeship laws to effectively re-enslave the children of their former slaves. The Freedmen's Bureau helped freedmen to fight to get their children back. I discuss this in my write-up of my ancestors from Somerset County, MD.

7. **Illnesses and deaths**
Example: There was a smallpox epidemic in 1873 in Jacksonville, FL, where my dad's family lived, which forced many people to temporarily flee the city. Also, the 1918 flu pandemic touched just about every community. Use mortality census records for this topic as well.

8. **Prominent people (both black and white)**
Example: Harry Hooks amassed a fortune as a freed black shoemaker in Hardin County, TN before the Civil War, which enabled him to purchase his wife and children.

9. **Major African-American churches, schools & businesses**
Example: My grandfather owned two successful pharmacies in the booming 1940s business district of Jacksonville, Florida, which in part explains why this family never migrated North along with so many others.

This is by no means complete, but perhaps its given you some ideas to get started. For those who have already started, tell me other topics that you have added to your family histories?

There are many ways now, thanks to technology, that we can keep getting smarter and better at genealogy. Learning creative methods of research and ways to use different groups of records (land records, court records, etc.) is what will make the difference in your ability to uncover your ancestors' past. Here's my list of ways to continue to sharpen your genealogy skills:

1. **Take a class.** There are local classes at many community colleges like this one at Howard Community College; check your local listings for the *non-credit* program. The National Archives offers a free genealogy lectures series each and every month, as well as a longer, more advanced fee-based class on using their records every year. The National Genealogical Society (NGS) has a free online refresher course for members, as well as fee-based training, covering topics such as *Working With Deeds*. The Institute for Genealogy and Historical Research (IGHR) operates a renowned weeklong genealogy class at Samford University in Birmingham, Alabama every year that fills up as quickly as it is announced. I take a few classes every year, of all kinds.

2. **Join a local genealogy group (or 2 or 3).** I can't stress the value of this enough. I'm constantly amazed at the number of people I meet who have been researching for years and are not connected to any local group. People perceive that because they don't live in the area they are researching, the local group won't be helpful but that's not the case. You need that energy and that connection—you'll learn things at every meeting because the eyes and ears are

multiplied to share the latest genealogy news, latest resources, websites, etc. It'll keep you inspired when you hit that brick wall. When your relatives are tired of hearing you talk about genealogy, your genealogy "buddies" will understand the excitement of your latest find.

3. **There are genealogy groups for almost everybody**. There's usually a group for your research county, but there are also regional groups, state groups and ethnic groups as well. For African-American research, find a local Afro-American Historical and Genealogical Society (AAHGS) chapter. I'm also in my state's genealogical society (Maryland) and in a professional genealogy networking group (the Association for Professional Genealogists). These groups are also an additional route to training, as most groups have speakers who give presentations on topics of interest. So get out and mix it up.

4. **Utilize the full spectrum of online resources.** Don't just limit yourself to Ancestry. You should be a member of the mailing list for each of your research counties and the message boards for your surnames (go to Rootsweb to sign up.) Read blogs. There are hundreds of quality genealogy blogs out there. For questions, you can always count on the collective knowledge of the folks at Afrigeneas. It's also a great place to keep abreast of all the great local stories about African-American history and genealogy. Stay plugged into your State Archives website as well as the

area historical and genealogical societies (may be two different groups). Resources are quickly digitized and uploaded to these sites, but you'll never know about them if you don't periodically browse the sites.

5. **Start going to annual genealogy conferences or one of the annual institutes.** The big ones every year are NGS and FGS (The Federation of Genealogical Societies), but there are any number of regional, state-level and local conferences as well. I didn't go to genealogy conferences the first few years I researched and I can tell you how my skill level jumped substantially when I started to attend regularly and learn from some of the field's best minds.

6. I highly recommend that as you progress, you start to read **professional genealogy journals** on a regular basis. You will learn about methodology and resources that will advance your thinking in big, big ways. I prefer NGS *Quarterly*, but as I mentioned in my previous post listing slavery related articles, there are many different genealogy journals and it's a matter of personal taste. There are also state-level genealogy journals like the one for Maryland. As a member of NGS, I get a subscription to NGS *Quarterly* as well as NGS *Magazine*, which is also an excellent publication. Membership in APG gets me the APG *Quarterly*. All these publications will contribute to your growth as a genealogist, whether you intend to pursue it as a business or simply are doing your own research.

7. **Read genealogy books.** This seems intuitive, but again, I encounter plenty of people who research for years and years and haven't read any of the many excellent books available. Most libraries have pretty good genealogy collections, or I am a big fan of purchasing used books from a website such as ABEBooks or Amazon.

Note: Appendix B contains my list of suggested books on various subjects.

FIGURE 150, ROBYN TEACHING CLASS

Slaveowner Tracking Chart

Family: Drew and Oakley Bynum **Location:** Lawrence County, Alabama
Date Compiled: October 7, 2009

Census	Name	Age	Birthpl.	Property	No. Slaves	Microfilm, Roll, Pg. #	Notes
1870	OH Bynum Oakley H	52 23	NC AL	7000RE/100 0PP		M593, R22, Pg. 112A	
1860	OH Bynum Effie L Mary Oakley Effie Anna Drury Susan Bynum	40 35 15 13 11 7 4 70	NC AL AL AL AL AL AL NC	170000/350 000	124	M653, R12, Pg. 1054B	
1850	OH Bynum Effie L Mary OH Jr Susan Bynum Z. Temlinson FAL Bynum	31 26 7 4 60 25 2	NC AL AL AL NC AL AL	36440	151	M432, R8, Pg. 449A	
1840	OH "Bynan" JA "Bynam"?	3m 20-30 1f 40-50 1m 20-30 1f 20-30			4	M704, R8, Pg. 192B	
1830	Drew S Bynum	1m 10-15 3m 15-20 1m 40-50 1f 40-50			61 1 free black m, 36- 45	M19, R1, Pg. 288B	William Watkins Neighbor

FIGURE 151, SLAVEOWNER CHART

The best way for me to interpret and analyze data has always been to represent that data as a drawing, picture, table or a chart. Even in engineering school, I could never solve an advanced mathematical problem if I couldn't visualize it first. We all have different learning styles and types of intelligence and its been a natural progression for

me to apply this knowledge to my genealogy. Of course, much of genealogy starts with descendant and ancestor charts and family grouping sheets.

The third step in the Genealogical Proof Standard involves *analysis and correlation* of your data. I find it easiest to create a table in Microsoft Word, although sometimes I will use Microsoft Excel. Here are some of the custom tables and charts I have created for my own research. The possibilities are endless and only limited by your imagination.

Birthplace Tracking Chart: organize birthplaces from a set of census records (for example, 1870-1930) in order to determine the likely place of birth.

Birthdate Tracking Chart: use a set of census records to estimate a birthdate range for individuals.

1870 Neighbor Chart: because analyzing the neighbors in 1870 is especially crucial for African-American research, I track them in a chart.

Tax Tracking Chart: self-explanatory.

Land Records Chart: I saw this in Emily Croom's book *Unpuzzling Your Past*. She made a chart where she traced each piece of land for an ancestor, and also recorded where that land went (i.e., showing the person selling the land, and showing who bought or inherited that same piece of land).

Slaveowner Tracking: I do lots of different slaveowner tracking. I have charts of "potential" slaveowners, showing their slaveholdings from census records. I have charts of their family structures, their deed transactions involving slaves, and of their entire probate processes. One is shown on the previous page.

Slave Charts: This is related to the slaveowner charts, but once I amass enough information on a group of slaves, I will typically chart them separately.

Family History Center Film Charts: I list all the microfilms I order from the FHC. I'd forget what I've already viewed if I didn't do this. I usually include the FHC film number, the dates I did the research, and any special notes or comments.

Of course, there are plenty of good websites online with blank charts of all types to use for your genealogical research. Cyndi's List has a category for Supplies, Charts, Forms, also Ancestry, Family Tree Magazine , and Rootsweb has assorted charts and forms. My favorite census forms are Gary Minder's at the Census Tools website. He's also got plenty of other useful forms. There are also a wide array of private vendors who offer these sorts of products, and I'd be remiss if I didn't mention my buddy Michael Hait and his terrific CD called Family History Research Toolkit, available from the Genealogical Publishing Company.

If you haven't expanded beyond the basic genealogy charts, I encourage you to take a look at some of these downloadable charts and also don't be afraid to create your own. You may see something in a new way or notice something you've never seen before.

6 SEPTEMBER 2013

My friend Aaron calls them artificial. They can also be called self-imposed brick walls. We say this to mean we have labeled something a brick wall that really isn't a brick wall. We call them that even though we haven't done our due diligence in terms of careful research. Consider these examples:

We declare the brick wall of not being able to find an ancestor in a census year but we haven't tried multiple spellings and pronunciations, haven't used wildcard searches, haven't searched surrounding counties, haven't searched other census websites other than Ancestry, haven't considered a migration out of state and biggest of all— haven't done a line-by-line search in the district or county we expect to find them in.

We declare a brick wall, but we have only been to one or two repositories in person, or worse still, have done all our research online.

We declare a brick wall, but have used books and websites to collect information without ordering and examining firsthand the original record.

We declare a brick wall, but we've only searched 2 or 3 TYPES of records such as census records, vital records and the "easy" databases on Ancestry (like World War I draft cards). We haven't even tried to search land records, court records, church records, maps, city directories, probate records, newspapers and other records.

We declare a brick wall, but we've only been searching for our direct ancestor and maybe his wife and children. We have not expanded to the group (or "cluster") of people that were associated with our ancestors and would significantly increase our chances for success.

We declare a brick wall, after jumping back several generations, and not doing extensive research within each generation on all the siblings and children of each sibling.

We declare a brick wall, but we're wearing cultural blinders. We aren't considering that people may have had children outside of or before marriage, or that they may appear in the records as a different race.

We declare a brick wall, but have never actually analyzed and correlated the evidence that we DO have. In fact, we don't know how to evaluate the evidence. We believe everything we see in print is factual, accurate and true. If two records give conflicting information, we have no idea which one is correct.

We declare a brick wall, and have never tried to find living descendants of any of the family members.

We declare a brick wall, but never stopped to consider our ancestor may have had multiple marriages. We also never actually verified the mother of each child separately from the father.

We declare a brick wall, but have never expanded our search to less common but potentially valuable records stored onsite at <u>universities,</u> historical and genealogical societies. And..

(my personal favorite) **We declare a brick wall,** but have never actually <u>read</u> a book on <u>genealogy methodology</u> or any of the thousands of teaching articles published in genealogy journals. We have progressed mainly by asking others what to do next instead of taking the time to learn ourselves "what to do next."

I could go on and on, but I think you get the point. Genealogy is a learned skill and a profession with <u>defined standards.</u> You get good at it by practice and by education. I *define "good" as using best practices for careful research and ultimately being able to discern clues that don't jump off the page.* That's what will set you apart from when you were a beginner. I look at evidence I gathered in earlier years and see things

now I couldn't possibly see then. You have to progress away from "looking up" people in databases and learn how to "look into" people's lives, which is a different animal altogether.

I have been guilty of many of these artificial brick walls myself and have had to overcome my <u>special tendency to declare someone dead</u> when I can't find them;) But I've gotten better over the years by constantly educating myself and learning about methodology and resources. I hope you will too. Tell me in the comments, which artificial brick walls you have been guilty of?

<u>Note</u>: This is the second most popular post on my blog. Bernice Bennett had me as a guest on her Blog Talk Radio, *Research at the National Archives and Beyond.* The interview can be heard in its <u>entirety at the show's link,</u> along with all of her other archived shows.

FIGURE 152, THE FAMOUS "BRICK WALL" IN GENEALOGY

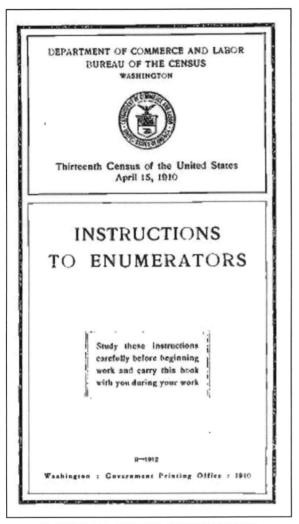

FIGURE 153, CENSUS INSTRUCTIONS

Censuses provide the framework for much of the family history research that we do. Every once in a while, it is useful to consult the instructions that were given to enumerators for a particular census year. The University of Minnesota has posted them online to the eternal gratification of all genealogists. We all know that not every enumerator followed the instructions to the letter, but I've also found that what we think was meant by a census question is not always that simple. As an example, let's look at how the instructions for defining "black" (colored, negro, etc.) evolved over time:

In 1860 and 1870, a blank space under Color implied "White": Color.– Under heading 6, entitled "Color," in all cases where the person is white leave the space blank; in all cases where the person is black without admixture insert the letter "B"; if a mulatto, or of mixed blood, write "M"; if an Indian, write "Ind." It is very desirable to have these directions carefully observed.

By 1880 that was no longer the case: Color–It must not be assumed that, where nothing is written in this column, "white" is to be understood. The column is always to be filled. Be particularly careful in reporting the class mulatto. The word here is generic, and includes quadroons, octoroons, and all persons having any perceptible trace of African blood. Important scientific results depend upon the correct determination of this class in schedules 1 and 5.

By 1900, there was no "Mulatto" category anymore: Color- Write "W" for white; "B" for black (negro or of negro descent); "Ch" for Chinese; "JP" for Japanese, and "In" for Indian.

By 1910, "Mulatto" was back, with a new definition for "black": Color or race.-Write "W" for white; "B" for black; "Mu" for mulatto; "Ch" for Chinese; "Jp" for Japanese; "In" for Indian. For all persons not falling within one of these classes, write "Ot" (for other), and write on the left-hand margin of the schedule the race of the person so indicated.

For census purposes, the term "black" (B) includes all persons who are evidently full-blooded negroes, while the term "mulatto" (Mu) *includes all other persons having some proportion or perceptible trace of negro blood.*

By 1920, there were other color/race choices:

Color or race.-Write "W" for white, "B" for black; "Mu" for mulatto; "In" for Indian; "Ch" for Chinese; "Jp" for Japanese; "Fil" for Filipino; "Hin" for Hindu; "Kor" for Korean. for all persons not falling within one of these classes, write "Ot" (for other), and write on the left-hand margin of the schedule the race of the person so indicated. For census purposes the term "black" (B) includes all Negroes of full blood, while the term "mulatto" (Mu) *includes all Negroes having some proportion of white blood.*

For both 1930 and 1940, the new word "Negro" got detailed (although with conflicting) guidelines, and notice the 'Other Mixed Races':

Color or race.-Write "W" for white, "B" for black; "Mus" for mulatto; "In" for Indian; "Ch" for Chinese; "Jp" for Japanese; "Fil" for Filipino; "Hin" for Hindu; "Kor" for Korean. For a person of any other race, write the race in full. Negroes.-A person of mixed white and Negro blood should be returned as a Negro, no matter how small the percentage of Negro blood. Both black and mulatto persons are to be returned as Negroes, without distinction. A person of mixed Indian and Negro blood should be returned a Negro, unless the

Indian blood predominates and the status as an Indian is generally accepted in the community.

Other mixed races.-Any mixture of white and nonwhite should be reported according to the nonwhite parent. Mixtures of colored races should be reported according to the race of the father, except Negro-Indian.

This nation's preoccupation with color, especially when that color was black, is evident. It is also apparent that centuries of miscegenation had forever changed what the definition of that would include. Take a look at some of the enumerator instructions and tell me what surprises you.

I got a real kick out of how detailed the instructions were for Occupation, as well as this note about getting information on certain classes of people in 1880:

The law requires a return in the case of each blind, deaf and dumb, insane or idiotic, or crippled person. It not infrequently happens that fathers and mothers, especially the latter, are disposed to conceal, or even deny, the existence of such infirmities on the part of children. In such cases, if the fact is personally known to the enumerator, or shall be ascertained by inquiry from neighbors, it should be entered on the schedules equally as if obtained from the head of the family.

Note: Elizabeth Shown-Mills, on her *Evidence Explained* website, has an excellent QuickLesson about the importance of knowing census instructions. See QuickLesson #9: " Census Instructions? Who Needs Instructions?"

FIGURE 154, ADAMS DEATH CERT

This is a phrase I've been using to refer to that Bermuda Triangle between 1880 and 1900…the Donut Hole. Now I like donuts just as much as the next person. But I'm not the first and sure won't be the last to lose relatives on either side of it. We all know about how the fire that destroyed a large percentage of the 1890 census. First, you'll want to be sure to check that your research area is not one that has a surviving 1890 census fragment. After that, you'll want to use all your genealogical sleuthing skills to ensure that the person "on the inside" of the 1880 donut is the same person you find "on the outside." Minus the frosting.

Consider this: a couple can have a child right after 1880 **that is grown and gone by 1900**. For example, according to her death certificate Julia Adams of Montgomery County, TN was born in 1881. However, if you look at her father Lucas Walker's household in 1900, she is not there. That's because she married James Adams in 1897 (next page).

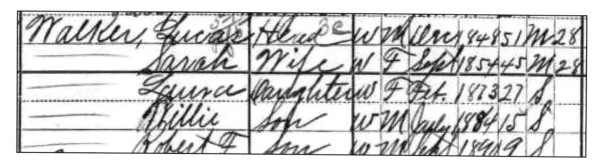

If you didn't find out about Julia from some other record or source, you would have missed her completely.

This example was meant to illustrate the point: it was easy to show because the parent was listed on the death certificate. But how many death certificates do we see that have no parents listed? Also, you would have never found the death certificate if you had not known this child existed AND their married name. In those cases, you'll miss an ancestor. So beware and be extra vigilant of those people born in the early 1880s "inside the donut." Tell me in the comments if any of you have "lost" an ancestor in the gap? If you found them, how did you verify that it was the correct person?

FIGURE 156, ADAMS MARRIAGE

FIGURE 157, BROOKE GROVE

I'd been wanting to re-visit my Prather family's historic cemeterys in Montgomery County, MD, not far from where I live. The church was historically called **Brooke Grove Methodist Church,** and is on Maryland's Inventory of Historic Properties. I discussed how useful these types of databases can be in a previous post.

Brooke Grove Church was started after the Civil War by a group of former slaves, several of whom had been enslaved together. Some were my Prather ancestors. Generations of the black community in this area are buried at this church. It's a beautiful, peaceful place, with large oak trees, only interrupted by modern development. I can only imagine what it was like then.

The history of the formation of area churches in the areas where your ancestors lived is also a nice thing to include in your family histories. Church was a large part of the lives of our ancestors. One of the non-population census schedules is called "Social Statistics." It did not track individuals but counted things like how many churches, schools and newspapers were in each community. Some of

these records are available on Ancestry.com. Also, look for archives for each denomination. For example, the archives for the United Methodist Church are stored at Drew University in New Jersey. Baylor University has a Baptist Studies Center for Research that posts a webpage with links to various archives for the Baptist denomination.

Part of the purpose of my visit to the cemetery is that I wanted to put into practice some of Elizabeth Shown Mills' guidance in her quicksheet, *"The Historical Researchers Guide to Cluster Research."* I have used the clustering technique many times in my research successfully, but Ms. Mills gives many more examples of its use that I'll probably spend a lifetime trying to do. Her quicksheet suggests using it at cemeteries; that means noticing who is buried near your ancestor, especially those with different surnames. They probably are relatives. I hadn't thought of that before.

The organization "Heritage Montgomery" published a wonderful PDF brochure about the historic African-American churches of the county.

FIGURE 158, MOCCABEE GRAVE

It was a gorgeous sunny day when I went, and I knew so much more about the community and its people. I could search the cemetery with brand new eyes and I saw connections everywhere. Now I could start looking for clusters of people. Martha Simpson had several siblings buried nearby, as shown in the photo above. The surname "Simpson" made them easy to notice.

However, right behind those Simpson headstones, were the headstones of Nicholas McAbee and his wife *"H.Leannah"*. At the time I didn't know it, but *"H. Leannah"* was **Harriet Leannah <u>Simpson</u>,** the sister of my ancestor Martha and wife of Nicholas. It makes sense now that they were buried right behind the other Simpsons; the "cluster" was right there. This was a big clue that could have helped me uncover their relationship earlier.

I began to map out the cemetery on a few sheets of paper and I got about halfway through before I ran out of energy. There are hundreds more people buried at the cemetery than have surviving

headstones today. Fortunately, now many of these headstones have been uploaded to Find-A-Grave.

Another thing I do is to cross-reference the information found on the headstones with death certificates and obituaries. I try to find the marriage records of couples in the cemetery as well. The further back in time you go, you will find some inconsistencies in dates that will need to be ironed out.

I also noticed the burials of many young and no doubt beloved children, evidence of the high mortality rates of the past. It still floors me that it so common for women to experience the deaths of their children.

What adventures have you had at the cemetery lately? The next time you go, study the "cluster"; write down the names of those buried nearest your ancestors. Those individuals could very easily be the parents or family of the wife, or sisters hidden under their married names.

24 JANUARY 2014

Following a repeatable process in our genealogy research can make the difference between success on the one hand, and being lost in papers and files years later with nowhere to go.

There are so many things I wish I could whisper to my 1997 self when I first set out on this path, although there are some things I'm proud that I did the "right" way, like interviewing relatives and reading everything related to genealogy I could get my hands on.

All of our research should start with a specific research question. These questions help us to create a focused plan of attack, and help us to focus on records likely to hold the answers we need. I want to use something from my own research to illustrate how to formulate those questions.

FIGURE 160, REV. DANIEL WATERS

The wonderful photo at left is **my great-grandfather Daniel George Waters,** born in 1875 on the Eastern Shore of Maryland in Somerset County. He was a minister with the Methodist church, as was his grandfather and several uncles and great-uncles. My father has told me many stories of him, mainly of how everybody was so afraid of him because he was very stern. Looking at this photo, I believe it!

Ministers moved as their assignments changed, so my grandmother grew up in towns all over the Eastern Shore of Maryland and Delaware. I enjoyed

hearing what that experience was like. It was a source of immense pride to be the child of a minister, but it came with high expectations for behavior. You can read about his Waters lineage on the "Paternal Ancestors" tab of my blog, then scroll down to Waters.

While I have amassed plenty of information on his paternal side, his maternal side research has been lacking. As a little background, Somerset County, Maryland had a large number of freed blacks before state emancipation in 1864. Daniel's mother's name, Mollie Curtis, was passed down via oral history.

I found her in several census records with her husband Samuel Waters, and I located their date of marriage. Recently I pulled Mollie's death certificate (next page). Her parents on the certificate are listed as George and Maria Curtis. Fortunately, George lived to be 90 and I was able to pull his death certificate as well.

All of the information I found places George Curtis' birth at approximately 1814. I was able to locate his family on the 1850, 1860, 1870, 1880 and 1900 census records for the county. He was also a landowner and appears on a county map of the area, and I pulled all their land records.

Although there are no other George Curtis' who are black and free in that county at that time, I still have a lot of research to do. That research begins by formulating questions.

FIGURE 161, CURTIS DEATH CERTS

Here are several questions these two records, in addition to the census, have led me to ask:

1) Does Manokin Cemetery, Somerset County, MD, have existing headstones or burial records?
2) What is the relationship, if any, of Clinton Collins, the informant on Mollie's death certificate?
3) Mollie is listed as a widow; does a death certificate exist for her husband Samuel Waters?
4) What is the relationship, if any, of George Hill, the informant on George Curtis' death certificate?
5) Mollie was born ca. 1859 according to this record; was she recorded as a freed black in the freedom certificates of the county?
6) Were George and his wife Maria recorded as freed blacks in the freedom certificates of the county?
7) How did Mollie Waters obtain her freedom?
8) How did George Curtis obtain his freedom?
9) What was the maiden name of George Curtis' wife, Maria?
10) When did George Curtis marry his wife Maria?

11) Is there a death certificate for Maria Curtis?
12) Are the family of George and Maria Curtis found in the records of the local black church?
13) Did John Curtis (white), with whom George Curtis is living in the 1850 and 1860 census, own and later free George Curtis?

I'm sure I'll have more over time, but notice how specific the questions are. Some will involve more work to answer, but each question builds upon the others, and allows me to gather the information I seek in a focused way. For some questions, I may be unable to find the answer. Those "negative" results (negative evidence)should also be recorded. Using my knowledge of the available records for Maryland in general and Somerset County in particular, I can put together a list of repositories and records I need to search to find the answers.

Have you created specific genealogy research questions? Tell me in the comments if you've been practicing this already.

9 FEBRUARY 2014

I have discussed the idea of **thoroughness** in our research before–the need to be diligent in searching out original records related to our ancestors. For example, we've all seen those shaky leaves on Ancestry. For a long time, I never clicked on them, but last year I found some treasures hidden within the 100 or so hints I had, so now I make a point to periodically investigate those leaves.

Earlier this week, I found a leaf for an ancestor named Syvoid Holt. The leaf linked to an outside website–in this case the Monroe County [Michigan] Historical Museum. Several of my ancestors, including Syvoid, migrated from Tennessee to Michigan to work for the Ford Motor Co., and settled in Detroit and its suburbs.

The Museum website has, among other items, an obituary database. Upon request, they will email an obituary found in their database for $1. What's notable here is that I *already knew* who Syvoid's parents were, his siblings, when and where he died, who he married and the names of his children.

But my philosophy is to order *any and all* original records related to my ancestors. So off my request went. The obituary is shown below. What I did not realize until I saw this is that I had never been able to locate the death certificate for his mother Vannie.

I had expected to find it in Tennessee but had no luck. This obituary revealed she had married a man surnamed Thurman and was alive as recently as 1969. I found that Vannie actually had married another man before Thurman in 1938, a man named Dan Cathey. Dan died the very next year.

That revelation led to finding Vannie's headstone on Find-A-Grave. Vannie is buried in the same cemetery as her two sons. Syvoid's obituary contained the key to unlocking the mystery of where and when his mother Vannie died. If I had dismissed this document because I already knew a lot of information about Syvoid, I wouldn't have found this. Aim to be thorough in your research.

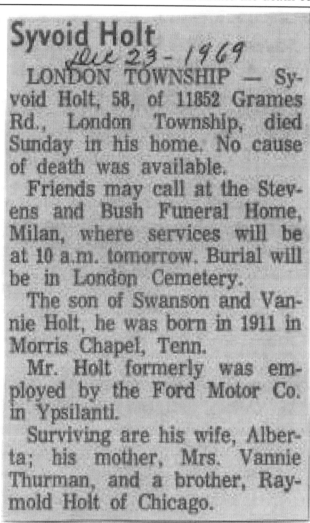

FIGURE 162, HOLT OBITUARY

JUNE 30, 2014

How do you document the slaveowner in your research? Here are two ideas from my own toolbox:

Create separate family trees for each slaveowning family within your genealogy software. Most people never use the feature available in most software to do this. I use Rootsmagic, but this capability is available in most all the recent software. Just create a "New File" for each family. (Rootsmagic has a free download if you'd like to test drive it for yourself.)

It is extremely important to keep track of the slaveowner and his family in order to trace how enslaved people were transferred to family members as they were inherited, gifted and sold. You'll want to include the wife's parents, since many men came into slaveownership through their wives, men like George Washington. Slaveowning families often married first cousins, and I have found it impossible to keep track of them without doing a separate tree. Then I can print it out and take it along with me on research trips.

Another idea is that for the people who were enslaved, I create a new "fact" called "Slaveowner." In Rootsmagic, each fact can include associated media, so I can scan in the slaveowner will, inventory, tax documents, bill of sale, etc. as I find them and link them to the entry. That way all the relevant documents are accessible within the program. I write the slaveowner's name in the "Details" tab, and there is plenty of room for Notes. I can add source citations, which are built into all the major genealogy software programs today. I can also have the "Slaveowner" fact print out when I run narrative reports on my family, along with all the other facts. I can do a "missing fact" report, and see which people are missing this fact. These are just a few of the many powerful ways genealogy software can assist us.

These practices have made slaveowner research a little more structured and organized for me, although I will never say it is easy.

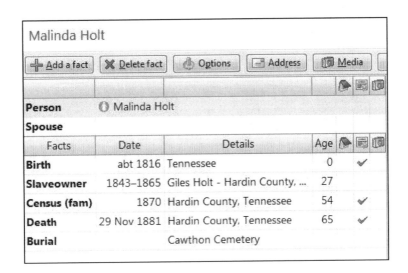

Person	Malinda Holt			
Spouse				
Facts	Date	Details	Age	
Birth	abt 1816	Tennessee	0	✓
Slaveowner	1843–1865	Giles Holt - Hardin County, ...	27	
Census (fam)	1870	Hardin County, Tennessee	54	✓
Death	29 Nov 1881	Hardin County, Tennessee	65	✓
Burial		Cawthon Cemetery		

FIGURE 163, SLAVEOWNER FACT

5A. CRIMINALS IN THE FAMILY

25 JUNE 2012

FIGURE 164, JOSEPH HARBOUR

Every family tree, whether we want to own up to it or not, has its share of *criminals, vagabonds, shysters, thieves, polygamists, deserters, roughnecks, liars and cheats.* While lots of things change, human behavior doesn't.

One of my shadier ancestors was Joseph Harbour (above), my 4th great grandfather, who was born in September 1852 in Hardin County, Tennessee. He actually even looks like he was up to no good, doesn't he? In the early years of my research, he was a mystery. He only appeared in the 1880 census, married to Hannah Barnes, with two children, Doss and Odie. I assumed he died after that. I've <u>since learned that we must always</u> <u>remember our assumptions</u> and be ready to revisit them in light of new evidence.

I've <u>blogged before about various types of court records,</u> and in my lecture on court records, Joseph is the star. Only when I finally got up enough nerve to venture into local court records did more details about his life emerge. It was amazing to me that he behaved this way during the post-Reconstruction era, where racial hatred and violence rose to unprecedented levels.

Joseph Harbour appeared in the criminal court records from at least 1882 to 1897. In 1882, he was charged with profanity. The court minutes alleged that he stood out in front of a church house and said:

"…let any [insert profanity] man report [me] that wants to and by God it won't be good for him…I am a [more profanity] on wheels…I dare any man to report me…"

I guess someone called his bluff and actually reported him. Sounds like he may have been drinking to me. The court records go on to show that Joseph left his first wife and children to marry another woman, Rachel Shannon. Before his marriage to Rachel, the court charged them both with "Lewdness" (one can only imagine what they were caught doing). Our ancestors were truly reality shows before reality shows came to be! For the next decade, Joseph proved to be a constant presence at the courthouse. Amazingly, Joseph escaped all the charges with fines, even the more serious charge of attempted manslaughter.

Joseph's escapades must have caused Rachel to contemplate whether taking Joseph from first wife Hannah was a good idea. By July of 1895, Rachel filed divorce papers against Joseph with the Circuit Court. Their divorce papers detail a violent and troubled marriage with both charging the other with adultery. In addition, Rachel stated that Joseph "threatened to kill her," while Joseph responded that "the child born during their marriage" was not his child. Their divorce was granted in 1896, after testimony from witnesses on both sides. I have heard of some crazy divorces in my time, but my goodness.

After the divorce, Joseph Harbour disappeared from the written records in Hardin County, however, some of his descendants remain living in the county today. Let me state for the record, they are lovely, lovely people;)

Now I understand why his first wife Hannah, in the 1900 census, reported her marital status in 1900 as a widow! That led me astray for many years. I guess he was dead *to her*.

July 1887	• Disturbing Public Worship
Nov 1887	• Attempted Manslaughter
Mar 1888	• Gaming
Jul 1891	• Selling Liquor W/o License
July 1894	• Larceny
Nov 1894	• Carrying Weapons

FIGURE 165, HARBOUR CHARGES

In July 2010, I was cleaning out my office and ran across some papers I'd printed years ago from one of the Southern Claims Commission Indexes. I had never found any relatives when I searched these before, <u>but I've posted about the great finds that are possible</u>. The particular indexed name I had was a white man who, oral history said, had fathered a child with my 4th great grandmother, Margaret Barnes in Hardin County, Tennessee. Her daughter Nannie is shown in the picture.

The man's name was Ben Rush Freeman. <u>I figured since Footnote(now Fold3) had most of the Southern Claims Commission files online</u>, I might as well look before tossing that piece of paper.

I can't adequately explain to you the astonishment and then rush of excitement as I pulled up Ben's 45+ page file and found that Margaret was one of his witnesses!

This was stunning because I only had information about Margaret from one court case, oral history, and census records. She was born in the early 1800s, so I had sort of given up the hope that I would find anything more about her.

The Southern Claims Commission was set up to repay loyal Southerners who had had property taken or destroyed by the Union Army during the Civil War. One had to have witnesses to attest to the damages, and many times, slaveowners used former slaves as witnesses.

Margaret testified to the fact that hogs were slaughtered, horses taken, and some other crops. The deposition provided her age, and stated that she was not owned by Mr. Freeman but worked for Mrs. Barnes.

FIGURE 166, NANNIE BARNES

Margaret Roberts had been a freedwoman in Hardin County, or a "bonded slave." She was "purchased" by John Barnes in 1838, and appeared on the census in his household in 1840 and 1850. By 1860, the census records her with the surname Barnes, John had died by then and she was living with his widow Elizabeth. Margaret was listed as a mulatto woman with several mulatto children. She appears in the 1870 census for the last time.

Another thing that makes this file pretty amazing is that her son, Campbell Barnes, also testified. Campbell was listed on the census record with his mother in 1850, but I could only locate a "Cam Barnes" living in neighboring McNairy County in 1880.

I thought this might be her son—and this file confirmed that it was, when it noted that he lived in McNairy County. His testimony also stated that he went away with the Union Army, and returned after the war (I haven't found him listed formally as a soldier).

When asked who he had been owned by, Campbell reiterates that he "was never a slave," but that his mother had been a free woman and was purchased by John Barnes as a young girl. Again, this confirmed information I had already discovered. This find also greatly increases the chance that Ben Rush Freeman was indeed the father of at least one of her children. She states in her file that she was

frequently sent over to help him by Mrs. Barnes. Shown below is part of the first page of Margaret's testimony.

What I've learned, and hopefully you can benefit from, is to also search these files for neighbors, relatives and associates of your slaveowner. I thought it interesting that many of Ben's close family members and friends also filed claims.

There were just tidbits here about Margaret, as the primary purpose of the testimony was to ascertain the facts about the lost goods. But every bit counts. I kept wishfully thinking, "Why didn't they ask her parent's names???!"

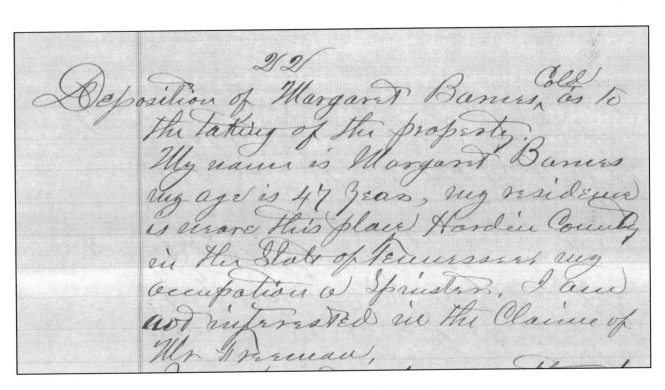

FIGURE 167, BARNES DEPOSITION

FIGURE 168, SIMPSON BIBLE ENTRIES

I am in a state of genealogic shock.

My ancestor Martha Simpson (right)was the wife of Levi Prather. I've been working hard in past years trying to unravel the complicated slave relationships in the Prather family of Montgomery County, Maryland. Finding Levi's slaveowner was hard work, so I hadn't focused much on Martha yet. Just recently, I started thinking perhaps Martha was freed before 1864. That was the year Maryland's state constitution freed its slaves.

I'd been able to find a sister of Martha's (Leanna) and a brother (James) living as free blacks in 1860, so it was logical to think that Martha had been free herself. But there was a better reason for my suspicion: we are fortunate to have a few pages of the Prather family bible, noting exact dates births and deaths of some of the Simpson family.

When I started to analyze these pages, it occurred to me that it would be unlikely that enslaved people would have known exact birthdates dating from the 1840s.

FIGURE 169, MARTHA SIMPSON

I did a search for Martha Simpson in 1860, and a woman with that name appeared living with the white William R. Warfield family—but in neighboring Howard County instead of Montgomery County (above).

The Howard County location surprised me, although it shouldn't have. We are always supposed to examine neighboring counties. I still wasn't sure this was MY Martha, even though the age matched. But here is yet another example of how use of the clustering technique can be helpful (i.e., looking for groups of people associated with your ancestors). I knew from studying Martha and Levi's 1870 census neighborhood in Montgomery Cty that they lived right in the middle of other black people with the surname—can you guess?– *Warfield*. So Martha living with a family of that surname made me feel like I was onto something. I decided to see if Martha was there in 1850, and Oh My Goodness. There they were, Martha and several of the siblings listed in my bible page—nice and neat and living as freedpeople in Howard County, Maryland in 1850! Even better—they were with (presumably) their mother

Louisa. The actual image is bad, so I will transcribe the entry:

Louisa Simpson, 33
Harriet L, 11
Mary E, 9
James W, 7
Joseph W, 5
Martha J, 4
Minta L, 3 [?]

This was an unusual case in that I knew the name of the father–Perry Simpson–and it was in fact the mother's name who had been lost to history. He may have been still enslaved in 1850, and perhaps that is why his name is not shown in the household.

But wait—it gets better. Howard County was formally organized relatively late—1851—from Anne Arundel County. Both Anne Arundel and Howard County have some combination of freedom certificates, manumission and chattel records available on the Archives of Maryland website. Just, WOW. It almost gets no better than that. Doing an online search of these records, I discovered a manumission from one Ann Dorsey dated August 1816, of the following enslaved people:

Lyd, age 30
Harriot, age 11
William, 10
Mary, 7
Belinda, 5
Eliza, age 3
**Louisa, 18 months

Witnesses to this transaction were Gustavus Warfield and Humphrey Dorsey. It is possible the "Louisa" in this list, who is a baby, could be the same Louisa found in the 1850 census who is the mother of my Martha Simpson. Of course, I've got alot of work to do onsite in repositories before I can conclude that because we all know nothing thorough can be done online. My first task is to figure out *which* Ann Dorsey this was, since the Dorseys were a large, prominent Maryland family and there were Anns all over the place. For right

now, I suspect it was the Ann whose maiden name was —Warfield.

I have also gathered that this enslaved community likely had roots in many of the "first families" of Anne Arundel and Howard County: Dorsey, Worthington, Simpson, Warfield, Chase, Hall, etc. Many former slaves with those surnames are living in the community near my Prathers in Montgomery County in the 1870s. I was also fortunate to find at Google Books a downloadable copy of *The Founders of Anne Arundel and Howard Counties"* written by Joshua Dorsey Warfield in 1905. There is a phenomenal amount of information in this book, and I'm just beginning to sift through it.

This is such a rewarding and absolutely thrilling discovery. I haven't been speechless in a long time. Martha was here–right under my nose the whole time.

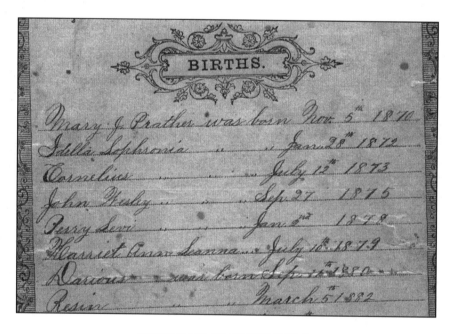

FIGURE 171, PRATHER BIBLE

1 MAY 2009

FIGURE 172, HARDIN COURTHOUSE

I knew Samuel and Louisa Holt's family well, but never guessed Felix was Louisa's child (Louisa is shown below). This court record doesn't name his father, but implies the father was white. What's written here is the kind of stuff we rarely ever find written anywhere else, and that's why court records are a rich source.

I don't recommend diving into court records at the very beginning of genealogical research; they are complicated and many aren't indexed. But when you're ready, **endless** possibilities await you in the dusty old record books of the courthouse!

FIGURE 173, LOUISA BARNES HOLT

I absolutely, positively LOVE court records. I should caveat that: I don't particularly like court records about *myself*, but historical court records in search of those ever-elusive ancestors are way, way cool. They are second on my "genealogical excitement" scale only to Civil War pension records.

Guess what I found tonight buried in the Hardin County Court Minutes that I ordered and viewed at my local Family History Center? Well, I had been wondering for years how this particular man, Felix Barnes, fit into the community. I have Barnes ancestors, but had never seen him in the household of any of my Barnes kinfolk. So tonight, I found a record of Felix being apprenticed. Take a look at his phrase:

"...the apprenticeship of Felix Barnes, minor child of Lou[isa] Barnes (now wife of Sam[uel] Holt) said boy being an illegitimate mulatto child."

All of us know about the horrid history in this country of slavery, racism, white supremacy, Jim Crow and the types of discrimination that persist to this very day. Violence was at the core of those systems. Far from being passive or willing subjects, African peoples and their descendants fought back in myriad ways as did Native Americans. That's why slave rebellion plots were often dealt with by using ever-increasing levels of depravity, such as burning bodies and cutting off heads.

The practice of lynching is what I call the *original American brand of terrorism*. I see a clear difference in these types of murders; they were meant to send a message to the community and to elicit a set of behaviors that maintain white rule. This is evident in the detailed files on lynching that the NAACP kept (and their subsequent push for legislation), as well as the efforts of brave journalists like Ida B.

Wells-Barnett. It must have been a frightening time in general, but especially to our ancestors who risked their lives to try to vote, buy land, educate their children or any of the other things that whites believed looked too much like being an actual citizen. I am glad I live in a time and place where I can have friends and family of all colors, ethnicities, religious beliefs and pretty much anything else.

Early in my research, oral history from Tennessee ancestors recalled the lynching of one of my Holt ancestors. Never did I think I would find documented proof, but I did. The local paper, which in the 1880s and 1890s was replete with mentions of race riots and lynchings in other parts of the country wrote the following in May, 1887:

"George Holt, col., who lived near Sibley met his fate by the rope route last Friday."

FIGURE 174, LYNCHING CLIPPING

I was shocked by the sarcasm and brevity of it. The authors had the audacity to write "Suicide" as the header to this sentence, which it was not. Later I discovered that George was the brother of my gggrandfather John W. Holt. He had a wife and young children, and owned hundreds of acres of land at the time of his death. This was a rural west Tennessee county that never had a large black population. Though slavery and racism existed here, the small African-American community must have been rocked by this act of terror. The reasons for the lynching are lost to time, although some of George Holt's descendants believe it had to do with a dispute over his land. Did he know his assailants? How did his family go on after that? How do you rebuild? Do you leave the area? Is revenge ever an option? His brother John W. later became one of the most prominent blacks in the county– land wealthy, a merchant and Postmaster. But even John's brother was not untouchable.

His descendants kept many interest documents from George's life. Years ago, I found George W. Holt's headstone in the local black cemetery. I remember the vines and roots had come out of the ground and were wrapped around the headstone, eerily reminiscent of the way he died. I got chills up my spine.

Today, I remember George Holt and all the others, who met their fate "at the hands of persons unknown." May they rest in eternal peace. For more on lynching, see the <u>Project HAL database</u>.

FIGURE 175, GEORGE'S MARRIAGE CERTIFICATE

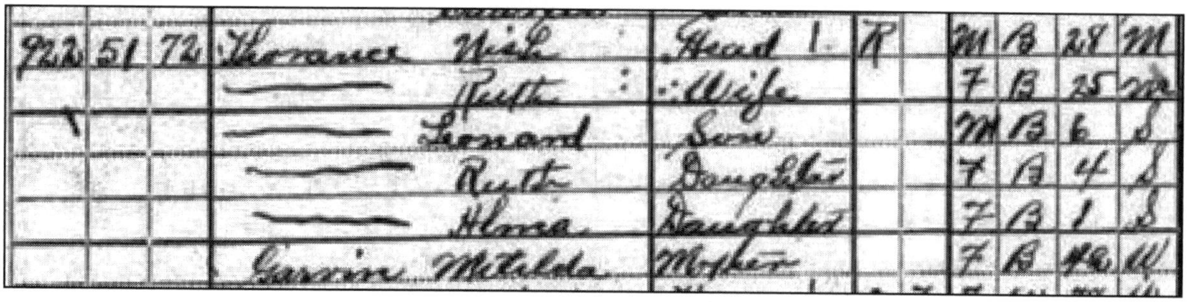

922	51	72	Thorance	Nish		Head	1		R		M B 28 M
				Ruth		Wife					F B 25 m
				Leonard		Son					M B 6 S
				Ruth		Daughter					F B 4 S
				Horea		Daughter					F B 1 S
			Garvin	Matilda		Mother					F B 46 W

FIGURE 176, 1920 THORANCE HOUSEHOLD

Sometimes I just don't take my own advice. My ggrandmother Georgia Harris' line has always been problematic for me. Awhile ago, I made some headway in tracing her roots not in Jacksonville (Duval County) Florida, as oral history said, but in Madison County, over 100 miles west of Jacksonville. I was able to find her previous marriage and discover she had other children. I also found Georgia's mother, Matilda, her stepfather, Perry Davis, and sister Ruth in Madison County. After that, the trail ran dry. I really wanted to find out what happened to Georgia's mother, Matilda.

I decided one day last week to research Georgia's only known sibling, Ruth Harris. Familysearch listed a marriage between Ruth Harris and a man named "Nish Torrence" in 1910. A search for his (thankfully) odd name in the 1920 census found the couple living in...drum roll...Philadelphia, Pennsylvania! Who was living with them? Drum roll #2...Ruth (and Georgia's) mother Matilda! By 1930, they had moved yet again and were living in Camden, New Jersey (below).:

FIGURE 177, 1930 TORRENCE HOUSEHOLD

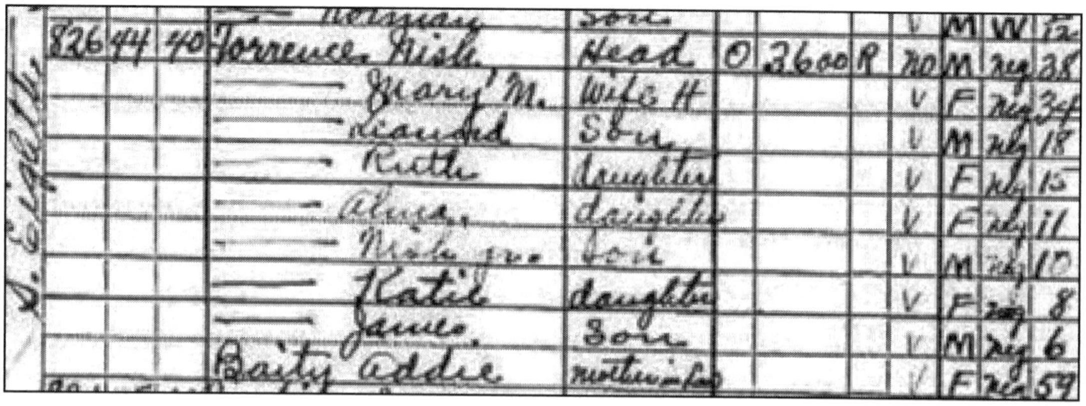

				Merriam		Son					M W F
826	44	40	Torrence	Nish		Head	O 2600	R	no	M neg 38
				Mary M.		Wife H			v	F neg 34
				Leonard		Son			v	M neg 18
				Ruth		daughter			v	F neg 15
				Alma		daughter			v	F neg 11
				Nish jr.		Son			v	M neg 10
				Katie		daughter			v	F neg 8
				James		Son			v	M neg 6
		Baity	Addie		mother-in-law				v	F neg 59

REGISTRATION CARD—(Men born on or after April 28, 1877 and on or before February 16, 1897)

SERIAL NUMBER   1. NAME (Print)   ORDER NUMBER

U 16*7   Nish   Tornce

826 S. 8th Street   Camden   Camden   NJ.

(THE PLACE OF RESIDENCE GIVEN ON THE LINE ABOVE WILL DETERMINE LOCAL BOARD JURISDICTION, LINE : OF REGISTRATION CERTIFICATE WILL BE IDENTICAL)

Same

57   Madison

May 25 1890   Florida

Mrs Mary Tornce   826 S. 8th St. Camden NJ.

Philadelphia Transfer Co.

50th + Jefferson St. Phila.   Phila.   Pa.

I AFFIRM THAT I HAVE VERIFIED ABOVE ANSWERS AND THAT THEY ARE TRUE   nish Tornce

By then, Nish was remarried to a woman named Mary Baity, and had several more children. Matilda was gone. I am still surprised that so many of my ancestors moved around as much as they did. They are all over the place. And that's a major reason many of us lose the trail. Nish worked on the railroad, and that was likely the reason behind their move. I get happy when ancestors move to a big city from a rural area, because that usually means more and better records. I am now focusing in on Philadelphia, between 1920-1930, and *hoping* to be able to find death certificates for Ruth Harris and Matilda Davis. (Update: I eventually found Ruth's death certificate in Philadelphia).

From the SSDI, it appears that Nish lived in Camden until he died in 1970. Nish's World War II draft card confirmed this is the right family (top).

Since I had the address, I went to Google Maps and found a picture of the home–it's the one in the center.

I am *hoping* also to find some Torrence descendants that may still live in Camden. This would be exciting since I've never met anyone even remotely associated with this line. To have some new cousins would be very cool. I'm still wondering why I didn't find this sooner–as many times as I have told my students, "when you get stuck, search sideways, search the siblings!"

FIGURE 179, CAMDEN HOUSE

FIGURE 180, JOHN AND MARY HOLT

I recently got around to transcribing my third great-grandfather John W. Holt's will. John lived in Hardin County, TN, and spent his childhood enslaved by Giles Holt, along with his mother Malinda and siblings. By the early 20th century, John W. Holt was said to be the wealthiest black in the county, owning hundreds of acres of land. At one point, he was Postmaster at the town bearing his name (Holtville) and had a school named Holtsville. He was also a merchant who owned a country store. A photo of John and his wife Mary Garrett is shown above.:

His standing in the community is also evident by the number of times he was named in other wills as executor, and he served as security in numerous land records. He first purchased over 200 acres of land with a brother and possible cousin only six years after the end of the Civil War in 1871.

His will, written in 1911, is one of the most detailed I have ever seen in all the years of my research. John died in 1925 and his will had 15 individual items and ran over six written pages. The level of specificity is what is most notable. He clearly had been well-schooled in estate and land matters,

although where and how he attained that knowledge remains a mystery. He names his son Troy as executor but wisely places his vast estate within a trust that is set to last for twenty years:

"Out of the rents and income of the estate, the trustee will, during the said period of twenty years, pay all taxes assessed against the estate, will keep the real estate in reason-able repair…

Troy (shown next page)was also the trustee, and was to use the proceeds from the trust to care for his mother Mary and other siblings, all who were named. John even detailed the meaning of his words, so there would be no doubt as to the purpose of his trust:

"…My object being to provide first, from the income of my estate, a support for my widow and minor children, that is for my widow as long as she lives and my minor children as long as they or any one of them are minors (whenever the word support is used it is intended to embrace and include all necessary food and clothing)…"

John W. Holt apparently had a bout with infidelity, which produced a son named Hundley. Hundley is mentioned throughout the will, his inheritance being only one half of what the other siblings would receive:

"...the remainder of said rents, profits and income in his hands be distributed by him annually amongst all of my children, equally, except that Hundley Holt shall be paid only one half of a child's share in said annual disbursements during said period of twenty years..."

John also directed that the trustee was not empowered to:

"sell, mortgage or otherwise dispose of any of the real estate for any purpose, and any such attempted disposition shall be void."

The repercussions were clear for disobeying this directive:

"...None of the beneficiaries under this will shall possess the power or authority to dispose of any part of my estate, herein willed and devised within said period of twenty years. No deed or bargain and sale can be made by either of them, no mortgage deed of trust or other transfer can be made, and no conveyance or alienation of any kind in anticipation can be made by either, but such power is expressly withheld, and any attempt on the part of either to so dispose of the same will operate as an immediate forfeiture of the interest in my estate."

This is an extraordinary example of the heights some of our formerly enslaved ancestors were able to reach because of education, industry and their own will to succeed.

FIGURE 181, TROY HOLT

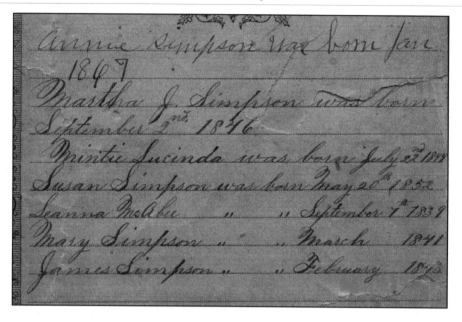

FIGURE 182, SIMPSON BIBLE

Getting better at genealogical research involves many things. One important skillset is understanding and learning how to find relationships when no document states the relationship. The early years of genealogy are filled with the "low hanging fruit" of census records, marriage and death records, online documents, etc. When that fruit runs out—which I assure you it will—are you equipped to keep uncovering relationships in your family? That skill involves learning new methodologies and ways of approaching your research, as well as finding little clues and piecing them together through analysis. Elizabeth Shown Mills calls it "harvesting clues." Here's a good, short example from my own research.

My 2nd great grandmother Martha Simpson was born a freed woman in Anne Arundel (later Howard) County, MD. I found her and her siblings living with their mother in 1850. She married Levi

Prather in Montgomery County, MD, birthed 12 children that survived to adulthood and lived there the rest of her life. I had a page from a family bible that recorded both Martha's siblings names (above).

When Martha's husband Levi died in 1894, Martha purchased 75 acres of land in 1897 from a man named Nicholas Moccabee and his wife. Martha lived in the same house with Nicholas and his wife in 1880, and lived next door to a widowed Nicholas in 1900, probably because she'd purchased some of their land.

These kind of connections should always arouse suspicion and curiosity in the diligent genealogist. Who was this couple–Nicholas and Harriet? Nicholas was also buried in the same cemetery as my ancestor Martha. So I decided to delve into Nicholas' life more deeply. An obvious impediment was his name, "Moccabee" which was spelled umpteen different ways.

152	154	Prather Martha	Head	B	F	Feb	1846	54	W	30	15	12	
		John H	Son	B	M	Sept	1875	24	S				
		Eugene	Son	B	M	Jan	1891	8	S				
		Lilcy	Daughter	B	F	Sept	1883	16					
		Ruth L	Daughter	B	F	Jan	1887	13	S				
153	155	Macabee Nicolas	Head	B	M	May	1839	61	M	35			
		Mary E	Daughter	B	F	Jan	1871	29	S				
		Louise V	Daughter	B	F	Dec	1874	25	S				
		Gorens, Walter	Servant	B	M	May	1882	18					
		Buckley Richard	Servant	B	M	July	1881	8					
		Carroll Benjamin	Servant	B	M	Oct	1887	13	S				

But take a look at what I found in land records— (these are the year and the grantor/grantee):

1876, Willie R. Griffith to Nicholas "Macbee" and wife Leanna
1896, Nicolas "Mackabee" to Harriet L. Mackabee
1897, Nicholas "Mackabee" and wife Harriet L. to Martha J. Prather
1897, <u>Harriet Leannah Mackabee</u> and husband Nicholas to Sandy Spring Bank

His wife's full name—her first and middle name—is only ever given in the last 1897 deed record above. His wife's name was "Harriet Leannah." With this critical clue, I unlocked the puzzle. I remembered Martha named one of her daughter's "Harriet (Ann) Leanna." If you go back to the bible records on the previous page, you'll also see the name of "Leanna McAbee." All of this provides evidence for one conclusion: Nicholas married Martha's sister, Harriet Leanna Simpson. Later, I found an obituary for Nicholas Moccabee that provided the full (though

misspelled) name of his wife-"Harriett Lena Simpson." (next page)

<u>Notice that no record told me directly that Harriet Leanna, Nicholas' wife, was Martha's sister.</u> But I could draw that reasonable conclusion from the compilation and analysis of the relevant evidence. Later when I went back to the cemetery, I also found "H. Leannah McAbee's" headstone right next to her husband Nicholas, and <u>in the same group of Simpson family headstones</u>.

A few months ago, I joyfully discovered a descendant of Harriet Leannah who still lived in Maryland. He and his family surprised me by accepting my invitation to attend our family reunion. I thought I would cry right there. Since then, I have gotten to spend time with their wonderful family and share all the things I have discovered. They shared priceless historical photographs, and the one I was most happy to see was the photograph here of Harriet Leannah Simpson. The two sisters have finally been reunited. Another ancestor–reclaimed..

FIGURE 184, HARRIET LEANNA SIMPSON

PROMINENT MINISTER DEAD

Was Born a Slave in Montgomery

County—Accumulated Property

—Has Son Teaching in Balti-

more.

Latonsville, Md., January 23rd—
The funeral of Rev. Nicholas McAbee
took place from Brook Grove Methodist Episcopal Church, Tuesday. It
was the largest funeral ever held in
this community, being attended by,
both colored and white. Mr. Mc-
Abee was one of the best known
members of this community, where
he lived for years. Mr. McAbee was
born in Montgomery county, near
this place, February 25th, 1838, and
was nearly 64 years of age at his
death. He became a member of the
M. E. church in 1856, and was li-
censed to preach in 1863. He was
married to Miss Harriett Lena Simp
son, in 1850. His wife died several
years ago, and he is survied by three
daughters and one son, Mr. W. H.
McAbee a teacher in the public
schools of Baltimore city. The funeral services were conducted by
Rev. A. L. Carter, assisted by Revs.
Elijah Ayers, of Sykesville, A. B.
Dorsey, of Rockville, and R. P. Lawson, of Sandy Springs Circuit.

FIGURE 186, JAMES HOLT FAMILY

I recently had one of those amazing moments in genealogy that reaffirmed my belief that I was *meant* to this work, c*alled* to do this work, by forces beyond my comprehension.

I posted awhile ago about breaking through a brick wall using black newspapers. I had been stuck trying to trace my ancestor James Holt. I am trying to find all the branches of the Holt family that left the area of Hardin County, Tennessee, and there were lots that left at various times and planted roots elsewhere.

Recently I was contacted by the granddaughter of James Holt. She had been searching for her roots online and found me. In fact, she went through Tim Pinnick, who wrote the Forward to this book, to find me. We had a tearful and joyous conversation, as we shared stories about our lives and our historical paths. I had reclaimed another family member. It gets even better--she shared the wonderful photo of James M. Holt and his family shown above.

My heart leapt as I gazed upon this ancestor of mine who had left Tennessee, the son of an enslaved woman named Judah. He blazed a trail across the states (in each census he is living in a different place) as a successful Methodist minister. Then he attended law school in Kentucky and eventually had a successful law practice in Indianapolis, Indiana.

Another photo of James Holt below shows him, I assume, in his law office surrounded by legal books. The story didn't end there. After talking more, I realized that one of my unidentified photos may have been the father of my newfound cousin. This is mainly because of her description of him as a police officer. Wonderfully–it turned out to be him (photo below).

She was thrilled to have a photograph of her father she had not seen before, and I couldn't believe this obscure photograph I hadn't looked at in years turned out to be him. Another unidentified kin– reclaimed! This experience just warmed by heart, and affirmed for me why I love genealogy so much.

FIGURE 187, HOLT AND SON

FIGURE 188, ALEC AND QUEEN HALEY

My maternal ancestors are from a rural southwestern county in Tennessee called Hardin County that most folks haven't heard of unless they're from there or have been following my blog. Many of my family members lived in a town called *Hooker's Bend*, which is fodder enough for another post, but Hardin County's largest city is Savannah (you didn't know there was one in Tennessee, did you?) Well, as the title of my post exposes, Alex Haley (the author of *Roots*) is Savannah's biggest celebrity and he plays a prominent role in the tourism brochures for the area.

Alex Haley grew up in Hening, Tennessee, which is several counties over in Lauderdale County. But the reason Alex is also Hardin County royalty is that his grandparents were prominent and well-known Savannah citizens from the end of the 19th through the early 20th century. They were Alec Haley and his wife Queen (above). They're also (stated with utter pride) in my family. His name is found in records written both ways, but I will call him "Alec" in this post to differentiate between him and his famous grandson.

The Holts are one of my Hardin County lines and they intermarried with Haleys in two places on my tree. My great-great-aunt, Madelina Holt, married Abner Haley. Abner was one of Alec and Queen's sons. Their other son, Simon, was Alex Haley's father. Another Holt ancestor married Julia Haley, who was the daughter of Abner Haley.

FIGURE 189, CHERRRY MANSION

Alec and his wife Queen were a fascinating couple. Alec's fame was mostly because he operated the ferry that took people across the Tennessee River to the city of Savannah when that was the quickest way to travel if your horse took too long. So he knew just about everybody in town, white or black. One year he saved a white woman who almost drowned, so after that, he was vaulted to forever sit amongst the echelons of "most beloved colored folk."

The Cherrys were one of the wealthiest families in Hardin County from the early-mid 1800s, and they owned what came to be known as the Cherry Mansion. The house is on the U.S. National Register of Historic Places. It sits on the edge of the Tennessee river and was where Alec Haley's ferry picked up passengers to "go 'cross the river.". His wife Queen worked in the Cherry mansion. Their house was about 100 yards from the Cherry Mansion. The Cherry Mansion (which still stands) was so grand that when General Grant brought the Civil War through Hardin County (eventually fighting in the Battle of Shiloh), he camped out at the Cherry Mansion.

When *Roots* and *Queen* shot Alex Haley to fame, there was a rush of visitors to Savannah. People sought out elderly folks, both white and black, to ask them their memories of the couple. This created a rich record of them passed down via oral history, in addition to the wonderful book written by Alex. All kinds of neat details emerged about the community, like the fact that people got baptized down at the river. One woman talked about when the circus came to town, how the elephants would swim across the river. Alec was described as a hard-working, smart, honest man who didn't like "no *ficety* kids."

Queen was a tiny woman, who claimed Captain Jackson was her father her entire life. Queen's "mental spells" were the stuff of legend–everyone knew of her time spent in the mental hospital at Bolivar. Her spells "made an indelible impression on everybody." One elder claims, "Miss Queen had fits, but she told us she acted that way to get what she wanted." Others agreed about how smart she was and how they loved to hear her witty sayings: talking once about a girl's dress being too short, Queen suggested she put a "condition" around the bottom of it–meaning a ruffle. Queen's spectacular way with gardening was noted: "She was crazy about flowers and her yard was beautiful. She had elephant ear plants all over the place." Stories like these are the kind I live for in genealogy.

216

By 1930, Abner and Madelina Holt Haley migrated to Detroit, Michigan, <u>part of the Great Migration of African-Americans to the North</u> to find better employment and escape the hardships of the South. A few years ago I joyfully got to meet several of my Holt and Haley ancestors who live outside Detroit. We exchanged pictures and information about our shared Tennessee roots.

I see my cousin Chris Haley more often since he's here in Maryland and does a lot of genealogy-related activities. Alex Haley was his uncle. Chris is also active with the <u>Kunte Kinte-Alex Haley Foundation.</u> He keeps the *Roots* message alive in his speaking engagements and reminds us of the wonderful gift Alex Haley left for all genealogists.

<u>Note:</u> This is by far my most popular blog post because of the enduring popularity of *Roots*. I get lots of hits on this post every year when *Roots* airs.

FIGURE 190, ROBYN AND CHRIS

FIGURE 191, 1870 SUGGS HOUSEHOLD

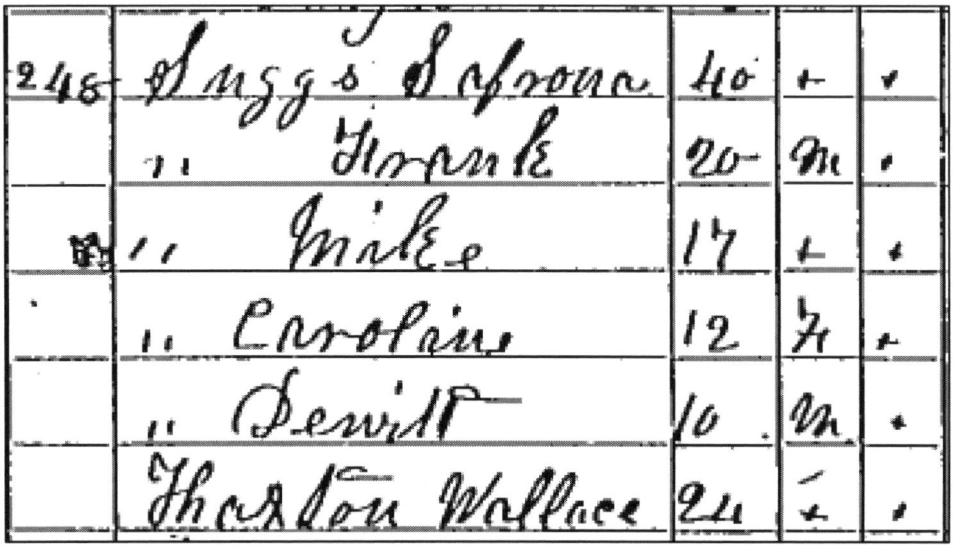

I'm building a case that just got stronger. I have posted before about my long odyssey researching the Fendricks family, my maternal great-grandmother's family. I had a breakthrough in August 2009 and found a duplicate death certificate earlier this year.

To summarize past research, I was at a standstill with my third great-grandfather Mike Fendricks and wife (Jane) Eliza. I found them newly married and living in Hardin County, TN in 1880. Census records indicate they were from Alabama. But, illustrating a common problem with migrations, I did not know the *county* in Alabama. In 2009, the breakthrough came when I developed enough skills to really use cluster research techniques. In short, this technique suggests researching the people your ancestor had close relationships with. Mike Fendricks, as an elderly man in 1920 was living in the household of a man named Dee Suggs, so I decided to research this Suggs family. You can read the lengthier original post for more details, but the research led me to Lawrence County, Alabama, and the census grouping shown above in 1870.

My hypothesis is that the mysterious "Dee Suggs" is the same man shown in the 1870 census household of Sofrona Suggs and called "Dewitt Suggs."

The fact that the 1870 census *does not state relationships* was a hindrance. I couldn't find Dee Suggs in Tennessee anymore after 1920. I had a hunch that perhaps he went back home to Alabama and that hunch paid off when I checked the Alabama Deaths database on Familysearch. I found him, and his mother was indeed "Fronie Suggs" (next page). Finding this death certificate was exciting.

It lends significant support to my hypothesis. Several African-Americans surnamed Suggs were centered around Russellville, Alabama, and buried at New Home Cemetery, so this opens a new research avenue for me.

The death certificate also identified Dee Suggs' father as "Obe[diah] Gholston," which illustrates another previous post topic, finding fathers who are not enumerated with the family in 1870. Obediah was located in several documents and was married to another woman and living in Franklin County, AL in 1880.

The evidence thus far supports a conclusion that the "Mike Suggs" in the household is my ancestor and probably Dee Suggs' brother, which explains why they both migrated to Hardin County, TN, why Mike was the witness on Dee Suggs' marriage license, and why Mike is living with Dee Suggs in 1920.

My next journey: thoroughly research all the children in the Sofrona Suggs household, and then start the search for the slaveowner.

FIGURE 192, DEE SUGGS DEATH CERT

Chapter 1E: Figure 9, Plantation in Vicksburg, MS, 1936. Library of Congress, Farm Security Administration, photo by Walker Evans, call no.: LC-USF342-008050-A.

Chapter 1G, Figure 14, Polly in Peanut Patch, ca. 1900-1905. Library of Congress, Prints and Photographs Online Catalog, Detroit Publishing Company, call no.: LC-D4-62096, reproduction no. LC-DIG-det-4a21461

Chapter 1I, Figure 18, Convicts Leased to Harvest Timber, 1915, Florida, Florida Department of State, Division of Library and Information Services, Reference Collection. Florida Photographic Collection, item no. RC12880

Chapter 1J, Figure 20, Henry Robinson [?], Ex-Slave, Library of Congress, Prints and Photographs Online Catalog, reproduction no. LC-USZ62-125158.

Chapter 1N, Figure 28, Ex-Slave Broadside, published by the Mutual Relief, Bounty and Pension Association, National Archives, Records of the Department of Veterans Affairs, RG15

Chapter 1R, Figure 38, Company E, 4th United States Colored Infantry at Fort Lincoln in Washington, D.C., bet. 1863-1866, Library of Congress, Prints and Photographs Online Catalog, photo by William Morris Smith, call no.: LC-B8171-7890, reproduction no. LC-DIG-cwpb-04294.

Chapter 1R, Figure 39, Christian A. Fleetwood, Library of Congress, Prints and Photographs Online Catalog, reproduction no. LC-USZ62-48685.

Chapter 1R, Figure 41, Sergeant Samuel Smith and Family, 1863-1865, Library of Congress, Prints and Photographs Online Catalog, The Liljenquist Family Collection, reproduction no. LC-DIG-ppmsca-36454.

Chapter 1S, Figure 42, Teamsters Near the Signal Tower, Bermuda Hundred, VA, 1864, Library of Congress, Prints and Photographs Online Catalog, reproduction no. LC-DIG-cwpb-02004.

Chapter 1V, Figure 50, The First Vote, 16 November 1867, photo by Alfred R. Waud, published in Harper's Weekly, Library of Congress, Prints and Photographs Online Catalog, reproduction no. LC-DIG-ppmsca-37947.

Chapter 1W, Figure 51, Freedmen's Union Industrial School, Richmond, VA, 1866, sketch by James E. Taylor, Library of Congress, Prints and Photographs Online Catalog, reproduction no. LC-USZ62-37860 DLC.

Chapter 1W, Figure 52, Family at the Hermitage, Savannah, GA, published by the Detroit Publishing Company, Library of Congress, Prints and Photographs Online Catalog, reproduction no. LC-D4-34666.

Chapter 1X, Figure 54, Slave Coffle Passing the Capitol, Library of Congress, Prints and Photographs Online Catalog, reproduction no. LC-USZ62-2574.

Chapter 3A, Figure 96, Cumberland Landing, VA Group of Contrabands at Foller's House, 14 May 1862, photo by James Gibson, Library of Congress, Prints and Photographs Online Catalog, call no. LC-B811- 383, reproduction no. LC-DIG-cwpb-01005.

Chapter 3A, Figure 97, Former Slave Walter Calloway, age 89, Birmingham, Alabama,1936-1938, Library of Congress, Manuscript Division, Slave Narratives from the Federal Writer's Project, 1936-1938, Works Projects Administration, digital id no. mesnp 010051.

Chapter 3B, Figure 101, Slaves Coming Into [Union] Lines, photo by Edwin Forbes, Library of Congress, Prints and Photographs Online Catalog, Gladstone Collection, reproduction no. LC-DIG-ppmsca-20762.

Chapter 3D, Figure 104, Slaves of the Rebel Genl Thomas F Drayton, May 1862, Hilton Head, SC, photo by Henry P. Moore, Library of Congress, Prints and Photographs Online Catalog, Gladstone Collection, reproduction no. LC-DIG-ppmsca-04324.

Chapter 3E, Figure 105, Andrew Johnson Reconstruction cartoon, 14 April 1866, published by Harper's Weekly, drawn by Thomas Nast, http://www.harpweek.com.

Chapter 3E, Figure 106, Freedmens Bureau Agent cartoon, 25 July 1868, published by Harper's Weekly, drawn by Alfred R. Waud, http://www.harpweek.com.

Chapter 3G, Figure 109, Slaves Reunion, 1911, Hilton Head, S.C., photo by Harris and Ewing, Library of Congress, Prints and Photographs Online Catalog, call no. LC-H261-3359, reproduction no. LC-DIG-hec-03547. Individuals shown: Lewis Martin, age 100, Martha Elizabeth Banks, age 104, Amy Ware, age 103, Rev. S.P. Drew, born free.

Chapter 3N, Figure 125, Blaindair Slave Quarters, 6651 Highway 175, Columbia, Howard County, MD, Historic American Buildings Survey, Library of Congress, Prints and Photographs Online Catalog, call no. HABS-MD-1149-A. Notes indicate a building date of approximately 1845.

Chapter 3P, Figure 130, Fugitive Slaves Fording the Rappahannock during Pope's Retreat, VA, August 1862, photo by Timothy H. O'Sullivan, Library of Congress, Prints and Photographs Online Catalog, call no. LC-B815-518, reproduction no. LC-DIG-cwpb-00219.

Chapter 3S, Figure 135, Slave Market of America Broadside, 1836, published by the American Anti-Slavery Society in New York, Library of Congress, Prints and Photograph Collections Online Catalog, Rare Book Collection, call no. broadside collection, portfolio 118, no. 26, reproduction no. LC-DIG-ppmsca-19705. The broadside depicts the slave markets of Washington, D.C.

Chapter 3V, Figure 139, Contrabands in Culpeper, VA, Library of Congress, Prints and Photographs Online Catalog, reproduction no. LC-DIG-cwpb-00821.

APPENDIX B: SUGGESTED BOOKS

GENEALOGY

"Evidence Explained: Citing Historical Sources from Artifacts to Cyberspace," by Elizabeth Shown Mills, 2009.

"Courthouse Research for Family Historians: Your Guide to Genealogical Treasures," by Christine Rose, 2004.

"The Sleuth Book for Genealogists: Strategies for More Successful Family Research," by Emily Croom, 2009.

"The Researcher's Guide to American Genealogy, 3rd Edition," by Val D. Greenwood, 2000.

"Red Book: American State, County and Town Sources, 3rd Edition," by Alice Eichhloz, 2004.

"The Source: A Guidebook of American Genealogy, 3rd Edition," by Loretto Dennis Szucs and Sandra Luebking, 2006.

"A Genealogist's Guide to Discovering Your African American Ancestors," by Emily A. Croom and Franklin Carter Smith , 2009.

"Black Roots: A Beginner's Guide to Tracing the African American Family Tree," by Tony Burroughs, 2001.

"Finding A Place Called Home: A Guide to African American Genealogy," by Dee Parmer Woodtor, 1999.

"Google Your Family Tree: Unlocking the Hidden Power of Google" by Daniel M. Lynch, 2008.

"The Family Tree Problem Solver" by Marsha Hoffman Rising, 2005.

"Genealogical Proof Standard: Building a Solid Case" by Christine Rose, 2009.

"Locating Your Roots: Discover Your Ancestors Using Land Records," by Patricia Law Hatcher, 2003.

"Finding and Using African-American Newspapers," by Timothy Pinnick, 2008.

"Mastering Genealogical Proof," by Thomas W. Jones, 2013.

"You Can Write Your Family History," by Sharon Carmack, 2009.

"Writing Your Family History: A Practical Guide," by Deborah Cass, 2012.

"The Complete Idiot's Guide to Writing Your Family History," by Lynda Stephenson

"From Slavery to Freedom: A History of African-Americans," by John Hope Franklin, 1988

"Slavery and the Making of America," by James Oliver Horton and Lois Horton, 2006.

"Bullwhip Days: The Slaves Remember," edited by James Mellon, 2002.

"The Slave Community," by John W. Blassingame, 1972

"Been In the Storm So Long: The Aftermath of Slavery," by Leon F. Litwack, 1980.

"Roll Jordan Roll: The World the Slaves Made," by Eugene Genovese, 1974.

"Runaway Slaves: Rebels on the Plantation," by John Hope Franklin and Loren Schweninger, 2000.

"Slaves Without Masters: the Free Negro in the Antebellum South," by Ira Berlin, 1992.

"Many Thousands Gone: The First Two Centuries of Slavery in America," by Ira Berlin, 2000.

"Freedom National: The Destruction of Freedom in the United States, 1861-1865," by James Oakes, 2014.

"The Rise of the House of Dixie: the Civil War and the Social Revolution that Transformed the South," by Bruce Levine, 2013.

"Complicity: How the North Promoted, Prolonged and Profited from Slavery" by Anne Farrow, Joel Lang and Jenifer Frank, 2006.

"The Black Family in Slavery and Freedom, 1750-1925," by Herbert Gutman, 1976.

"Ar'n't I a Woman? Female Slaves in the Plantation South," by Deborah Gray White, 1999.

"The Peculiar Institution: Slavery in the Antebellum South," by Kenneth M. Stampp, 1956.

"American Negro Slave Revolts," by Herbert Aptheker, 1983.

"Slavery: A Problem in American Institutional and Intellectual Life," by Stanley Elkins, 1959.

"Slave Testimony: Two Centuries of Letters, Speeches, Interviews and Autobiographies," by John W. Blassingame, 1977.

"We Are Your Sisters: Black Women in the Nineteenth Century," edited by Dorothy Sterling and Mary Helen Washington, 2007

"Back of the Big House: The Architecture of Plantation Slavery," by John Michael Vlach, 1993.

"Blacks Who Stole Themselves: Advertisements for Runaways from the Pennsylvania Gazette, 1728-1790," by Billy G. Smith, 1989.

"Ebony and Ivy: Race, Slavery and the Troubled History of America's Universities," by Craig Steven Wilder, 2013

"Compensated Emancipation in the District of Columbia: Petitions Under the Act of April 16, 1862," by Dorothy S. Provine, 2009.

"Black Masters: A Free Family of Color in the South," by Michael P. Johnson, 1986.

AFRICAN-AMERICAN HISTORY

"From Slavery to Freedom: A History of African Americans," 2 Volumes, John Hope Franklin

"Before the Mayflower: A History of Black America," by Lerone Bennett, 1993.

"Life Upon These Shores: Looking at African-American History, 1513-2008," by Henry Louis Gates Jr., 2011.

"Children of Fire: A History of African Americans," by Thomas C. Holt, 2011.

"The Warmth of Other Suns: The Epic Story of America's Great Migration," by Isabel Wilkerson, 2011.

"Homecoming: The Story of African-American Farmers," by Charlene Gilbert and Quinne Eli, 2000.

"Remembering Jim Crow: African-Americans Tell About Life in the Segregated South," edited by William H. Chase, Raymond Gavins and Robert Korstad, 2008.

"Voices of Emancipation: Understanding Slavery, the Civil War and Reconstruction through the U.S. Pension Bureau Files," by Elizabeth Regosin and Donald R. Shaffer, 2008.

"A Class of Their Own: Black Teachers in the Segregated South," by Adam Fairclough, 2007.

"Reconstruction: America's Unfinished Revolution, 1863-1877," by Eric Foner, 2002.

"Red Summer: The Summer of 1919 and the Awakening of Black America," by Cameron McWhirter, 2012.

"Slavery By Another Name: The Re-Enslavement of Black Americans from the Civil War to World War II," by Douglas A. Blackmon, 2009.

"My Face is Black Is True: Callie House and the Struggle for Ex-Slave Reparations," by Mary Frances Berry, 2006.

"Free at Last: A History of the Civil Rights Movement & Those Who Died in the Struggle," by Sara Bullard and Julian Bond, 1994.

"After the Glory: The Struggles of Black Civil War Veterans," by Donald Schaffer, 2004.

FAMILY HISTORY-RELATED NON-FICTION

"Somerset Homecoming: Recovering a Lost Heritage," by Dorothy Spruill Redford, 1980.

"The Hemingses of Monticello: An American Family," by Annette Gordon-Reed, 2009.

"All God's Dangers: The Life of Nate Shaw," by Theodore Rosengarten, 1974.

"Celia, A Slave," by Melton A. McLaurin, 1999.

"The Sweet Hell Inside: The Rise of an Elite Black Family in the Segregated South," by Edward Ball and Edwina Whitlock, 2002.

"The Seed of Sally Good'n: A Black Family of Arkansas, 1833-1953," by Ruth Polk Patterson, 1996.

"Woman of Color, Daughter of Privilege: Amanda America Dickson, 1849-1893," by Kent Anderson Leslie, 1996.

"The Sweeter the Juice: A Family Memoir in Black and White," by Shirlee Taylor Haizlip, 1995.

"The Hairstons: An American Family in Black and White" by Henry Weincek, 1999.

"Slaves in the Family" by Edward Ball, 1999.

"Arc of Justice: A Saga of Race, Civil Rights and Murder in the Jazz Age," by Kevin Boyle, 2005.

"Not in My Neighborhood: How Bigotry Shaped a Great American City," Antero Pietila, 2000.

"Family Properties: How the Struggle Over Race and Real Estate Transformed Chicago and Urban America," by Beryl Satter, 2010.

If you're new to genealogy research, congratulations! You are about to undertake a long (and it will be *long*) but fulfilling and fascinating journey along your family's roots and branches. To take on the responsibility of tracing and recording your family history is a serious and meaningful endeavor. My blog discusses all aspects of genealogy research, but I wanted to include a special section of small suggestions for beginners. I want you to be able to benefit from the mistakes many of us made early on, including me of course.

1) Read. The best thing you could do before you start researching is to read one of the beginning genealogy books. I highly recommend you start with: *"The Complete Idiot's Guide to Genealogy, 3rd Edition,"* by Christine Rose and Kay Ingalls. Despite the title, it's written by two heavy hitters in the field. For those researching African-Americans, I recommend *"Black Roots: A Beginner's Guide to Tracing the African American Family Tree"* by Tony Burroughs. The reason I stress this for all beginners is that it will save you precious time. You will learn what records are available and what information they provide. You will learn the importance of recording where you find your information. People who don't start off this way will *absolutely waste time* on things like searching for the 1890 census, searching for enslaved people before 1870 or wondering why you can't find the 1960 census. These books are easy to read and well worth it.

2) Join a Local Genealogy Group. The value of belonging to a local genealogy group cannot be underestimated. You will be inspired and have a group of people to support you and help you navigate the genealogy waters. Some genealogy groups will provide mentors to help guide you through the research process and help you when you hit the inevitable brick wall. The group does not have to be in the same area you are researching. It should be somewhere local to where you live so you can attend meetings on a regular meeting. It does not matter whether anyone is researching in your particular area; it is the support; the guidance; and learning about the common methods and sources that everyone uses.

3) Interview your Family. The very first step most recommend is to interview your family members (i.e., gather oral history) so you can have some information to start your research with. Begin with the elders in your family, but there may be others who can provide insight. Face-to-face interviews are great, but don't hesitate to have a phone interview. There are numerous websites that can provide sample oral history questions. A Google search on "oral history interviews" will pull up not only questions, but other advice about conducting the interviews. Most importantly: *Do not wait.* Every genealogist can tell you a story about putting off talking to a relative who then died. And don't neglect to collect family memorabilia–every family has boxes with old church or school programs, old ID cards, all sorts of stuff that will help your research. Go digging around in the attic. With permission of course!

4) Reach out to Continue Learning. Take advantage of all of the other opportunities there are to learn: take free classes in your area perhaps at the local library, look for non-credit genealogy courses at a local community college and subscribe and read some of the excellent genealogy blogs online. All of these will help you to grow your skills in ways that will enrich your research. Over time, you'll get better and better at solving some of the tough puzzles you will come across over the years.

5) Go Slowly. Start with yourself and research back in time, one generation at a time, slowly. Plan to research all siblings (not just your direct ancestors) in every generation. That's all your aunts and uncles on both sides and yes, all your great-aunts and great-uncles too. You'd be surprised how much more you'll discover by widening your focus beyond your direct ancestors.

6) This Book. In this book, you may want to start with Chapter 3, Evidence Analysis and Chapter 4, Research Tips. Those posts are wide-ranging and will be easily understandable to beginners. As your research progresses, you can move on to the other chapters.

Good luck and welcome to the journey of a lifetime!

22218017R00135

Made in the USA
Middletown, DE
29 July 2015